Through the Maze

Statistic...
Computer Applic...

William K. Akard

Through the Maze

Statistics with Computer Applications

Margaret Platt Jendrek

Miami University of Ohio

Wadsworth Publishing Company

Belmont, California

A Division of Wadsworth, Inc.

Sociology Editor: Sheryl Fullerton
Production: Mary Forkner, Publication Alternatives
Designer: Al Burkhardt
Copy Editor: Kathleen Engelberg
Technical Illustrator: Carl Brown
Cover: Al Burkhardt

Printed in the United States of America

2 3 4 5 6 7 8 9 10—89 88 87 86 85

Library of Congress Cataloging in Publication Data

Jendrek, Margaret P.
    Through the maze.
    Includes index.
    1. Social sciences—Statistical methods—Data
processing.   2. Statistics—Data processing.
3. SPSS (Electronic computer system)   I. Title.
HA32.J46   1984   310′.28′54   84-13188
ISBN 0-534-03921-9

contents

v

chapter **15**

chapter **16**

preface

Social science students need to be able to interpret statistics and use statistical computer packages. In fact, some claim that by 1987 over eighty percent of all jobs will require a working knowledge of computers. No book provides students with instruction as well as extensive examples and quizzes in both statistical interpretation and computer use. Current texts cover either statistics, with an emphasis on computation, or computer programming. That's why I wrote this book! I wanted a book for my research methods students that would:

1. Present the conceptual foundations of basic statistics
2. Guide students in the interpretation of statistics
3. Present the computer as an important data analysis tool
4. Guide students in using a popular social science computer package, the *Statistical Package for the Social Sciences* (SPSS^x)
5. Guide students through computer projects that require statistical interpretations
6. Allow students to work at their own pace

This text was written to attain these objectives, and it is unique in four respects. First, it includes *many* examples and checkpoints. This approach allows students to learn materials at their own pace. Some students may need to work through the material several times, yet others may only need to review a few sections. In either case, the material is presented in such a way that students receive continuous feedback about their grasp of the subject.

Second, the book is designed to guide students through the interpretation of statistics and the use of the computer via a popular social science program, SPSS^x. Social science students are notorious for being "math, statistics, and computer shy." Yet their ability to interpret statistics and use computers is among their most marketable skills. This book teaches these skills and provides students with practice.

Third, whereas some books examine several computer packages and others teach one computer language, few existing books teach the basics of just one computer package. In one course students can meaningfully learn only one computer package.

Fourth, concept quizzes and computer application exercises appear throughout each chapter. *Concept quizzes* test students on definitions and concepts presented in the chapter. The "hands-on" *computer exercises* test both programming and interpretive skills. The "hands-on" exercises are based on a *data set* (on cards) provided to instructors who adopt the book. The data set includes variables of interest to people in education, political science, psychology and sociology.

Acknowledgments

My sincerest thanks to my colleague Ted Wagenaar. He read every chapter and offered constructive comments and moral support. The constructive comments offered by the following reviewers truly improved the book: Kristine L. Anderson, Florida Atlantic University; Kenneth J. Berry, Colorado State University; David W. Chilson, Bowling Green State University; Lawrence G. Felice, Baylor University; David B. Graeven, California State University, Hayward; Gary D. Hampe, University of Wyoming; Joseph Healey, Christopher Newport College; David A. Nordlie, Bemidji State University; and Wornie L. Reed, Morgan State University. I am grateful to the Literary Executor of the late Sir Ronald Fisher, F. R. S., to Dr. Frank Yates, F. R. S., and to the Longman Group Ltd., London, for permission to reprint Tables III and IV from their book, *Statistical Tables for Biological, Agricultural, and Medical Research* (6th edition, 1974). I do have a husband and daughter. I suspect there were days and weeks when they wondered if they had a wife and mother. I thank them both for giving me the undisturbed time I needed to create the book.

Margaret Platt Jendrek

To Gene and Emily

chapter 1

An Introduction to the Computer

Welcome to the social scientist's computer world! For some of you this is a familiar world. For others, it's a new and magical world. This chapter familiarizes the new user with the computer and reviews computer terms for the old user.

After completing this chapter, you should be able to do the following:

1. Define selected computer terms
2. Use selected computer terms
3. Describe the four parts of the computer
4. Explain why computers cannot run the world
5. Explain why social scientists use computers

Why Use a Computer?

Read today's newspaper and notice the number of computer advertisements. Read a paper from 20, 10, or even 5 years ago, and you will not see computer advertisements. In recent years the computer has entered every phase of our lives (including our newspapers!). For example, schools computerize student lists; banks computerize customer statements; employers computerize payrolls; supermarkets computerize checkouts; and dating services computerize love and romance. Incredible? Yes and no. Yes, when we're speaking of the rapid developments in computer technology. No, when we're speaking of why we computerize.

The computer is a machine directed by a set of instructions to save, retrieve, and manipulate data. For the social scientist the computer is a valuable research tool. The computer makes it possible to handle large quantities of information quickly and accurately. For example, adding the ages of 3000 respondents, a simple calculation, may take a person several hours. The same calculation may take a computer less than one second!

Remember, however, that the computer is simply a machine. An automobile is also a machine. When driving a car, you are responsible for selecting the route. If you select a direct route you quickly arrive at your destination. If you select an indirect route you arrive later. If you select a poor route you may never arrive at your destination at all. In a similar way, you direct the computer. A **program** is a set of sequential directions that you give the computer. A top-notch **programmer**, a person who writes computer programs, is someone who directs the computer to do a job in a quick and efficient manner. A poor program is written by a programmer who meanders through the task. A really bad program does not do its intended job; the programmer, *not* the computer, goofed in the instructions!

Another term for the programs that run the computer is **software**. The physical equipment that makes up the computer is termed **hardware**. You can think of your favorite chocolate-chip cookie recipe as a program, a set of sequential directions for baking cookies. Your blender and oven are the hardware needed to bake the cookies.

Before considering how a computer works, let's discuss the difference between **data** and **programs**. Data refers to the information that we want to manipulate or analyze. In the chocolate-chip cookie example, the chips, flour, salt, sugar, baking soda, and eggs are the data. Social scientists frequently collect data on a sample of individuals. Demographic data often include the age, income, sex, and education of respondents. If we want to know the average age of our respondents, we need a program that can calculate an average. When we process our age data through a program that calculates an average, we get the average age of our respondents. Notice that the same program can be used to calculate the average income of our respondents. Although the data may change, the program remains the same; it was written to calculate an average.

The Parts of a Computer

To understand how a computer works one must be familiar with its four major parts: **input, storage, CPU,** and **output** devices. The input, storage, and output devices are called **peripheral devices**. They are external to the computer. Input devices enable us to feed information (programs or data) into the computer. Storage devices allow us to keep this information for later recall. The computer communicates the results of our program's execution to us through output devices. The CPU is the computer. The relationships among the four parts are illustrated in figure 1-1. Let's examine each device in more detail.

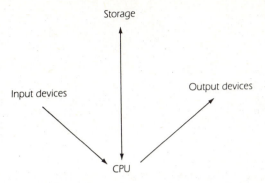

Figure 1-1 The four major parts of a computer.

Input Devices

Input devices enter data or programs into the computer. Typical input devices include the **card reader** and the **computer terminal**. The card reader inputs to the computer information contained on computer cards. As shown in figure 1-2, a computer card contains 80 columns. Each column is composed of the numbers 0 to 9. Information is punched onto cards by a **keypunch** machine, a machine that resembles a typewriter. The keypuncher types the program or data information at a keyboard, and the machine punches holes in the card's columns and rows. Information punched on cards is then input into the computer via a card reader. A typical card reader can process about 1000 cards per minute.

Alternatively, data or programs may be input from a terminal into the computer. Whereas a card reader acts as a mediating device between the computer card and the computer, the terminal is hooked directly to the computer. Two commonly used terminals are the **hardcopy** terminal and the **CRT** (cathode-ray tube). The hardcopy terminal looks like a typewriter. Users type their program or data at the terminal, sometimes called a console, and see the information printed on paper, the hardcopy. A CRT terminal resembles a typewriter with a small television screen. Users type their program or data at the terminal's console and see it displayed on a screen. Both types of terminals input data or programs directly into the computer. Working on a CRT tends to be faster than working on a hardcopy terminal because screen printing is more rapid than hardcopy printing. However, you don't usually get a hardcopy of your work at a CRT.

Storage Devices

Storage devices enable the computer to keep your programs and data. Without storage devices you would have to input your data or program into the computer every time you wanted to do a calculation or manip-

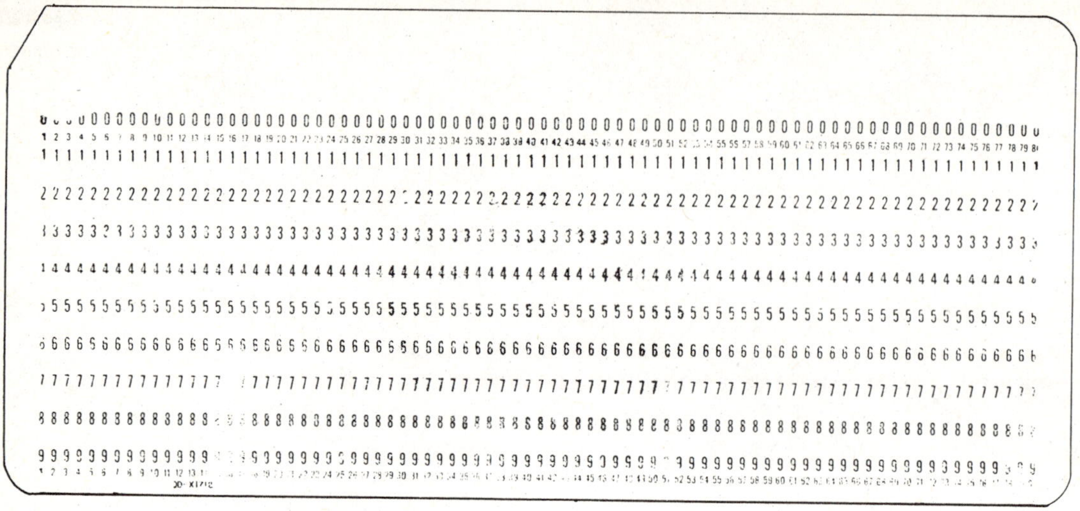

Figure 1-2 A computer card.

ulation. Storage devices permit data or programs to be stored compactly and reread quickly by the computer. Frequently used storage devices include **cards, disks, tapes,** and **core.** You can save and retrieve information from any one of these storage devices.

If you typed your data or program onto cards, you clearly retain the physical record of your work. Stored permanently on the cards, your program or data will be retained until you throw the cards away. Tape storage is similar to the storage of music on audio-cassettes. The information is retained until you erase or record over the tape. Disk storage is also similar to the use of audio-cassettes. Physically, however, disks resemble phonograph records. Information stored on disk is saved until you either erase or write over the disk.

Cards, disks, and tape are storage devices that are external to the computer; they are peripherals. There may be times when you want to store information in the computer itself, in what is called core. Core is usually a temporary form of storage. The information is kept in the computer's memory and not on an external device. Thus, you must tell the computer to set aside some memory for your data or program. In terms of speed, it is quicker to run information from core than from disk, from disk than from tape, and from tape than from cards. There is, however, a trade-off between speed and cost. Core costs more than disk. Core space is limited in size, and all computer programs must be run in core. Therefore, though limited in size, core is in high demand. Disk storage costs more than tape, and tape costs more than card storage.

Central Processing Unit

CPU stands for central processing unit. The CPU is the brain of the computer. It is the overall coordinator of a computer system. The CPU performs all the desired manipulations and calculations as directed by the program. For example, the CPU can retrieve information from storage, execute the steps in the program, and output the program's results to the proper device. The CPU ensures that the program is run and that the steps are followed in the sequence specified by the programmer.

Output Devices

Most input devices can also be used as output devices. After running a program, you want to see the results. Output devices allow you to view results. Typical output devices include cards, terminals, and line printers. You may tell the computer to do some manipulations or calculations and punch the results on cards. Or you may sit at a terminal and have the computer print the information on either a screen (CRT) or a line printer. If the line printer is not attached to your terminal, you will probably have to walk to a computer science building to pick up the hardcopy. A typical line printer prints 1000 lines per minute. Some printers produce more than 20,000 lines per minute! The printed output is called hardcopy or **printout**. Review figure 1-1 to see the links among the four parts of the computer: input devices, storage devices, CPU, and output devices.

Computer Programs

Throughout this chapter I've referred to computer programs, sets of sequential instructions telling the computer exactly what to do. How do you tell a computer what to do? Computers must be given instructions in a language they understand. In the United States, we speak English. If we ask people to do something in French or German, usually nothing happens, because the communication is not understood.

The same language barrier exists for our communications with the computer. Languages such as FORTRAN, COBOL, and BASIC were developed to allow us to communicate with the computer. Some of you may be thinking that you're having enough trouble learning French or Russian without having to learn a computer language too. Don't worry—you don't need to learn a computer language to communicate with the computer. A special kind of program, a prepackaged program, allows us to "talk" to the computer in English! We will be working with the prepackaged program called SPSS[X], the Statistical Package for the Social Sciences.

Before turning to SPSS[X], however, we need to examine the idea of data in more detail. After all, we write programs to store, retrieve, manipulate, and do calculations on data. The next chapter focuses on social science data: what it is and how to input it into the computer. In chapter 3 we begin SPSS^x programming.

C H E C K P O I N T

1. Match an entry in column A with one or more entries in column B. Answers to most checkpoints are located in the back of the book, but don't look! Try the exercise first.

A	B
a. Keypunch machine	**1.** Displays output on a screen
b. Card reader	**2.** An input device
c. CRT terminal	**3.** Punches holes in cards
d. Disk	**4.** A storage device
e. Tells the computer to calculate an average or print a table	**5.** Hardware
	6. Software

Check the one *best* answer for each of the following questions.

2. A person who writes software is called a(n)
   a. author
   b. programmer
   c. program
   d. writer

3. Which of the following devices is *not* external to the computer?
   a. peripheral devices
   b. disks
   c. CPU
   d. All of the above are external to the computer.

4. It is quicker to run information from
   a. core than disk
   b. disk than core
   c. tape than core
   d. card than disk

5. The part of the computer that actually performs the manipulations and calculations is called the
   a. storage device
   b. input device
   c. output device
   d. central processing unit

chapter 2

Data: An Introduction to Variables

At this point in your academic career you know that each discipline has its own "language." In foreign language courses you literally learn another language (French, German, Spanish, and so on). You also learn "new languages" in math, sociology, and music courses. These new languages are composed of symbols (for example, a sigma means summation, or a d' refers to the first derivative) and terms (structural-functionalism, reference group, G clef, augmented chords, and so on).

In this chapter you will begin to learn the data or variable language of research. Upon completion of this chapter, you should be able to do the following:

1. Define the term *variable*
2. Give examples of variables
3. Define the term *attribute*
4. Give examples of attributes
5. Define the four levels of measurement
6. Give examples of variables measured at each level
7. Code variables
8. Input data into the computer

Variables and Attributes

Social scientists collect and do research on data. Data are typically collected and analyzed in variable form. A **variable** is a phenomenon that can take on different values from case to case or time to time. Examples of variables often used in social science research include income, education, race, age, family size, and sex.

The values or categories of the variable are called **attributes**. For example, the attributes on the variable gender are male and female. Attributes on the variable educational attainment might include no formal education, first grade, second grade, third grade, fourth grade, . . . four years college, and so on. Or, educational attainment might be measured with the following attributes: none, elementary school, junior high school, high school, college, and so on.

Notice that there are at least two categorization schemes for the variable educational attainment. The difference between the two schemes reflects a difference in the level at which the variable was measured. Oops, we're jumping ahead! Before discussing level of measurement, let's check what we've just read.

C H E C K P O I N T

1. The list below contains both variables and attributes. Place a V next to the *variables* and an A next to the *attributes.*

Plumber	Educational level
Female	Republican
Religion	Political party preference
Occupation	Jewish
High school	Gender

Two criteria must be remembered when developing an attribute scheme for a variable. The attributes must be **mutually exclusive** and **exhaustive**. Mutually exclusive means that each response fits into only one category (attribute). There is no overlap. Exhaustive means that there is a category (attribute) for every response. For example, the attributes for the variable gender are male and female. The attributes are mutually exclusive and exhaustive. People are either male or female. They cannot be both. Thus, the criterion of mutually exclusive is fulfilled. All possible genders are included in the scheme, thereby fulfilling the criterion of exhaustive.

Let's examine an attribute scheme for the variable religion. Suppose the attributes were Catholic, Jewish, Methodist, Protestant, and other. Are these attributes mutually exclusive and exhaustive? No. What's the problem? The attribute scheme is exhaustive. All possible religions have been included—the attribute other includes all religions not specifically listed. The attributes are *not,* however, mutually exclusive. Methodist is a denomination within Protestantism. A respondent could check both Protestant and Methodist and thereby violate the mutually exclusive criterion.

CHECKPOINT

2. Class standing is a commonly used demographic variable in research done on students at universities and colleges. If the attributes on the variable are freshman, sophomore, junior, and senior, are they mutually exclusive and exhaustive?

Levels of Measurement

Nominal variables are variables whose attributes have the qualities of being mutually exclusive and exhaustive only. Examples of nominal variables commonly used in social research include sex (male, female), political party preference (Democrat, Independent, Republican, other), and religion (Catholic, Jewish, Protestant, other). Notice that the attributes in all three schemes are mutually exclusive and exhaustive.

Ordinal variables are those whose attributes are mutually exclusive, exhaustive, *and* ordered or ranked. For example, ordinal variables include social class (low, middle, upper) and class standing (freshman, sophomore, junior, senior, graduate student). The attributes for both variables are mutually exclusive and exhaustive, and they exhibit a ranking. For example, juniors have lower class standing than seniors and higher class standing than sophomores.

Interval variables have attributes that are mutually exclusive, exhaustive, and ordered *and* contain a standard unit of measurement. An example of an interval variable is IQ (for example, 60, 120, 180). Someone with an IQ of 120 scored 60 points higher than someone with an IQ of 60. Similarly, someone with an IQ of 180 scored 60 points higher than someone scoring 120. Furthermore, the distance between the IQ of 60 and 120 is the same as the distance between the IQ of 120 and 180, 60 points. That is, the units are equal.

Ratio variables have attributes that are mutually exclusive, exhaustive, and ordered and contain a standard unit of measurement *and* a true zero point. Examples of ratio variables used in social research include number of siblings (0,1,2,3, and so on), income ($0, $500, $10,000, and so on), and number of times married (0,1,2, and so on). The ratio level is the highest level of measurement. At this level we can state that someone with an income of $10,000 makes twice as much money as someone with an income of $5,000.

Now let's return to the earlier example of educational attainment. In one scheme, education had the attributes no formal schooling, first grade, second grade, third grade, and so on. In the second scheme, the attributes were none, elementary school, junior high school, high school, and so on. The difference between these schemes was the level at which the variable, educational attainment, had been measured.

What levels do the two schemes reflect? Nominal? Both schemes have attributes that are mutually exclusive and exhaustive. Nominal is not the level, however, because the attributes in both schemes have some additional features. Are they ordinal? In both schemes the attributes are ranked. Someone completing third grade has had more formal schooling than someone completing first grade. Similarly, someone who has finished college has had more formal schooling than someone who completed junior high school. So there is a ranking to the attributes in both schemes. Are they interval? The unit of measurement in the first scheme is grade; someone completing tenth grade has completed two more grades than someone finishing eighth grade. Is there a unit of measurement in the second scheme? *No.* The level of measurement for educational attainment (none, elementary school, junior high school, and so on) is therefore ordinal.

Let's continue with the first scheme. There is a true zero point. Respondents may not have completed any formal education. Therefore, measuring educational attainment with the attributes of none, first grade, second grade, third grade, and so on, illustrates the ratio level of measurement. So the difference between the schemes is indeed the level of measurement. Identify the level of measurement for the variables in the following checkpoint.

C H E C K P O I N T

3. For the following variables, place an N next to those that are nominal, an O next to those that are ordinal, an I next to those that are interval, and an R next to those that are ratio.
   a. Number of times voted Republican (0,1,2, and so on)
   b. Family size (small, medium, large)
   c. Type of beer (Schlitz, Budweiser, Coors, other)
   d. Attitude toward drafting women (strongly agree, agree, undecided, disagree, strongly disagree)
   e. Marital status (never married, married, widowed, divorced, separated)
   f. Family size (number of siblings)

Thus far we have defined and described variables, attributes, and the four levels of measurement. We do research on variables. We require the attributes on variables to be, at a minimum, mutually exclusive and exhaustive. We can measure variables at four different levels depending upon our choice of attributes.

The Importance of the Level of Measurement

It is important to be clear about the level at which you have measured a variable. The analyses discussed in this book frequently depend upon measuring at a particular level. In general, if you have measured at the ratio level, the highest level, you can perform analyses developed for that level and analyses developed for the lower levels. Similarly, if you measure at the interval level, you can utilize techniques developed for the interval, ordinal, or nominal level. Working with an ordinal variable means that techniques developed for ordinal or nominal variables are permissible. Measuring variables at the nominal level means you can use analyses or statistics intended only for the nominal level. In summary, you can always use analytical techniques intended for a lower level of measurement. You should not use analytical techniques intended for a higher level of measurement.

There is, however, a trade-off in analyzing variables measured at a higher level with a lower-level technique. The additional information conveyed at the higher level is ignored. Thus, measuring educational attainment at the ratio level and analyzing it with a statistic developed for ordinal data means that you are treating educational attainment as if it had been ordinally measured.

Before analyzing data, however, you must be able to input the data into the computer. We will discuss that next.

Getting Data Ready for the Computer

From the previous chapter, we know that input devices are used to transfer the data collecting on our desk to the computer. Two frequently used input devices are the card reader and the terminal. So now what do we do?

Coding Attributes

First, let's **code** the data. Coding refers to the assignment of a **number** or a **numeral** to the attributes of a variable. Numbers and numerals look the same—1, 2, 3, and so on—but they are different. Arithmetic operations can be performed on numbers but not on numerals. Although they look like numbers, numerals are simply symbols. You use numerals all the time. When watching a football game and cheering for "numbers" 44 and 89, are you really cheering for "number" 133, or are you cheering for the two people wearing jerseys with the symbols 44 and 89? Of course you're cheering for the two players and *not* the number 133. The numbers on the jerseys are really numerals. How does this distinction help us? Think about the fact that data are in variable form.

Nominal variables simply classify. The attributes male and female are categories on the nominal variable gender. How would you code the attributes? We could assign 1 to male and 2 to female. Or, we could assign 2 to male and 1 to female. Or, we could assign 6 to male and 22 to female. Any one of these coding schemes would be permissible because the nominal level of measurement simply classifies. There is no order to the attributes. The coding scheme assigns numerals as symbols for the various categories. After all, if we assigned a 1 to the attribute male and a 2 to the attribute female, we could not add two males together to obtain a female! So, at the nominal level we arbitrarily assign numerals to attributes.

At the ordinal level there is an order to the attributes. For example, suppose you were working with the variable class standing (freshman, sophomore, junior, senior). What coding scheme would you use? Would you feel comfortable with 1,2,3,4? How about 4,3,2,1? Or how about 2,3,4,1? The first two schemes seem okay, and the last one is awful. Why? The first two coding schemes reflect the order exhibited by the attributes. The codes in the first scheme (1,2,3,4) increase as class standing increases. In the second scheme (4,3,2,1), the codes decrease as class standing increases. In the third scheme (2,3,4,1), however, there is no order to the code assignment. The codes do not reflect the order exhibited by the attributes.

When working with ordinal data, therefore, we assign codes to reflect the order of the attributes. Are these codes numerals or numbers? Research methodologists are currently debating this question. In this book, however, we will take a conservative approach and treat ordinal codes as numerals. After all, as with males and females, if freshmen were assigned the code of 1 and sophomores the code of 2, two freshmen would not equal one sophomore.

At the interval and ratio levels of measurement, variables have a unit of measurement. These codes represent numbers! To code interval and ratio data, we typically code the reported information. For example, if income data were collected at the ratio level, and responses included $10,000, $43,500, and $6,335, we would code them as 10000, 43500, and 6335. Similarly, if age data were collected, we could easily code responses of 20, 35, and 42 years as 20, 35, and 42.

C H E C K P O I N T

4. Code the attributes for the following variables:
   a. Number of times voted Republican (0,1,2, and so on)
   b. Family size (small, medium, large)
   c. Type of beer (Schlitz, Budweiser, Coors, other)

   d. Attitude toward drafting women (strongly agree, agree, undecided, disagree, strongly disagree)

   e. Marital status (never married, married, widowed, divorced, separated)

   f. Family size (number of siblings)

Coding Data Onto Cards/Terminal Lines

After the data is coded, the next step is either to keypunch it onto cards
in preparation for the card reader or to type it into a terminal. The
process of punching data onto cards will be discussed here in detail and
terminal input will be discussed briefly. The later uses the same logic
as card punching.

   As described in chapter 1, the computer card is 80 columns long
and has rows numbered from 0 to 9. Think of each column or combination of columns as a variable and the rows as the attributes of the
variable. For example, suppose you had the following variables and attributes: gender—(1) male, (2) female; education—coded as years of
school completed, with possible codes of 0 to 25 grades; religion—(1)
Catholic, (2) Jewish, (3) Protestant, (4) other. How would you transfer
responses on these three variables to a computer card?

   Suppose we use one computer card (record) for each respondent.
Let's set aside column 1 on the computer card for the variable gender.
When a respondent is male we keypunch a 1 in column 1, and when
the respondent is female we punch a 2 in column 1. In looking at the
codes for education, we notice they can run from 0 to 25. Therefore,
we need two columns to represent the variable education. Let's desig-
nate columns 2 and 3 for education. If a respondent said he or she had
a tenth-grade education, we'd keypunch a 1 in column 2 and a 0 in
column 3. If 16 grades were completed, we'd punch a 1 in column 2
and a 6 in column 3. If the respondent completed eighth grade, we'd
punch a 0 in column 2 and an 8 in column 3.

   For religion we need only 1 column, so let's assign column 4 to
religion. For respondents indicating that they are Jewish we keypunch
a 2 in column 4. Respondents indicating that they are Protestant get a
punch of 3 in column 4. After all the variable information for each
respondent is keypunched, our data are ready for the computer. A data
card for a respondent who was male, a college graduate, and Catholic
is shown in figure 2-1. If this were typed on a terminal, the terminal
line would show the numbers 1161.

   Notice that we worked with one record (card) per respondent. If
you need more than 80 columns to represent the variables, you will
need more than one record (card) for each respondent. A good practice
in coding data is to allocate columns for a respondent identification
number and a card number. The identification number is a unique
number assigned to each respondent, and the card number simply

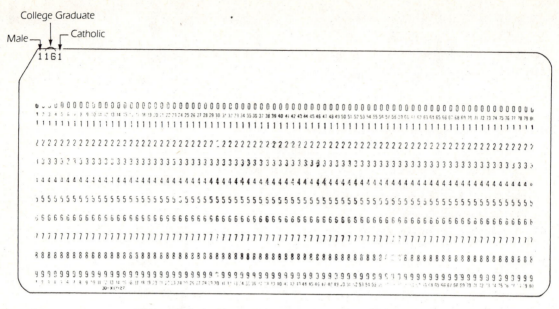

Figure 2-1 A data card for a male, Catholic, college graduate.

numbers the cards. For example, if you had 3500 respondents and four cards of information per respondent, you might set aside columns 1–4 and column 5 on each computer card for a respondent identification number (0001 to 3500) and the card number (1–4). Why do this? Suppose you dropped the data deck. Imagine trying to reassemble 14,000 cards (3500 × 4) in the proper order without that information!

C H E C K P O I N T

5. You collected data on the following variables for 320 respondents. Allocate card columns to these variables.

   a. Identification number

   b. Card number

   c. Sex (male, female)

   d. Political party preference (Democrat, Republican, other)

   e. Age (age at last birthday)

   f. Education (last year in school completed)

   g. Number of siblings

If you prefer working at a terminal, treat each line on your screen or printer as if it were 80 columns long. Each line therefore represents a computer card, and you can proceed in the fashion already described. Once the data are ready for the computer, we need a program to tell the computer what to do with the data. But before we get started on writing programs with SPSS[x] try the following checkpoint.

C H E C K P O I N T

6. You collected data on respondent's age (age at last birthday), education (last year in school completed), birth sign (Libra, Gemini, and so on), gender, and belief in UFOs (strongly believe, believe, undecided, disbelieve, strongly disbelieve) for 452 respondents.

   a. At what level is each variable measured?

   b. Code the variable's attributes.

   c. Assign card columns/terminal columns to each variable.

   d. Show the computer cards/terminal lines for the following five cases:

   Case 1: 21 years old, completed high school, Capricorn, male, strongly believes in UFOs

   Case 2: 54 years old, college graduate, Scorpio, female, undecided on UFOs

   Case 3: 10 years old, completed fourth grade, Libra, male, believes in UFOs

   Case 4: 38 years old, completed high school, Gemini, female, strongly disbelieves in UFOs

   Case 5: 32 years old, college graduate, Gemini, female, believes in UFOs

chapter 3
An Introduction to SPSS^X Programs

In chapter 2 we coded data for computer input. We are now ready to write programs to manipulate and analyze the data. Many of the examples and problems used in this text are based on the data set described in Appendix A. The data have already been coded and are ready for your use. Check with your instructor for specific information on how to access the data, since I cannot give you this information.

The reason I cannot give you these specifics is that they are computer or system dependent. As you know, there are many different brands and models of computers on the market (Hewlett-Packard, IBM, UNIVAC, and so on). Each computer brand, computer model, and installation (the site where a computer is located) has its own unique way of telling the computer how to access data and run programs. The unique way of telling a computer how to do something is accomplished with **system language**. Although the SPSS^X program remains the same, the specifics of accessing the SPSS^X package or retrieving data depend upon the computer brand and model, as well as the installation. Therefore, since the specifics are computer dependent, your instructor will explain the system language needed to access the data and the SPSS^X package.

In this chapter you will begin to learn the SPSS^X language. Remember, SPSS^X is not system dependent. What you learn about SPSS^X will work on any computer that has the SPSS^X software. In this chapter we will examine selected SPSS^X commands for defining data when the data are connected to the SPSS^X program. In addition, we will discuss some commands that enable you to control the appearance of your printout.

The chapter is divided into three sections: general SPSS^X information, data definition commands, and printout control commands. In the next chapter we will discuss selected data transformation and file manipulation commands. Upon completion of this chapter, you should be able to do the following:

1. Explain the basic format for an SPSS^X command
2. Explain selected data definition commands
3. Write data definition commands
4. Explain selected printout control commands
5. Write printout control commands

General SPSS^X Information

All SPSS^X commands begin in column 1 of a computer card or terminal line. Commands continue for as many cards/lines as are necessary. The continuation cards/lines *do not* begin in column 1. The continuation lines must be indented *at least* one column. Therefore, you may continue on card/line 2, column 2, or card/line 2, column 6, and so on. Where you actually choose to begin the continuation is simply a matter of style. For example, although the appearance of the following two MISSING VALUES commands differ, they give the computer identical information:

```
MISSING VALUES RACE (7,8) ED (97,98,99) SALARY (99999999)

MISSING VALUES RACE (7,8)
 ED(97,98,99)
 SALARY (99999999)
```

By the way, you're right if you're thinking that we haven't discussed the MISSING VALUES command. We will, shortly!

Commands and Specifications

Most SPSS^X commands have two parts, a **command keyword** and a **specification field**. The command keyword tells the computer that you wish to use a certain procedure. The specification field indicates which information you want used. For example, someone may tell you, "Run." You naturally respond, "Where?" "Run" is the command and the answer to "where?" is the specification. Your friend could respond, "Run to first base," or "Run to the store," or "Run to the library," and so on. The command (run) remains unchanged; the specification (first base, store, library, and so on) changes.

More methodologically, you may have data on 12 variables and wish to have frequency counts on only three. To obtain tallies, you would use the command keyword FREQUENCIES. You would name the three variables to be tallied in the specification field. Later in the analyses you may wish to have tallies on two more variables. What do you do? You use the FREQUENCIES command again and change the specification field to name the two other variables. By the way, the FREQUENCIES command will be discussed in chapter 5.

Defaults

Many SPSS^X commands have what are called **defaults**. Defaults are the instructions assumed by SPSS^X when you give either incomplete or no specifications. For example, as mentioned earlier, you may have a great deal of information on each case. You may have so much data that five records are required to code the information for each respondent. You must tell SPSS^X that you have five records per respondent. If you do not, SPSS^X will assume that there is one record of data per case. One record is the default for SPSS^X. Clearly, if SPSS^X assumes one record per respondent and you have five, there is a big problem! However, if you really have one record of data per case, you do not need to make the record number specification. SPSS^X's default for record number is one, and that fits your data. Now that you have a grasp of SPSS^X commands in general, what should we tell the computer?

Data Definition Commands

The first thing we want to do is tell the computer about the data. We want to tell it how we coded the data, where the data are located, and so on. To do this, SPSS^X contains several data definition commands: DATA LIST, VARIABLE LABELS, VALUE LABELS, and MISSING VALUES. The DATA LIST and MISSING VALUES commands enable us to describe the data set to the computer. The VARIABLE LABELS and VALUE LABELS commands help make the computer output more readable. Let's examine each one in detail.

Data List Command

The DATA LIST command is used to assign names to variables and to describe the location and format of the variables. A typical DATA LIST command reads as follows:

```
DATA LIST FILE=INLINE RECORDS=2
 /1 ID 1-3 SEX 4 RACE 5
 /2 ED 10-11 SALARY 12-19(2)
```

What have we told the computer? First, we told the computer that our data set is part of the SPSS^X program. How did we do that? The specification FILE=INLINE tells the computer that the data is included as part of the program. If we omit the specification FILE=INLINE,

SPSS[X] will assume that the data are attached to the program, because that's the default. So when the data are attached, the command

```
DATA LIST FILE=INLINE RECORDS=2
```

is equivalent to

```
DATA LIST RECORDS=2
```

But what do we mean by an attached data set? We mean that the data are part of the SPSS[X] job. For example, if our data were on cards, it would mean that we keypunched our SPSS[X] program, added the data cards, and submitted the combined deck to the card reader.

Second, we told the computer how many records (cards) there are for each respondent. In this example the specification RECORDS=2 indicates two cards for each respondent. If we omitted the RECORDS=2 specification, SPSS[X] would assume one record per case. One record is the default.

Third, we told the computer that the data is in **fixed format**. Fixed format means that, for each case, each variable is located on the same card and in the same columns. Using the above DATA LIST, this means that, for all respondents, sex is coded on card 1, column 4, and education data are coded on card 2, columns 10 and 11. There are other ways to format data. In this text, however, fixed format data are assumed. Notice that you do not see the term *fixed format* in the above data list. Why? SPSS[X] assumes fixed format data as its default. If you are working with data in another format, you must specify otherwise. Check the sources in the bibliography for assistance.

Thus far we have used the DATA LIST command to tell the computer about our data file—that it's part of the SPSS[X] job, that there are two records per case, and that the data are in fixed format. Now we need to tell the computer about our variables.

Variable definition information begins with the slash. The number after the slash indicates the record (card) to be described. The /1 means that we are describing the data contained on card 1. Next, we named three variables on card 1—ID, SEX, and RACE. Attached to these names are the column(s) in which the variables were coded. Thus, we told the computer that columns 1, 2, and 3 (1–3), column 4, and column 5 would be called ID, SEX, and RACE, respectively. We have now completely described the information on the DATA LIST command for card 1.

Now let's examine card 2. How do we do that? The /2 tells the computer to turn to card 2. Notice that on card 2 we chose to have the computer ignore the information contained in columns 1 through 9. For some reason that data did not interest us. So we began card 2's description with column 10. Card 2, columns 10 and 11 (10–11) contain the ED variable and columns 12,13,14,15,16,17,18, and 19 (12–19) contain SALARY data. But what is that (2) after 12–19?

The (2) tells the computer that the last two columns, 18 and 19, follow an implied decimal point. For example, suppose a respondent listed $15,300.45 under salary. How would we have coded that, and how would we tell the computer to read it? Did you say 01530045 starting in column 12? Great! If not, recall from chapter 2 that we would have coded a 0 in column 12, a 1 in column 13, a 5 in column 14, a 3 in column 15, a 0 in column 16, a 0 in column 17, a 4 in column 18, and a 5 in column 19.

Notice that we did not code the dollar sign, the comma, or the decimal point. We know that salary data is expressed in dollars, and therefore the dollar sign is omitted. We also know that $15,300.45 and 15300.45 are equivalent expressions, and therefore we do not code the comma. The decimal point is important. In the DATA LIST command we specify that two numbers come after a decimal point with the (2) specification. The 12–19(2) information tells the computer that columns 18 and 19, the last two columns, follow an implied decimal point. A variable coded on the DATA LIST card as 10–14(3) would indicate that columns 10, 11, 12, 13, and 14 contain the variable's data and that there is an implied decimal after column 11. If the codes 87625 and 22987 appeared in those columns, they would actually represent the numbers 87.625 and 22.987.

In summary, with the DATA LIST command we tell the computer that the data file is attached to the SPSSˣ program, and we specify the number of records/cards per respondent, the names of our variables, and the record and columns in which each variable is located. Some guidelines for this command include the following:

1. Variable names can be no longer than eight characters.
2. In general, variable names should begin with a letter of the alphabet. There are exceptions to this guideline, but that would take another book!
3. Names should be selected that have meaning for you. For example, EDUCATION is too long, nine characters. But the two-character ED probably conveys the same meaning.

C H E C K P O I N T

1. Interpret the following DATA LIST command:

```
DATA LIST FILE=INFILE RECORDS=3
 /1 ID 1-5 SEX 6 RACE 7 AGE 8-9 SALARY 10-17(2)
 /2 PRACTICE 5 FIRM 6 YEARS 7-9(1)
 /3 SAT 1
```

2. Write a DATA LIST command for the AGE, SIBS, WRKSTAT, REGION, SMOKE, and TRAUMA variables contained in Appendix A.

MISSING VALUES Command

The MISSING VALUES command is used to remove codes associated with certain attributes on a variable(s) from the analysis. A typical MISSING VALUES command reads as follows:

```
MISSING VALUES RACE(7,8) ED(97,98,99)
 SALARY (99999999)
```

What have we told the computer? We told it to omit the 7 and 8 codes on the RACE variable, the 97,98, and 99 codes on the ED variable, and the 99999999 code on the SALARY variable from the analysis. But why should we ignore these codes and "throw away" data?

The MISSING VALUES command does not throw data away. There are times when an attribute(s) on a variable, and therefore a code, will be irrelevant for your analysis. For example, it may be that codes 7 and 8 on RACE represent refused to answer and no answer, respectively. If you planned to compare white and nonwhite respondents, you would not be able to do anything with people who either refused to answer or simply did not answer the race question. You could not categorize them on race, and therefore you would want to exclude the codes for refused to answer and no answer from your analysis.

The same logic may hold for ED and SALARY. The 97,98, and 99 codes may coincide with don't know, refused to answer, and no answer for the education variable. The 99999999 code may correspond to refused to answer on SALARY. If you planned to compare the "average" educational levels of whites and nonwhites or the "average" salary for various educational levels, you need education and salary data. When data are lacking or of no interest, we exclude data from the analysis by using the MISSING VALUES command to declare codes as missing.

Do not assume, however, that you will always declare don't know, refused to answer, and no answer as missing. If you planned an analysis to compare the sex of those who refused to give salary data with those who did respond, you would not define refused to answer on SALARY as a missing value. If you did, you wouldn't be able to do the intended analysis. Remember that the decision to declare a code as missing is based on what codes you need for the analysis. Guidelines for the MISSING VALUES command include the following:

1. You can only declare values as missing for variables that were previously named in the DATA LIST command.
2. Be sure to match names. For example, if you called the education variable ED in the DATA LIST command, you cannot call it EDUC on the MISSING VALUES card. If you do, the program will abort in confusion!
3. No more than three values can be declared as missing per variable. So, for ED we could declare (97,98,99) as missing, but declaring (96,97,98,99) as missing would result in an error message. We could,

however, specify a range of missing values by using the THRU key-word. For example, (96 THRU 98,99) or (96 THRU 99) results in the codes of 96, 97, 98, and 99 being declared missing,

4. You may use commas or spaces to separate codes, but in either case, values must be enclosed in parentheses. Thus, (96,97,98) and (96 97 98) are equivalent expressions.

C H E C K P O I N T

3. Interpret the following MISSING VALUES command:

```
MISSING VALUES AGE (98,99) SALARY (99999997,99999998)
 PRACTICE(4) FIRM(6,7)
```

4. Write the MISSING VALUES command for the AGE, SIBS, and TVHOURS variables contained in Appendix A. You're right—you can't do a MISSING VALUES command unless you know what attributes are to be considered missing! Suppose you were interested in knowing whether actual age and number of siblings affects the number of hours spent watching TV. Now write the command.

VARIABLE LABELS Command

The VARIABLE LABELS command is used when the eight-character variable name used in the DATA LIST card is insufficient to recall the variable fully. A typical VARIABLE LABELS command reads as follows:

```
VARIABLE LABELS ED "RESPONDENT'S EDUCATION"
 SALARY "R'S GROSS INCOME"
```

What have we told the computer? We told the computer to attach the label RESPONDENT'S EDUCATION to the variable ED. Why do this? After all, we know that ED represents education. Well, we could have an ED1 in the same data set, representing the respondent's spouse's education. The label appears in the printout to remind you that ED, not ED1, represents the respondent's education. The salary label reminds us that the SALARY variable represents gross income. We could have a variable SALARY1 that contains information on net income. The VARIABLE LABELS command helps us to identify our variables easily.

The following VARIABLE LABELS command would not work. See if you can figure out why.

```
VARIABLE LABELS ED "RESPONDENT'S EDUCATION" SALARY "R'S
 GROSS INCOME"
```

It wouldn't work because you cannot split the label onto a continuation card unless you include a plus sign. The following command and continuation card would work:

```
VARIABLE LABELS ED "RESPONDENT'S EDUCATION" SALARY
  "R'S" + "GROSS INCOME"
```

Guidelines for the VARIABLE LABELS command include the following:

1. The variable you assign a label to must have been previously defined in the DATA LIST command.
2. Labels can be no longer than 40 characters including spaces.
3. Labels cannot be continued onto another line unless the continuation is preceded by a plus sign.

C H E C K P O I N T

5. Interpret the following VARIABLE LABELS command:

```
VARIABLE LABELS AGE "AGE AT LAST BIRTHDAY" SALARY "NET
  + INCOME FROM LAW PRACTICE" PRACTICE "DOMINANT TYPE OF
  + CASES" FIRM "NUMBER OF ATTORNEYS IN FIRM"
  + YEARS "YEARS SINCE LAW SCHOOL GRADUATION"
```

6. Write a VARIABLE LABELS card for the SIBS, INCOME, MEMNUM, and WRKSTAT variables contained in Appendix A.

VALUE LABELS Command

The VALUE LABELS command is used to name the codes or attributes on the variables. The logic behind this command is similar to that behind the VARIABLE LABELS command. It aids your memory by attaching the code labels to the printout. A typical VALUE LABELS command reads as follows:

```
VALUE LABELS SEX 1 'MALE' 2 'FEMALE'/
  RACE 1 'NONWHITE' 2 'WHITE' 3 'REFUSED'
```

What have we told the computer? We've told it that for the variable SEX, a code of 1 stands for male and a code of 2 represents female. We stated that codes of 1, 2, and 3 on RACE represent nonwhite, white, and refused, respectively. Notice that variables are separated with a slash. Guidelines for this command include the following

1. The variable whose codes you are assigning labels to must have been defined in the DATA LIST command.
2. Labels can be no longer than 20 characters, including spaces.
3. Labels must be enclosed in quotation marks or apostrophes.

1 'NONWHITE' 2 'WHITE' 3 'REFUSED' is equivalent to 1 "NONWHITE" 2 "WHITE" 3 "REFUSED".

4. Slashes are used to separate value labels for one variable from another. In the above example, the labels for SEX and RACE were separated by a slash.

C H E C K P O I N T

---

7. Interpret the following VALUE LABELS command:

```
VALUE LABELS SEX 1 'FEMALE' 2 'MALE'/
RACE 1 'WHITE' 2 'NONWHITE'/
FIRM 1 'SOLE' 2 'TWO TO FIVE' 3 'SIX OR MORE'
4 'REFUSED'
```

8. Write a VALUE LABELS command for the SEX, WRKSTAT, MARITAL, and DEGREE variables contained in Appendix A.

9. Would a VALUE LABELS command that included labels for the AGE and SIBS variables contained in Appendix A be helpful? Why or why not?

We have examined two SPSS^x commands that enable you to describe your data to the computer: DATA LIST and MISSING VALUES. Two other commands, VARIABLE LABELS and VALUE LABELS, allow you to document your output. Only one of these commands is required for an SPSS^x run. The other three are useful, but the program would run without them. If you guessed that the DATA LIST command is the required command, you're correct. This command describes the data to the computer. The VARIABLE LABELS and the VALUE LABELS commands assist your memory. The MISSING VALUES command is useful only if you wish to exclude codes from the analysis. Although the DATA LIST command is the only required command, I recommend that you assist your memory by utilizing the other commands!

When the raw data are attached to the SPSS^x program, two other commands are required, BEGIN DATA and END DATA. The BEGIN DATA command appears before the first data card as its name implies, and the END DATA command follows the last data record. A typical setup for an SPSS^x run is as follows:

```
SYSTEM LANGUAGE cards (see your instructor)
DATA LIST
VARIABLE LABELS
VALUE LABELS
MISSING VALUES
```

```
FREQUENCIES (we will discuss this soon)
BEGIN DATA
01034567
02345679
03216744
04789999
05389875
       .
       .
       .
END DATA
```

The cards beginning with 01, 02, 03, 04, 05, ., ., and . are the data cards.

Printout Control Commands

In addition to data definition commands, there are commands that allow you to control some characteristics of your printout. They are TITLE, COMMENT, NUMBERED, UNNUMBERED, and EDIT. None of these commands is required for a run, but you will find that they help to make your printout more readable.

TITLE Command

The TITLE command enables you to print a title at the start of each printout page. This is a very useful command if you plan to do more than one computer run or run several procedures in one run. Instead of thumbing through pages of printout, you can look at the name of the run and know whether you have the printout you want. The general form for this command is as follows:

```
TITLE "MY FIRST SPSSˣ FREQUENCIES RUN"
```

The above title tells the computer to start each printout page with the header MY FIRST SPSSˣ FREQUENCIES RUN. Guidelines for this command include the following:

1. The title can be no longer than 60 characters.
2. Quotation marks or apostrophes can be used to enclose the title. If quotation marks are used on the outside, apostrophes are used within the title, and if apostrophes are used on the outside, double apostrophes are used within the title. The command

    ```
    TITLE 'LAWYERS''S INCOME'
    ```

    is equivalent to the command

    ```
    TITLE "LAWYER'S INCOME"
    ```

3. You can use as many TITLE commands in a run as you want.

COMMENT Command

The COMMENT command enables you to add descriptive statements about your program. It is useful for refreshing your memory or assisting others in examining your printout. A typical COMMENT command reads as follows:

```
COMMENT TREATING THE REFUSED TO ANSWER AS MISSING VALUES
```

NUMBERED and UNNUMBERED Commands

The NUMBERED and UNNUMBERED commands can be used to number the lines in your printout. Some programming languages automatically reserve columns 73–80 for line numbering. Other programming languages use columns 73–80 for their data and program. The NUMBERED command means that you have reserved 73–80 for numbering, and the UNNUMBERED command means that data or program information is stored in those columns. If, for example, you have data extending into column 75, you would want to use the UNNUMBERED command. The NUMBERED and UNNUMBERED commands stand alone; there are no specifications. One of these commands is the default option at your computer site. Check with your instructor for that information.

EDIT Command

The EDIT command enables you to check the syntax of other commands without actually running the program. Although this command can be placed anywhere in the program, only commands appearing after the EDIT command are actually checked. I therefore recommend that you use this as your first command. All succeeding commands will be checked for spelling, some consistency, and so on. The EDIT command should allow you to catch and correct errors before executing your program. EDIT is a one-word command. When you are finally ready to execute the program, you *must* remove the edit card.

C H E C K P O I N T

10. The following SPSS^x program makes use of all the commands described in this chapter. It also includes the FREQUENCIES command, which we will discuss in chapter 5. Interpret the commands and specifications used in this run.

```
EDIT
UNNUMBERED
TITLE "A FREQUENCIES RUN ON THE OCCUPATIONAL MOBILITY
  DATA, 1983, N=2500"
DATA LIST RECORDS=5/
 1 ID 1-4 SEX 5 RACE 6 AGE 7-9(1)/2 ED 10-11 PAED 12-13/
 3 MAED 12-13 SIBS 14/4 ROCC 8 POCC 9 MOCC 10/5 STATUS 8
 INCOME 9
MISSING VALUES AGE(997,998,999) ED(98,99) PAED(98,99)
 MAED(98,99) SIBS(7,8,9) ROCC(9) POCC(9) MOCC(9)
 STATUS(9) INCOME(5)
VARIABLE LABELS ED "R'S EDUCATION" PAED "R'S FATHER'S ED"
 MAED "R'S MOTHER'S ED" SIBS "ANY SIBLINGS"
 ROCC "R'S OCCUPATION" POCC "R'S FATHER'S OCCUPATION"
 MOCC "R'S MOTHER'S OCCUPATION" STATUS "SUBJECTIVE STATUS"
 INCOME "DID R PAY INCOME TAX IN 1983?"
VALUE LABELS SEX 1 'MALE' 2 'FEMALE'/
 RACE 1 'WHITE' 2 'NONWHITE'/
 AGE 997 'DON'T KNOW' 998 'NO ANSWER' 999 'REFUSED'/
 SIBS 1 'YES' 2 'NO'/ROCC 1 'BLUE COLLAR' 2 'WHITE COLLAR'/
 POCC 1 'BLUE COLLAR' 2 'WHITE COLLAR'/
 MOCC 1 'BLUE COLLAR' 2 'WHITE COLLAR'/
 STATUS 1 'LOW' 2 'MIDDLE' 3 'HIGH' 9 'NO ANSWER'/
 INCOME 1 'YES' 2 'NO' 3 'DON'T RECALL' 5 'REFUSED'
FREQUENCIES (to be discussed)
BEGIN DATA
000112234...
000222324...
000312456...
000421999...
000512435...

      .
      .
      .

2500312456
END DATA
```

chapter 4
Selected SPSS^X Data Transformation and System File Commands

In the last chapter we examined several SPSS^X data definition and printout control commands. Those commands enable you to begin data analysis. Many times, however, data analyses require the transformation of variables—that is, the creation of new variables from variables already existing in the data, or the modification of already existing variables. After transforming data, we typically keep the changes. System files are often used to save the data transformations.

In this chapter we examine selected data transformation and system file commands. Upon completion of this chapter, you should be able to do the following:

1. Explain what is meant by data transformation
2. Describe situations in which you would want to transform data
3. Explain selected data transformation procedures
4. Write data transformation commands
5. Describe selected system file commands
6. Write system file commands

Selected Data Transformation Commands

Data transformations are a routine part of data cleaning and data analyses. For example, keypunch or coding errors may appear in the data. These errors need to be corrected before an analysis is begun. You can use the computer to make the corrections. Or, for another example, you may decide that instead of comparing workers' incomes at every educational level, you want to compare income data for people who did not complete high school with those who did complete high school. SPSS[x] data transformation commands allow you to do these transformations quickly and efficiently. Popular data transformation commands include the RECODE, COMPUTE, and SELECT IF commands.

RECODE Command

The RECODE command allows you to collapse the categories or revise the coding scheme of a variable previously defined in the DATA LIST command. You can make changes on a code-by-code basis, or you can alter codes for a range of values.

For example, suppose your data set included a two-column variable, ED, coded as last year in school completed. A 00 code meant no formal schooling, a 01 code meant completion of first grade, a 08 code meant completion of eighth grade, a 16 code meant completion of college, and so on. Suppose you decide that you really want to compare the incomes of people with less than a high school education with those who completed high school, with those who completed some college, with college graduates, and with those who completed postgraduate education. What do you do? Your data were collected to reflect last year in school completed, not to indicate less than high school, high school, some college, and so on. Do you need to collect more data?

First, don't despair. Your data are good, and you don't have to collect more. Think about the level of measurement discussion in chapter 2. The original two-column ED variable was measured at the ratio level. You now want to treat ED as an ordinal variable. Can it be done? Yes. Remember, you can always collapse a higher level of measurement to a lower level of measurement. Use the following RECODE command to collapse categories on the variable ED:

```
RECODE ED (0=1) (2=1) (3=1) (4=1) (5=1) (6=1)
  (7=1) (8=1) (9=1) (10=1) (11=1) (12=2) (13=3)
  (14=3) (15=3) (16=4) (17=5)
```

We have now told the computer to recode the variable ED by recoding the 0 code to 1, the 2 code to 1, the 3 code to 1, the 4 code to 1, and so on. We have, therefore, grouped the original codes of 0 to 11 together and coded them as 1. We have then coded 12 as 2, 13 to 15 as 3, 16 as 4, and 17 as 5. The codes of 1,2,3,4, and 5 correspond to the attributes less than high school, high school, some college, and so on. Notice that there is no (1=1) in the recode statement. The 1 is already coded as 1.

You may be thinking that the RECODE command requires quite a bit of typing, and fortunately, the SPSS[x] programmers agreed. There are specifications that shorten the command. The following RECODE command is equivalent to the previous command:

```
RECODE ED (0 THRU 11=1) (12=2) (13,14,15=3) (16=4)
  (17=5)
```

Instead of recoding on a code-by-code basis, we have told the computer via the THRU specification to take the codes 0 through 11 (0,1,2,3,4,5,6,7,8,9,10, and 11) and code them as 1. Instead of typing (13=3) (14=3) (15=3), we shortened our work by typing RECODE (13,14,15=3). Can you think of another way of doing that same recode? Good, (13 THRU 15=3) works. Notice that SPSS^x will accept codes of 1, 2, 3, and so on, in place of 00, 01, 02, and so on. Whenever the variable name ED appears in your program after you have used the RECODE command, the reference is to the new, recoded ED variable.

Sometimes you want to utilize both the old and the newly recoded variable in your analysis. To do this requires one addition to the RECODE command. The following RECODE command recodes the variable ED into a new variable, ED1, and saves the old ED variable with its coding scheme.

```
RECODE ED (0 THRU 11=1) (12=2) (13,14,15=3) (16=4)
  (17=5) INTO ED1
```

The addition of the INTO specification and the new variable's name results in the retention of both the old and the new coding schemes. You can now use either variable, ED or ED1, in your analysis.

Guidelines for the RECODE command include the following:

1. The recode is performed from left to right. The RECODE command FAM (0=1) (1=2) (2=3) recodes the 0, 1, and 2 codes to 1, 2, and 3. Moving from left to right, 0's were recoded to 1's, 1's were recoded to 2's, and 2's were recoded to 3's. The end result of this recode is that cases originally coded on FAM as 0, 1, 2 are now coded as 1, 2, 3. Think through, from left to right, how you want the final codes to look as the values are recoded only once per RECODE command.

2. Values of a variable not mentioned in the RECODE command are left unchanged. Suppose, for example, the variable FAM had codes 0,1,2,3,4,5. What does the following RECODE command tell the computer?

```
RECODE FAM (0,1,2=1) (3=2)
```

It says to recode the 0 and 2 codes to a 1 code and change the original 3 code to a 2 code. The original codes of 4 and 5 remain as 4 and 5.

3. You may recode more than one variable at a time by separating the variables with a slash. For example, the following RECODE would alter the codes for the ED and AGE variables:

```
RECODE ED (0 THRU 11=1) (12=2)/AGE (0 THRU 12=1)
  (13 THRU 19=2) (20,21=3)
```

The original 0,1,2,3,4,5,6,7,8,9,10, and 11 codes on ED would become 1, and the 12 code would become 2. On the AGE variable, the original ages of 0,1,2,3,4,5,6,7,8,9,10,11, and 12 would be recoded as 1. The codes 13,14,15,16,17,18, and 19 would be recoded as 2, and the codes 20 and 21 would become 3.

CHECKPOINT

1. Is there a difference between the following two RECODE commands? Explain.

```
RECODE TIME (0=1) (1=2) (2=3)
RECODE TIME (2=3) (1=2) (0=1)
```

2. Explain the following RECODE commands:

   a. RECODE SAT (0,2=1) (3=2) (4,5=3)

   b. RECODE SAT (0,2=1) (3=2) (4,5=3) INTO SAT1

   c. RECODE INCOME (0 THRU 10000=1) (10001 THRU 20000=2) INTO LOWMID/FUN (7,8=9)

3. Using the SIBS and INCOME variables in Appendix A, write a RECODE command to

   a. regroup SIBS into the following categories: only child, 1–3 siblings, 4–8 siblings, 9–11 siblings, and 12 or more siblings.

   b. create a new variable that regroups INCOME into the following categories: less than $9,999, $10,000 to $19,999, and $20,000 or more. Group the refused, don't knows, and no answers together in the new variable.

MISSING VALUES and the RECODE Command: The last checkpoint exercise raises an important question. What happens if you're recoding a variable that has a code declared missing in a missing values command? Is that code automatically treated as missing in the transformed variable? No. You will have to declare the newly recoded variable's values as missing in another MISSING VALUES command. There are, however, at least two ways of declaring a recoded variable's values as missing.

Let's work with the TVHOURS variable located in Appendix A. Suppose we had declared the don't know and no answer responses as missing. Now we decide that we really want to compare people who watch four or fewer hours of TV with people who watch five or more hours. Furthermore, we still want to exclude the don't knows and the no answers from the analysis. What do we do? One option is to use the following series of commands:

```
MISSING VALUES TVHOURS(98,99)
RECODE TVHOURS (0 THRU 4=1) (5 THRU 18=2) INTO NEWTV
MISSING VALUES NEWTV(98,99)
```

What have we told the computer? We told it that the codes of 98 and 99 for TVHOURS were missing values. We then recoded TVHOURS and retained the new version as a variable called NEWTV. NEWTV is the two-category variable of interest. Since we did not mention the 98 and 99 codes on the recode statement, they were left unchanged. Note, however, that their missing value status was not retained. Therefore, we wrote another MISSING VALUES command to declare the codes of 98 and 99 as missing on NEWTV.

A second way of handling missing values on a RECODE command is to use the MISSING specification. This specification recodes all previously declared missing values into a newly specified value. You must still, however, declare the new value as missing in another MISSING VALUES command. The following commands illustrate the use of the MISSING specification:

```
MISSING VALUES TVHOURS(98,99)
RECODE TVHOURS (0 THRU 4=1) (5 THRU 18=2) (MISSING=5)
 INTO NEWTV
MISSING VALUES NEWTV(5)
```

What have we told the computer? With the first MISSING VALUES command we told the computer that the 98 and 99 codes on TVHOURS are missing. Next, we told the computer to recode TVHOURS into a two-category variable, NEWTV. The (MISSING=5) specification tells the computer to take all the codes declared as missing for TVHOURS, 98 and 99, and set them equal to the value 5. The second MISSING VALUES statement tells the computer to treat the code of 5 on NEWTV as missing.

C H E C K P O I N T

4. Using the MEMNUM variable from Appendix A, explain what set A and B instructions tell the computer. Is there a difference between these two sets of instructions? If yes, what is it? If no, why not?

Set A Instructions

```
MISSING VALUES MEMNUM(99)
RECODE MEMNUM (0,1,2=1) (3 THRU 6=2) (7 THRU 18=3)
 INTO ORGS
```

Set B Instructions

```
MISSING VALUES MEMNUM(99)
RECODE MEMNUM (0,1,2=1) (3 THRU 6=2) (7 THRU 18=3)
 INTO ORGS
MISSING VALUES ORGS(99)
```

COMPUTE Command

The COMPUTE command is used to create a new variable from variables already in your data. For example, suppose you had data on the number of live births (NBIRTH) and the number of women in the population between 15 and 44 (NWOMEN) for 45 countries. If you were a demographer or someone interested in population, you might want to examine the general fertility rate (GFR) for the 45 countries. The general fertility rate compares countries on the number of births per 1000 women between the ages of 15 to 44. Why 15 to 44? Those are considered the prime childbearing years. Although you may not have the variable GFR in your data, it can easily be calculated. Here is the formula for the GFR:

$$\text{GFR} = \frac{\text{number of births}}{\text{number of women aged 15-44}} \times 1000$$

We now have a choice. We could let the computer calculate the GFR, or we could sit down with a hand calculator and do the calculations ourselves. What should we do? Let the computer do the work! We can do the same things a computer does; after all, we program the computer. However, the computer will be quicker. In addition, we won't have to recheck each calculation. To tell the computer to calculate GFR, use the following COMPUTE command:

```
COMPUTE GFR=(NBIRTH/NWOMEN)*1000
```

What have we told the computer? We told it to take the two variables already in our data, NBIRTH and NWOMEN, divide (/) NBIRTH by NWOMEN, and then multiply (*) that result by 1000. Upon completing the arithmetic for each country, the computer is to call the resulting number GFR. We have now added a new variable, GFR, to our data.

How did we know that the / symbol meant division? Why doesn't the expression for GFR say to multiply the number of women by 1000 and then divide that result into the number of births? To answer those questions, let's look at the arithmetic operations that can be used in the COMPUTE command and the order in which operations are carried out.

Arithmetic Operations and Functions: The following arithmetic operations can be performed in the COMPUTE command:

- Addition   +
- Subtraction   −
- Multiplication   *
- Division   /
- Exponentiation   **

In addition to these operations, SPSS^X has several built-in numeric functions. For example, you can easily perform the following operations:

- Base 10 logarithm   LG10
- Sum up values   SUM
- Square root   SQRT

There are other functions. Check the sources listed in the bibliography for a complete listing of the functions.

C H E C K P O I N T

---

5. Interpret the following COMPUTE commands:

    a. COMPUTE HOURS= DAY1 + DAY2 + DAY3

    b. COMPUTE AGESQ = AGE * AGE

    c. COMPUTE INCOME = GROSSINC/12

The Execution of Operations: When writing a computer command, you must carefully consider the order in which you want the mathematical operations performed. Typically, SPSS^X performs functions first, then exponentiation, then multiplication and division, and then addition and subtraction. How would the following COMPUTE statement be executed?

COMPUTE GFR = NBIRTH/NWOMEN*1000

Two arithmetic operations are to be performed, division (/) and multiplication (*). SPSS^X performs division and multiplication at the same level. Therefore, the computer simply reads the statement from left to right. This means that NBIRTH is divided by NWOMEN, and the resulting number is multiplied by 1000. Suppose, however, that you want to multiply NWOMEN by 1000 and then divide that number into NBIRTH. What do you do?

Parentheses are used to control the order in which operations are executed. Operations in parentheses are performed first. Operations are then executed from left to right with functions performed first, exponentiation next, multiplication and division next, and addition and subtraction last. Therefore, the following compute statement would solve your problem:

COMPUTE GFR = NBIRTH/(NWOMEN*1000)

The parentheses result in the multiplication (*) of NWOMEN by 1000. Once the operation in the parentheses is performed, the computer reads the statement from left to right. NBIRTH is, therefore, divided (/) by the previously calculated number. The result is called GFR. Remember, the above COMPUTE statement was used for illustrative purposes only. It should *not* be used to calculate GFR—the parentheses are in the wrong place!

C H E C K P O I N T

6. Explain the following COMPUTE statements. Do they give different results? Why or why not?

```
COMPUTE INCOME=(SALARY + DIVIDEND + INTEREST)/12
COMPUTE INCOME= SALARY + DIVIDEND + INTEREST/12
```

7. The sex ratio is a commonly used variable in social research. The sex ratio is defined as the number of males per 100 females. If a school had a sex ratio of 92, there would be 92 males per 100 females. A formula for calculating sex ratio is the following:

$$\text{Sex Ratio} = \frac{\text{number of males}}{\text{number of females}} \times 100$$

Write a COMPUTE command to tell the computer to create a SEX RATIO variable.

Missing Values and the COMPUTE Command: Suppose we used the COMPUTE statement in checkpoint question 6, above. How does the computer handle missing values? What value will be assigned to the INCOME variable if values are declared missing on SALARY, DIVIDEND, or INTEREST?

If a variable used in a COMPUTE command has a code declared missing, the computer almost always assigns a system-missing value to the newly computed variable. In the above example, if either SALARY, DIVIDEND, or INTEREST had a declared missing value, the variable INCOME would be assigned a system-missing value for that case. But what's a system-missing value?

Until this point we've been discussing **user-defined** missing values. You, the user, declare values as missing using the MISSING VALUES command. Anytime the computer encounters a flagged value, it treats it as a missing value. There are, however, missing values that are **system-missing values**. When SPSS^x encounters a code in the data that was not mentioned on the DATA LIST command, it automatically assigns a period to that value. Or, if there is a blank in your data, SPSS^x automatically assigns a period to the blank. Periods are the system's missing value code. Just as you may assign a 9 code to don't know and then declare the 9 as missing, the computer uses the period as the missing value code. Periods are automatically treated as missing values and appear in the printout like any other missing value code.

System-missing values are important in the COMPUTE command. In most instances, if values are missing on any one of the variables used in a computation, the computed variable is assigned a system-missing value. If a compute expression cannot be evaluated (for example, dividing by 0), the computer automatically assigns a system-missing value to that case.

For example, suppose we had the following SALARY, DIVIDEND, and INTEREST data:

- Case 1: $12,000, $50, $32
- Case 2: $20,000, $100, $65
- Case 3: Refused, $85, $300
- Case 4: $82,000, refused, don't know

Suppose you defined refused and don't know as missing via the MISSING VALUES command. How will the computer evaluate the following COMPUTE statement for the four cases?

```
COMPUTE INCOME=(SALARY + DIVIDEND + INTEREST)/12
```

Case 1 is straightforward. The parentheses indicate that the addition is performed first. The resulting number is then divided by 12. INCOME for case 1 is $1006.83. Case 2 is calculated similarly, and its value on INCOME is $1680.42. Case 3 has a missing value on SALARY, refused. Its INCOME value is, therefore, a period (.). Case 4 also has an INCOME value of period (.). Why? It has missing values on DIVIDEND and INTEREST.

CHECKPOINT

8. Using the CONEDUC, CONPRESS, and CONLEGIS variables in Appendix A, write a COMPUTE command that creates a new variable, CONFID. CONFID is obtained by adding the other three variables. What values can the new variable assume? What do these values indicate? Suppose DK and NA were declared missing. What values could the new variable assume? Evaluate CONFID for the following three cases when DK and NA have been declared missing on CONEDUC, CONPRESS, and CONLEGIS:

	CONEDUC	CONPRESS	CONLEGIS
Case 1:	1	8	3
Case 2:	3	3	3
Case 3:	1	3	2

SELECT IF Command

Strictly speaking, the SELECT IF command is not a data transformation command. However, it is a useful command for data manipulation. The SELECT IF command allows us to select cases based on some criteria. For example, suppose you coded the variable RACE as 1 = nonwhite and 2 = white. What would you do to look at the income distribution for whites and nonwhites separately? Use the following SELECT IF commands, and separate them with the FREQUENCIES command (we *will* get to this shortly!):

```
SELECT IF (RACE EQ 1)
FREQUENCIES
SELECT IF (RACE EQ 2)
FREQUENCIES
```

The first SELECT IF command selects only the nonwhite cases; the criterion was RACE = 1. The second SELECT IF command selects only the white cases; the criterion used was RACE = 2.

The relation used in the above SELECT IF commands was the EQ or equal relation. Cases were selected if they equaled the specified criteria. Other relations can be used in the SELECT IF command, including the following:

- NE—not equal to
- LT—less than
- GT—greater than
- GE—greater than or equal to

The criteria for selection can be simple or complex statements. For example, using the SEX variable in Appendix A, we could select only the females with this command:

```
SELECT IF (SEX NE 1)
```

If SEX is not equal (NE) to 1, it must equal 2, and therefore we select the females. Can you think of any other way(s) to select females using the SELECT IF command? How about one of these?

```
SELECT IF (SEX EQ 2)
```

Or

```
SELECT IF (SEX GT 1)
```

Complex SELECT IF commands use AND or OR to join variables. For example, if you wished to do an analysis on females aged 21 or older, you could use the following SELECT IF command:

```
SELECT IF (SEX EQ 2 AND AGE GE 21)
```

Cases will be selected only if they fulfill *both* criteria, SEX equals 2 *and* AGE greater than or equal to 21. A different set of cases would be selected if you used the OR link.

```
SELECT IF (SEX EQ 2 OR AGE GE 21)
```

The computer would select cases in which *either* statement was true, SEX equals 2 *or* AGE greater than or equal to 21. A very different selection!

C H E C K P O I N T

---

9. Using the variables in Appendix A, evaluate the following SELECT IF commands:

   a. `SELECT IF (INCOME LT 9)`

   b. `SELECT IF (SIBS GE 1)`

   c. `SELECT IF (REGION EQ 1 AND MARITAL NE 5)`

   d. `SELECT IF (REGION EQ 1 OR MARITAL NE 5)`

10. Using the variables in Appendix A, write a SELECT IF command to examine cases in which the respondent is married (MARITAL) and working full-time (WRKSTAT).

11. Using the variables in Appendix A, write a SELECT IF command to examine cases in which the respondent completed either high school or a bachelor's degree (DEGREE).

System File Commands

Once you define the data you do not need to repeat that process each time you do a computer run. Instead, you can keep an SPSS^x **system file**. A system file contains data and SPSS^x programs. Two commands are needed to work with system files, the SAVE and GET commands.

SAVE Command

The SAVE command is used to tell the computer to save the file as a system file. If you save data, all data, including data transformations, are saved. If you save a program, you need not carry a deck of cards to the card reader each time you wish to do a run. Most researchers save system files and modify the program part for new runs.

System files are typically saved on either disk or tape, two storage devices discussed in chapter 1. Check with your instructor for the type of storage device you will use and the system language needed to specify that device. A typical SAVE command reads as follows:

```
SAVE OUTFILE=MYFILE
```

What have we told the computer? We told it to save a file called MYFILE. As long as the file name does not exceed eight characters, you may name your file anything you want. The OUTFILE name is a required part of the SAVE command.

Other specifications you may wish to use on the SAVE command include KEEP, DROP, and MAP. The KEEP and DROP names are truly descriptive of what they do. Think for a minute about what these sub-commands might do. Remember that you're saving data.

KEEP tells the computer to retain only the variables listed, and to save them in the specified order. For example, the following SAVE command tells the computer to KEEP four variables (RACE, SEX, EDUC, and SALARY), in that order, on a file called MYFILE:

```
SAVE OUTFILE=MYFILE/KEEP RACE,SEX,EDUC,SALARY
```

You could add the MAP specification at the end of SALARY. That would allow you to see the names of the variables being saved. If you have been working with several files, you may lose track of what you're doing. The MAP specification helps to insure that you're keeping the variables you wish to keep. The addition of the MAP specification results in the following SAVE command:

```
SAVE OUTFILE=MYFILE/KEEP RACE,SEX,EDUC,SALARY/MAP
```

DROP, as you probably expect, tells the computer to drop variables from the file. For example, you may be working with ten variables and need to keep only six on the system file. The following SAVE command would be useful:

```
SAVE OUTFILE=MYFILE/DROP ABORTION,AGE,INCOME,MARITAL
```

Using the above command, you told the computer to keep a system file called MYFILE and to exclude the ABORTION, AGE, INCOME, and MARITAL variables from that file.

Some guidelines for the SAVE command include the following:

1. The file name cannot exceed eight characters.
2. If you are working on an IBM computer, the file name must match the name used in the system language commands. Check with your instructor for additional information.
3. If you are working on a computer other than an IBM, the OUTFILE name must match the name used in SPSS^X'S FILE HANDLE command. Let's examine the FILE HANDLE command for those of you working on a non-IBM computer

When working with SPSS^X system files, you need the FILE HANDLE command. This command assigns a unique name (handle) to each file that you read or write on. This will be important if you read or write on more than one file in a run. The file handle can be no longer than eight characters. A typical FILE HANDLE command reads as follows:

```
FILE HANDLE MYFILE/file specifications
```

What have you told the computer? You named a file MYFILE. The file specifications are computer specific. Once again, you need additional instructions from your instructor about how to fill in the file specifications. This command is placed before the DATA LIST command.

C H E C K P O I N T

12. Explain the following SAVE commands:
    a. SAVE OUTFILE=FIRST/KEEP SAT,JOB1,INCOME1
    b. SAVE OUTFILE=JOBS/KEEP JOB1,JOB2,JOB/MAP
    c. SAVE OUTFILE=HOURS

GET Command

After you save a system file, the way to access it is via the GET command. The GET command enables you to read a previously created system file. The GET command reads all previously saved value labels, variable labels, missing values, data transformations, and raw data. You must specify a FILE on the GET command. A typical GET command reads as follows:

```
GET FILE=MYFILE
```

The above command tells the computer to retrieve a system FILE called MYFILE. For those of you working on an IBM computer, remember that the file names used on the SAVE and GET commands must match the names used on the system language commands. If you are working on another brand of computer, the file names used on the SAVE and GET commands must match the FILE HANDLE command.

C H E C K P O I N T

13. Explain the following GET commands:
    a. GET FILE=TIME
    b. GET FILE=HOURS

In the last two chapters we have examined selected SPSS^x computer commands to transform data and manipulate files. There are more SPSS^x commands, but the ones we have discussed should enable you to do most computer analyses. At this point, we need to examine the kinds of analyses we want to do and the SPSS^x procedure commands to do them. Before turning to procedures, however, let's interpret two sample runs.

C H E C K P O I N T

14. Run#1

```
TITLE "AN EXAMPLE OF SAVING AN SPSSˣ SYSTEM FILE"
FILE HANDLE NONIBM
COMMENT REMEMBER IBM USERS DON'T NEED A FILE HANDLE
 COMMAND
DATA LIST RECORDS=3/
 1 ID 1-3 CARD 4 SEX 5 ED 6-7/3 ID 1-3 CARD 4 OCCUP 5-6
 INCOME 7-14(2) HOURS 15-17(1)
MISSING VALUES ED(98,99) OCCUP(99) INCOME(99999999)
 HOURS(998,999)
VALUE LABELS SEX 1 'MALE' 2 'FEMALE'
VARIABLE LABELS ED "LAST YEAR COMPLETED" OCCUP "R'S
 OCC"
 INCOME "MONTHLY NET" HOURS "WEEKLY WORK HRS"
COMPUTE HRLYINC=INCOME/HOURS
RECODE ED (0 THRU 11=1) (12=2) (13 THRU 15=3) (16=4)
 INTO NEWED
MISSING VALUES NEWED(98,99)
VALUE LABELS NEWED 1 'LESS THAN HS' 2 'HS' 3 'SOME
 COLLEGE' 4 'COLLEGE'
FREQUENCIES
BEGIN DATA
0011...
0012...
0013...
0021...
0022...
0023...
  .
  .
  .
END DATA
SAVE OUTFILE=TRIAL/KEEP HRLYIN,NEWED,SEX
```

15. Run #2

```
TITLE "RETRIEVING A SAVED SYSTEM FILE"
GET FILE=TRIAL
SELECT IF (SEX EQ 2)
FREQUENCIES
```

Now I think it's about time we discussed the FREQUENCIES command, don't you?

chapter 5

Univariate Analyses: Frequency Distributions

The last four chapters focused on computers and social science data. Let's put that information to work and do some data analysis. The next three chapters examine **univariate** analyses, which involve the analysis of one (uni-) variable. In chapters 8 through 11 we will explore **bivariate** analyses, involving the analysis of two (bi-) variables. **Multivariate** analyses, involving the analysis of three or more (multi-) variables, are the focus of chapters 12 through 15.

You read the results of univariate analyses all the time. Open a magazine or newspaper. What's the current unemployment rate? How many children are there in a typical American family? Are most Americans pro abortion? Are city dwellers afraid to go out alone at night? Answers to such questions require univariate analysis. The variables analyzed include unemployment rate, number of children, attitude toward abortion, and fear of crime, respectively.

Upon completion of this chapter, you should be able to do the following:

1. Define the term *univariate analysis*
2. Give examples of univariate analysis
3. Define the term *frequency distribution*
4. Give examples of frequency distributions
5. Describe bar charts and histograms
6. Write SPSS^X programs to obtain numeric and graphic frequency distributions

Why Do Univariate Analyses?

Most research begins with univariate data analysis. Researchers must be sure the data are clean before beginning data analysis. Once the data are clean, most researchers like to know the characteristics of each individual variable.

Clean data does not refer to scrubbing data cards in rock-laden streams. Nor does it refer to hanging data tapes on a line to dry! Rather, **data cleaning** refers, in part, to checking the legitimacy of data codes. For example, suppose you collected data on the variable gender and coded male as 1 and female as 2. In the process of analyzing the data, you find a 3 and 4 code on gender. You never assigned codes of 3 or 4 to gender! What happened? *Dirty data.*

To find out where the 3 and 4 codes came from, first check the DATA LIST command. Did you indicate the correct column(s) for each variable? If you read gender in column 5 instead of column 4, that's the problem. Fix it by rewriting the DATA LIST command. If, however, the DATA LIST command looks correct, the illegitimate codes could be coding or keypunching errors.

Whatever the cause of the error, you need to correct it. You certainly don't want to analyze meaningless data codes! How do you learn about code errors in the first place? Since proofreading all the codes on your terminal hardcopy or data cards is tedious, let the computer do the work—do a univariate analysis.

A second reason for doing univariate analysis is to become familiar with your variables. It makes little sense to talk about a relationship between gender and salary, a bivariate analysis, if you don't know the sample's salary distribution. Careful researchers know the characteristics of individual variables before examining relationships between variables.

A third reason for doing univariate analysis is to answer a particular research question. For example, if you want to know how long, on the average, couples date before marrying, do a univariate analysis. Ask people the number of months and years they dated their spouse before marrying. A single variable, time dated, is examined to answer the research question.

One or more of these three reasons is responsible for the fact that most data analysis begins with univariate analysis. In fact, most research begins with an examination of frequency distributions.

The Frequency Distribution

A frequency distribution counts (tallies) how often each attribute (code) on a variable occurs. For example, if you count the number of females and the number of males in one of your classes, your counts produce the frequency distribution for that class's gender. If you count the number of left-handed students and the number of right-handed students, your tallies now give the frequency distribution for the variable preferred hand. A frequency distribution indicates how often each attribute on a single variable occurs.

When working with large samples, we give the job of counting to the computer by using a FREQUENCIES command. The FREQUENCIES command produces a table of counts and percentages for the named variable(s). A typical FREQUENCIES command reads as follows:

```
FREQUENCIES VARIABLES=AGE ED HOURS
```

In the FREQUENCIES command, you need only name the variables whose attributes are to be counted. The above command requests three frequency distributions, for AGE, ED, and HOURS, respectively. If you want the frequency distributions for all the variables declared on a DATA LIST command or saved on a file, you use the keyword ALL:

```
FREQUENCIES VARIABLES=ALL
```

Let's apply this information to the data in Appendix A. The following SPSS[x] program was used to obtain frequency distributions for CHILDS, SEX, and MAWORK:

```
TITLE "TESTING THE FREQUENCIES COMMAND"
DATA LIST RECORDS=1/
 1 CHILDS 15 SEX 17 MAWORK 19
COMMENT TRY THIS RUN.
 REMEMBER, NONIBM USERS MAY NEED A FILE HANDLE COMMAND.
 EVERYONE NEEDS TO CHECK WITH HIS OR HER INSTRUCTOR FOR
  THE SYSTEM LANGUAGE.
 THIS RUN ASSUMES THAT THE DATA IS PART OF THE SPSS[x]
 JOB. IT DOES NOT ASSUME A SYSTEM FILE.
MISSING VALUES CHILDS(9) MAWORK(0,8,9)
VALUE LABELS SEX 1 'MALE' 2 'FEMALE'/
 MAWORK 0 'NO LIVE WITH MA' 1 'YES' 2 'NO'
VARIABLE LABELS CHILDS "CHILDREN EVER HAD"
 MAWORK "MA EVER WORK FOR A YEAR AFTER MARRIAGE"
FREQUENCIES VARIABLES=CHILDS SEX MAWORK
BEGIN DATA

   .
   .(data cards)
   .

END DATA
```

The resulting printout is shown in table 5-1. Let's look at it together. Notice that labels are attached to the CHILDS and MAWORK variable names. The SEX variable does not have a variable label; its name was considered self-explanatory. Value labels appear for the attri-

Table 5-1 / Example Printout: Frequency distributions for CHILDS, SEX, and MAWORK

CHILDS   CHILDREN EVER HAD

VALUE LABEL	VALUE	FREQUENCY	PERCENT	VALID PERCENT	CUM PERCENT
	0	64	25.7	25.8	25.8
	1	45	18.1	18.1	44.0
	2	64	25.7	25.8	69.8
	3	33	13.3	13.3	83.1
	4	18	7.2	7.3	90.3
	5	12	4.8	4.8	95.2
	6	6	2.4	2.4	97.6
	7	2	.8	.8	98.4
	8	4	1.6	1.6	100.0
OUT OF RANGE		1	.4	MISSING	
	TOTAL	249	100.0	100.0	

VALID CASES   248   MISSING CASES   1

VALUE LABEL	VALUE	FREQUENCY	PERCENT	VALID PERCENT	CUM PERCENT
MALE	1	112	45.0	45.0	45.0
FEMALE	2	137	55.0	55.0	100.0
	TOTAL	249	100.0	100.0	

VALID CASES   249   MISSING CASES   0

MAWORK   EVER WORK FOR YEAR AFTER MARRIAGE

VALUE LABEL	VALUE	FREQUENCY	PERCENT	VALID PERCENT	CUM PERCENT
NO LIVE WITH MA	0	19	7.6	MISSING	
YES	1	127	51.0	57.2	57.2
NO	2	95	38.2	42.8	100.0
	8	3	1.2	MISSING	
OUT OF RANGE		5	2.0	MISSING	
	TOTAL	249	100.0	100.0	

VALID CASES   222   MISSING CASES   27

butes on SEX and MAWORK. No labels are attached to the CHILDS variable. Why? Its attributes are numbers (0,1,2, and so on); the assignment of labels would be redundant (zero, one, two, and so on).

The VALUE column represents the attribute's code, the code you assigned to put the data onto the computer. For example, code 1 on SEX corresponds to the male attribute and code 2 to female. Whenever you encountered a male respondent, you assigned a 1, and whenever you encountered a female respondent, you assigned a 2. Code 4 on CHILDS represents 4 children. Whenever respondents indicated that they had four children, you coded that as a 4.

Next is a column entitled FREQUENCY. As you probably expect, this column indicates the count for each attribute. Looking at this column for SEX indicates that there are 112 males in the sample and 137 females. The frequency column on MAWORK indicates that 19 people did not live with their mother, 127 had mothers who worked for pay for at least one year after their marriage, and 95 respondents had mothers who did not work.

The next column, PERCENT, gives each attribute's percentage of the sample. That is, each attribute's frequency is divided by the sample size, and the resulting number is then multiplied by 100. For example, 45 percent (112/249 $\times$ 100) of the sample is male and 55 percent (137/249 $\times$ 100) is female. Looking at the CHILDS variable, we learn that 25.7 percent of the respondents never had a child, and that 1.6 percent have had eight or more children.

The next column, VALID PERCENT, matches the PERCENT column for the SEX variable but differs from the PERCENT column for the CHILDS and MAWORK variables. Any ideas? Valid means that only the valid cases are included in the percentage calculation; cases with missing values have been excluded. No missing values were declared for SEX, and therefore the VALID PERCENT matches the PERCENT column; the percentages were calculated with 249 in the denominator. However, for CHILDS and MAWORK, the 9 code and the 0, 8, and 9 codes, respectively, were declared missing. The word MISSING is placed in the 9 and the 0, 8, and 9 VALID PERCENT categories for CHILDS and MAWORK. The VALID PERCENT calculation is based on 248 cases for CHILDS and 222 cases for MAWORK.

CUM PERCENT stands for cumulative percentage. A summation of the percentages in the VALID PERCENT column appears in this column, beginning in the category with the lowest code. All percentages are added together; the final sum must be 100 percent because all valid cases are included in the percentages. For example, the CHILDS CUM PERCENT column indicates that 44 percent of the sample had one child or fewer and that 83.1 percent of the sample had three children or fewer. Looking at the CUM PERCENT on SEX, we find that 100 percent of our sample was female or less. Does that make any sense? No. You cannot interpret the CUM PERCENT column for nominal or, strictly speaking, ordinal variables. CUM PERCENTS are used on interval or ratio data, such as CHILDS.

What do we know about CHILDS, MAWORK, and SEX from their frequency distributions? First, the data appear clean. All printout codes match the codes appearing in Appendix A. Suppose, for a minute, that we did have dirty data. Suppose the frequency distribution for SEX looked like this:

SEX

VALUE	FREQUENCY . . .
1	112
2	135
3	1
7	1

What would you do? How would you locate the two "peculiar" cases? Think about the commands discussed in the last two chapters. Remember, you want to pick out cases having a 3 and 7 code on SEX. Try the following commands:

```
SELECT IF (SEX EQ 3 OR 7)
FREQUENCIES VARIABLES = ID
```

What have we told the computer? We told it to select cases having either a 3 or 7 code on SEX. Working with the selected cases, we told the computer to print the ID frequency distribution. Do you see why it's important to include a respondent identification number? That number uniquely identifies each case. It enables you to check the original data for the sex of the selected cases. By the way, don't look for an ID number in this data set. The data are clean and it was omitted.

As long as we're pretending, suppose the computer gave the numbers 10 and 132 in the ID frequency listing. Assume that after looking at the original data, you learn that both cases are female. How do you make the corrections? Try the following command:

```
RECODE SEX(3,7=2)
```

The RECODE command tells the computer to change the 3 and 7 codes on SEX to the correct and meaningful 2 code. Without the ID number, we would need to go through the data manually to locate the problem and correct it, an extremely tedious task. In this case, however, the data are clean.

What else do we know about the variables? One respondent did not answer the CHILDS question, 0.4 percent of the sample. Ignoring that case, we know that 25.8 percent of the respondents have no children, 18.1 percent have one child, 25.8 percent have two children, and so on. Most respondents, 69.8 percent, have two or fewer children. In fact, the frequency distribution indicates that the likelihood of having an additional child continues to decline after three.

Notice, however, that in comparison to respondents reporting seven children, the number of respondents reporting eight children increases slightly. This does not mean that having eight children is more common than having seven! Remember, the 8 category includes eight or more children (8, 9, 10, 11, and so on). A category that includes several attributes is called a **grouped data** category. The other categories (1, 2, 3, . . ., 7) represent ungrouped data; there is a single value in each category.

The frequency distribution on SEX indicates that the sample is predominantly female, 55 percent. That statistic includes the entire sample; everyone responded to the sex question.

Eight respondents, 3.2 percent of the sample, did not answer the MAWORK question. An additional 7.6 percent did not live with their mothers. Of those living with their mothers (222), 127 said she did work and 95 claimed she did not work. Most respondents, 57.2 percent, had mothers who worked for pay for at least one year after they were married.

We learned quite a bit about our variables by examining their frequency distributions. We learn similar information by studying a variable's graphs. Before doing that, however, try doing some univariate frequency analyses.

C H E C K P O I N T

1. Using the data in Appendix A, write and run an SPSS^X program to examine the SIBS, RELIG, and RACE frequency distributions. Exclude don't knows and no answers as missing values. Do we have dirty data? What information do we have about the variables?

2. A friend asks whether most of your respondents are married. Using Appendix A data, answer your friend's question. Remember, you must write and run an SPSS^X program.

3. Look at the frequency distribution for INCOME for only the males in the sample. To do this you will need to write and run an SPSS^X program

Graphing Frequency Distributions

Some people claim that a picture is worth a thousand words. Well, I suppose these same people think that a graph is worth a thousand numbers! Stop groaning! Let's look at graphs, or pictorial representations, of the frequency distribution. Numeric frequency distributions easily convert to graphic form. Two popular graphs are the **bar chart** and the **histogram**.

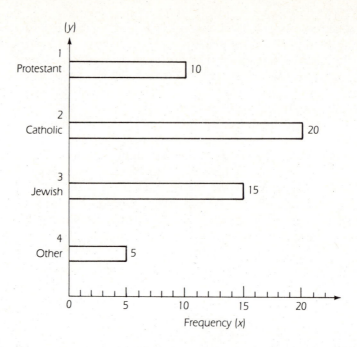

Figure 5-1 Example of a bar chart for the variable religion, N = 50.

In a bar chart, each bar corresponds to an attribute. The length of the bar corresponds to the frequency of that attribute. For example, a bar chart for religion coded as Protestant (1), Catholic (2), Jewish (3), and other (4), might resemble the graph in figure 5-1. The graph tells us that there are 10 Protestants, 20 Catholics, 15 Jews, and 5 others in the sample. People who "dislike" numbers or who want to scan the data quickly can easily see that there are more Catholics in the sample than members of any other religion: the bar is longest for Catholic.

The histogram provides similar information. As with the bar chart, the length of a histogram "bar" indicates the frequency of an attribute. Figure 5-2 shows the histogram for religion. It too indicates that there are 10 Protestants, 20 Catholics, 15 Jews, and 5 others in the sample. What differentiates a bar chart from a histogram?

You can construct a bar chart and a histogram for any variable. However, the level at which you measure variables usually determines whether you select the bar chart or the histogram. Bar charts are typically used on nominal and ordinal variables. Histograms are usually constructed for interval and ratio variables.

Let's examine some bar charts and histograms in more detail. To obtain a bar chart or histogram in SPSS[x], simply add that specification to the FREQUENCIES command. Requests for a bar chart and a histogram read as follows:

```
FREQUENCIES VARIABLES=MAWORK/BARCHART/
FREQUENCIES VARIABLES=MAWORK/HISTOGRAM/
```

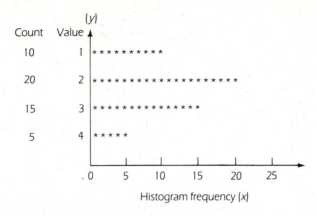

Figure 5-2 Example of a histogram for the variable religion, N = 50.

The first FREQUENCIES command requests a bar chart for the MA-WORK variable, and the second FREQUENCIES command requests a histogram for that variable. You cannot request a bar chart *and* a histogram on one FREQUENCIES command. To look at the histogram and bar chart for SEX and CHILDS, use these commands:

```
FREQUENCIES VARIABLES=SEX CHILDS/BARCHART=SEX CHILDS
FREQUENCIES VARIABLES=SEX CHILDS/HISTOGRAM
```

The first FREQUENCIES command produces the frequency distributions and bar charts for SEX and CHILDS. The second FREQUENCIES command produces only the histograms. The resulting bar charts and histograms appear in figures 5-3a and 5-3b. Do you notice any difference between the two?

Although the two produce the same information, the histogram is particularly useful for examining variables with a large number of codes—the interval and ratio variables. Bar charts, however, are suited for variables with few attributes—the nominal and ordinal variables. Remember, bar charts and histograms provide you with information similar to that given in a frequency distribution. However, some people prefer graphics, and others prefer the frequency distribution.

C H E C K P O I N T

4. Write and execute an SPSS^X program to examine the histogram or bar chart for the AGE and RACE variables in Appendix A. Which did you select for AGE? Why? Which did you select for RACE? Why?

5. What do the graphs tell you?

CHILDS   CHILDREN EVER HAD

VALUE LABEL	VALUE	FREQUENCY	PERCENT	VALID PERCENT	CUM PERCENT
	0	64	25.7	25.8	25.8
	1	45	18.1	18.1	44.0
	2	64	25.7	25.8	69.8
	3	33	13.3	13.3	83.1
	4	18	7.2	7.3	90.3
	5	12	4.8	4.8	95.2
	6	6	2.4	2.4	97.6
	7	2	.8	.8	98.4
	8	4	1.6	1.6	100.0
	9	1	.4	MISSING	
TOTAL		249	100.0	100.0	

CHILDS   CHILDREN EVER HAD

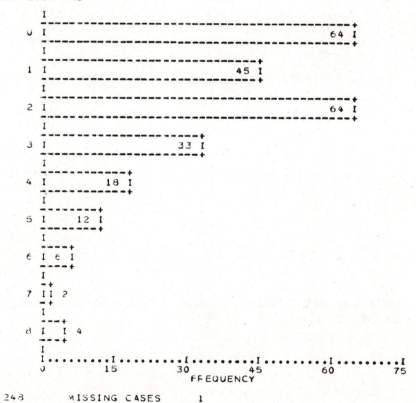

VALID CASES   248   MISSING CASES   1

Figure 5-3a Bar charts for SEX and CHILDS.

SEX

VALUE LABEL	VALUE	FREQUENCY	PERCENT	VALID PERCENT	CUM PERCENT
MALE	1	112	45.0	45.0	45.0
FEMALE	2	137	55.0	55.0	100.0
	TOTAL	249	100.0	100.0	

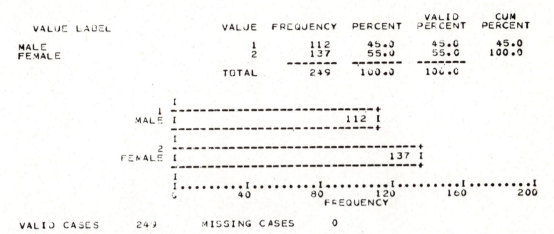

VALID CASES   249   MISSING CASES   0

Figure 5-3a continued

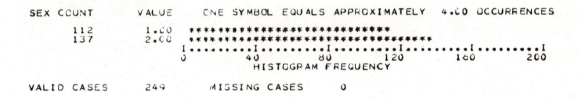

SEX COUNT   VALUE   ONE SYMBOL EQUALS APPROXIMATELY   4.00 OCCURRENCES

```
    112      1.00   ************************************
    137      2.00   **************************************************
             I.........I.........I.........I.........I.........I
             0        40        80       120       160       200
                         HISTOGRAM FREQUENCY
```

VALID CASES   249   MISSING CASES   0

CHILDS   CHILDREN EVER HAD

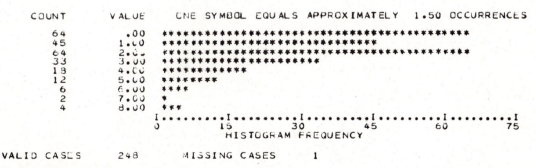

```
    COUNT      VALUE      ONE SYMBOL EQUALS APPROXIMATELY   1.50 OCCURRENCES
      64       .00    ********************************************************
      45      1.00    ******************************************
      64      2.00    ********************************************************
      33      3.00    **********************
      18      4.00    ************
      12      5.00    ********
       6      6.00    ****
       2      7.00    *
       4      8.00    ***
              I.........I.........I.........I.........I.........I
              0        15        30        45        60        75
                          HISTOGRAM FREQUENCY
```

VALID CASES   248   MISSING CASES   1

Figure 5-3b Histograms for SEX and CHILDS.

After looking at the frequency distributions or graphic displays of variables, we usually examine summary measures that describe distributions. The univariate summary measures that we will discuss are the measures of central tendency and of dispersion. These measures are the focus of the next two chapters on univariate analyses.

chapter 6

Univariate Analyses: Measures of Central Tendency

As the title of this chapter indicates, we're still working with one variable. In the last chapter we looked at numeric and graphic distributions on one variable. These distributions indicated the distribution of cases on the variable's attributes, and they also alerted us to the existence of dirty data. What else do we need to know about a single variable? We need to know what the "average" or "typical" case is for the variable. To describe the average or typical case, we examine measures of central tendency.

Upon completion of this chapter, you should be able to do the following:

1. Explain the concept of central tendency
2. List three measures of central tendency
3. Define three measures of central tendency
4. Select the most appropriate measure of central tendency for your data
5. Write SPSS^X commands to calculate the desired measure of central tendency

Measures of Central Tendency

Your instructor is returning your first exam. You look at your grade. After you mentally applaud or scold yourself, what question pops into your mind? The one I hear most often is, "What was the average grade?" On an exam I gave, I answered that question with three different numbers: 82, 78, and 75. All three numbers were correct, and all three numbers answered the question!

Workers strike for higher wages. They claim they're underpaid, since the average salary is $14,000. Management says that's nonsense, since the average salary is $21,000. Both are correct!

This is very unsettling. How could I give my students three different "averages" for one exam? How could management and workers be correct in their calculations of the average salary and yet differ by $7,000? The truth is, there are three measures of central tendency: the mean, the median, and the mode. Each measure indicates how the data clusters. Yet each measure is calculated on a different basis and therefore takes slightly different information into account. Let's examine each in more detail.

The Mode

The **mode** is defined as the most frequently occurring value in a distribution. You calculate a mode by looking at a variable's frequency distribution. As the definition states, you look for the most frequently occurring value. The attribute having the largest frequency is the variable's mode.

When we examine the frequency distributions described in chapter 5, we find that the mode for SEX is code 2. Code 2 corresponds to female, and therefore the modal attribute is female. We found the mode by noting that there were more females, code 2, than males, code 1. Two attributes have the highest frequency on CHILDS, 0 and 2. That means that CHILDS is a bimodal distribution; it has two modes. The 0 and 2 correspond to the attributes no children and two children.

The Median

The **median** is defined as the value that splits the distribution in half. Half the cases fall below the median, and half the cases fall above the median. The median is the value of the middle case. How do we calculate a median?

Suppose we knew the ages of five people: 16, 18, 25, 34, and 49. To determine the median age, we find the case that has half the values above it and half below it. There are five cases. The third case falls in the middle. Its value is 25, and so the median age is 25.

Suppose we had gender data on the same five people. We knew they were male, female, female, male, male. What's the median? What case has half the values above it and half the cases below it? There are still five cases, so the third case falls in the middle. Its value is female, so the median is female. Right? Wrong! There is no median!

Think about what it means to say that a case is in the middle of a variable's frequency distribution. It means that you must be able to order attributes from low values to high values. Recall from chapter 2 that the ordering of attributes requires, at a minimum, a variable measured at the ordinal level. Sex (male, female) is a nominal, *not* an ordinal, variable. Therefore, you cannot calculate a median for sex. We'll discuss level of measurement further below.

The Mean

The **mean** is defined as the sum of all values on a variable divided by the number of cases. For example, the mean age for the five people listed above is 28.4 years. The mean was obtained by adding together all the respondents' ages, 142, and dividing that number by the number of cases, 5. Could we calculate the mean sex? No. Although code 1 represents male and code 2 female, in this case 1 plus 1 does not equal 2! You cannot add two males together to get one female. Remember from chapter 2 that some codes are numerals, not numbers. Sex is a nominal variable; its codes are numerals, and numerals cannot be added. Before turning to the level of measurement discussion, let's check what we've discussed so far.

C H E C K P O I N T

1. Match the words in column A with one or more statements from column B.

   A

   a. Mean

   b. Mode

   c. Median

   B

   1. Is the value with the largest frequency

   2. Sums all the values together and divides by the number of cases

   3. Is the value of the middle case

   4. Requires that cases be arrayed from low to high values

   5. Indicates how cases cluster

Comparing the Measures of Central Tendency

Having defined the three measures of central tendency, let's now consider why we select one rather than another. A major difference among the three measures was hinted at above—level of measurement. The level at which you measure variables determines, in part, which measure of central tendency is most appropriate.

The mode can be calculated for any variable. It indicates the most frequently occurring attribute. The median requires the ordering of attributes from low to high values. Therefore, an ordinal level of measurement must be attained to calculate a median. The mean requires data to be at least at the interval level. In order for values to be added and divided, codes must be numbers. As discussed in chapter 2, codes are numbers at the interval level of measurement. A summary of the relationship between level of measurement and measure of central tendency appears in table 6-1.

Let's return to the first example in this chapter. I reported three different measures of central tendency for one exam, 82, 78, and 75. You now know why they were all correct. The mode was 82, the median was 78, and the mean was 75. Of all the different grades received on the exam, more students received an 82 than any other grade. The score that split the distribution in half was 78; half the students got a higher grade, and half got a lower grade. When all exam scores were added together and divided by the number of students taking the exam, the result was 75.

I could legitimately report all three measures to my students, because exam grade measured in points, 0 to 100, is a ratio variable. All three measures of central tendency can be calculated on a ratio variable. All three measures give slightly different information, and in this case all three measures gave a different number.

The mode indicates the most frequently occurring grade. Ignored in this statistic is an examination of any other grade. The mode focuses on only one category, the one with the largest frequency. The median requires the ordering of attributes from low to high values. Once arrayed, the median reports only the middle case's value. Values on cases other than the middle case are ignored. The mean calculation takes all cases into account; the value on every case is added to every other case.

What statistic should I have reported to the class? Remember, we want to report a measure that best indicates how the data cluster. The *first rule of thumb* is to report the measure that makes the most use of the level at which the variable was measured. If we measured at the interval or ratio level, we report the mean. For an ordinal variable, we report the median. If we have a nominal variable, we can only report the mode. There is, however, another consideration in the selection of a measure of central tendency.

Let's return to the strike example. Management reported an average salary of $21,000, and workers claimed an average salary of $14,000. Both are correct. Management calculated the mean income. They added together all employees' incomes, including the two big bosses' incomes of $650,000, and divided by the number of employees. The workers calculated the median income, the income that split the distribution in half.

Both figures are mathematically correct, but the median gives a better indication of the typical employee income. Why? Think about the distribution of cases. The two big bosses have incomes that are very different from other employees' incomes. In calculating the mean, the big incomes are added together with the others. The mean is thus pulled in the direction of extreme cases, in this instance, the extremely high incomes. The median, however, is the value of the middle case; half the incomes are above it (including the incomes of the big bosses), and half are below it. Although both statistics, $21,000 and $14,000, are

Table 6-1 / Level of Measurement and Measures of Central Tendency

	Mode	Median	Mean
Nominal	Yes	No	No
Ordinal	Yes	Yes	No
Interval	Yes	Yes	Yes
Ratio	Yes	Yes	Yes

mathematically correct, the median gives a more accurate picture of the typical income for workers.

The *second rule of thumb* is, when selecting a measure of central tendency for interval or ratio data, to look at the distribution of cases on the variable. If there are a few extreme cases, consider reporting the median. If, however, cases are spread across the distribution, report the mean. How do you know about the spread of cases? You can either look at the frequency distribution, as discussed in the last chapter, or look at measures of dispersion, to be discussed in the next chapter.

Before moving on, let's check what we've been discussing. Then we'll learn how to use the computer to obtain measures of central tendency.

C H E C K P O I N T

2. Without knowing the variables' distributions, what measure of central tendency do you think would be most appropriate for the following variables?

   a. Family size (small, medium, large)

   b. Race (white, nonwhite)

   c. Attitude toward abortion (pro, con)

   d. Social class (low, middle, upper)

   e. Educational attainment (none, first grade, second grade, third grade, and so on)

   f. Educational attainment (less than high school, high school, some college, more than college)

   g. Number of siblings (0,1,2, and so on)

Measures of Central Tendency: Computer Calculations

The computer can be used to calculate measures of central tendency. To do that, you add a STATISTICS specification to the FREQUENCIES command. For example, to obtain the mean, median, and mode for the variable CHILDS, use the following:

```
FREQUENCIES VARIABLES = CHILDS/
    STATISTICS = MEAN MEDIAN MODE
```

If you want only the mean, simply ask for the mean:

```
FREQUENCIES VARIABLES = CHILDS/
    STATISTICS = MEAN
```

Let's add a STATISTICS request to the FREQUENCIES command used in chapter 5:

```
FREQUENCIES VARIABLES = SEX MAWORK CHILDS/
    STATISTICS = MEAN MEDIAN MODE/
```

The printout appears in table 6-2. How would you interpret the printout?

Let's consider the rules of thumb. At what level is each variable measured? SEX and MAWORK are nominal variables. That means that only their modes can be interpreted. As already discussed, the mode for SEX is female, code 2, and the mode for MAWORK is yes, code 1. Notice that the printout contains medians and means for MAWORK and SEX. This is because the computer is simply a machine. It does not know that SEX is a nominal variable in which a 1 represents male and 2 a female. You, the researcher, must interpret the resulting statistics!

It is unclear how to classify CHILDS. Some researchers treat it as a ratio variable; there is a true zero end-point, a unit of measurement, an order to the categories. Other researchers treat CHILDS as an ordinal variable; we don't know the values of the cases located in the eight or more grouped data category. For that category we do not, therefore, have a unit of measurement.

In either case, we can interpret the median and the mode. The mode is printed as 0.000. That value does not correspond to any value on CHILDS. Looking at the frequency distribution on CHILDS, we find that the most frequently occurring values are 0 and 2, no children and two children. The computer does not report a mode for a bimodal distribution such as CHILDS. The median is 2; that is, the value that splits the distribution in half is 2. Half the respondents have more than two children and half have fewer.

If we treat CHILDS as a ratio variable, we can continue to interpret its mean. The mean is 1.96. Summing all 248 valid cases together and dividing by 248 gives the arithmetic average, 1.96. On the average, people have 1.96 children.

C H E C K P O I N T

3. Write and run an SPSS^X program to examine measures of central tendency for the TVHOURS, SPKATH, SPKCOM, and SPKHOMO variables in Appendix A. Exclude the don't knows and no answers from the analysis. In this

Table 6-2 / Example Printout: Measures of Central Tendency

```
CHILDS CHILDREN EVER HAD
   MEAN  1.960   MEDIAN  2.000    MODE    .000


SEX
   MEAN  1.550   MEDIAN  2.000    MODE   2.000


MAWORK
   MEAN  1.428   MEDIAN  1.000    MODE   1.000
```

NOTE: The request for measures of central tendency yields this information in addition to the information shown in table 5-1.

run, create a new variable, TVNEW. To construct TVNEW, collapse the categories on TVHOURS such that code 1 = less than three hours, code 2 = three to six hours, code 3 = seven hours or more. Once again, exclude the don't knows and no answers from the analysis of TVNEW.

4. Interpret the statistics obtained from the previous exercise. Are the same measures of central tendency useful for TVHOURS and TVNEW? Explain why or why not.

In this chapter we examined measures of central tendency. These measures describe in a single number how the data cluster around some central value. In the next chapter we will discuss measures that describe the spread of data around a central value.

chapter 7

Univariate Analyses: Measures of Dispersion

Your instructor returned your first exam and reported the mean, mode, and median. What's your next question? The one I often hear is, "What were the highest and lowest scores?" This question actually probes a more general question: "Now that I know my grade and the average, how did my grade compare to everyone else's?" One answer to that question is obtained by looking at the frequency distribution for exam grades. After all, the frequency distribution shows how often each exam grade occurred. If, however, you want one number to answer the question, you use a measure of dispersion.

Upon completion of this chapter, you should be able to do the following:

1. Explain the concept of dispersion
2. List three measures of dispersion
3. Define three measures of dispersion
4. Interpret three measures of dispersion
5. Describe the normal curve
6. Use the normal curve to interpret standard deviation
7. Write SPSS^X programs to calculate measures of dispersion

Measures of Dispersion

Measures of dispersion describe, with a single statistic, the spread of cases on a variable. For example, suppose 78 was the mean grade on your exam. If asked about the spread of exam grades around the mean, your instructor could respond in at least three ways: no spread, some spread, or a lot of spread. No spread means that everyone received a 78; the high and low scores were 78. Some spread might mean grades in the 70s and 80s; the high grade was 82, and the low grade was 74. A lot of spread may mean exam grades in the 40s, 50s, 60s, 70s, 80s and 90s. The high grade was a 98, and the low was 40. You would probably feel very different about receiving an exam grade of 78 in each of these three situations.

Imagine receiving a 78 when there was no variation in exam scores. You would probably find it difficult to believe that everyone in the class obtained a 78 on the exam. In fact, you might wonder if the papers had actually been graded! In the second case, your 78 is indicative of how everyone is doing. All your classmates are performing at about the same level; there was little deviation in the grades. In the third case, a lot of spread, it seems as if everyone is performing at a different level. Some students are doing extremely well, and some extremely poorly. Your grade appears "average."

Measures of dispersion turn the phrases "a lot of spread," "some spread," and "no spread" into single summary statistics. Three popular measures of spread or dispersion are range, standard deviation, and variance. Let's look at each in more detail.

The Range

The **range** is an easily calculated measure of dispersion. It is obtained by subtracting the low value in a distribution from the high value. For example, the range for an age distribution in which the youngest person is 16 and the oldest 52 its 36 (52 − 16). Sometimes researchers report the range as 16 to 52. Instead of doing the subtraction, they report both the low and the high values.

Notice that the range takes only the most extreme scores on a variable into account. Given the following grade distributions, what is the range?

- 22, 86, 86, 86, 87, 87, 92, 92, 93, 95, 96
- 22, 22, 23, 24, 25, 26, 45, 45, 54, 65, 96

It's 74, or 22 to 96, in both cases, and yet the distributions look very different. How is the difference in the distributions reported? The presentation of a frequency distribution, graph, or measure of central tendency should be used in conjunction with the range to show that the distributions are different. Because the range takes only extreme values into account, researchers often report a variable's standard deviation or variance.

The Standard Deviation

The **standard deviation** indicates how much, on the average, the scores depart from the mean. The calculation of the standard deviation entails the subtraction of the variable's mean from *every* score. The complete formula appears in Appendix B.

Suppose you were examining the variable age and found that the mean was 54 years and the standard deviation 2 years. How would you interpret these statistics? The interpretation is that, on the average, respondents' ages depart from the mean age of 54 by 2 years. Some respondents may be 56, others 35, and still others 72. Yet the average age is 54, and, on the average, respondents' ages depart from that mean by 2 years. If the mean were 54 and the standard deviation 4 years, it indicates that, on the average, respondents' ages depart from the mean by 4 years. The larger the standard deviation, the larger the spread or dispersion around the mean. What does a standard deviation of 0 indicate? There is no spread; all cases have the mean score.

Variance

Variance is a third measure of dispersion. Variance is simply the square of the standard deviation. If the standard deviation is 2, variance is 4. If the standard deviation is 5, variance is 25.

Since variance is the square of the standard deviation, it too measures how cases spread around the mean, and it too includes all cases in its calculation. Unlike the standard deviation, however, variance is not expressed in the same units as the original variable. That is, if the variance for an age distribution were 9, that is interpreted as 9 *square years*. The standard deviation for that same distribution would be 3 years. You may find square years a difficult concept and therefore prefer to interpret the standard deviation!

C H E C K P O I N T

1. Match the words in column A with one or more statements from column B.

A	B
a. Standard deviation	**1.** Indicates the low and the high value
b. Range	**2.** Indicates how scores depart from the mean
c. Variance	**3.** Takes into account only the extreme scores
	4. Is the square of another measure of dispersion
	5. Indicates the spread of cases on a variable

Interpreting Standard Deviation: The Normal Curve

The **normal curve** is a useful device for interpreting the standard deviation. The normal curve is a special curve. On it, the mean, mode, and median all have the same value. The normal curve is, therefore, a perfectly symmetrical distribution; the most frequently occurring value (the mode) is the value that splits the distribution in half (the median), and that value equals the sum of all values divided by the number of cases (the mean). A picture of a normal curve appears in figure 7-1.

The normal curve was not devised by a demonic statistician. Although it is a hypothetical distribution, many naturally occurring phenomena approximate the normal curve. For example, where I live, a plot of the year's temperatures resembles the normal curve. There are very few subzero days, slightly more days in the teens, more in the 20s, more in the 30s, more in the 40s, more in the 50s, and the bulk in the 60s. Moving away from the average 60s, there are fewer days in the 70s, even fewer in the 80s, fewer still in the 90s, and mercifully even fewer exceeding 100 degrees. Thus a plot of temperatures produces a normal curve.

Two statistics perfectly describe any normal curve, the mean and the standard deviation. Departures from central tendency, the mean, are described in standard-deviation units. Researchers talk about a +1 standard-deviation departure from the mean, or a +2 departure, or a +1.7 departure, and so on. Departures can also occur in the negative direction: a −1 standard-deviation departure from the mean, or a −2 standard-deviation departure, or a −1.7 standard-deviation departure.

As shown in figure 7-1, positive departures indicate movement to the right of the mean. Therefore values on the variable increase relative to the mean. A negative standard deviation indicates a score below the mean. Movement is to the left of the mean. What does a standard deviation of 0 indicate? There is no departure from the mean; the score is the mean. How does the normal curve help to interpret a variable's standard deviation? Let's look at an example.

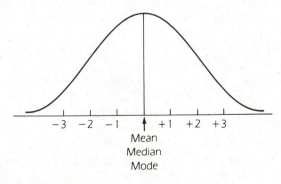

Figure 7-1 The normal curve.

Suppose that while returning exams, your instructor announced that 78 was the average grade and that the standard deviation was 5. Furthermore, your instructor said that the normal curve would be used to assign letter grades. What does that mean?

First, sketch a normal curve. The mean, mode, and median equal 78. In every sense of the term, the average grade is 78. Since a grade of C represents average, we know that people receiving 78s receive Cs. What else do we know? The standard deviation was 5. Moving 1 standard-deviation unit to the right of the mean corresponds to a grade of 83, or 78 + 5. Remember, 1 standard-deviation unit in this example equals 5 points! Moving +2 standard-deviation units to the right of the mean results in a grade of 88, or 78 + 2(5). Moving −2 standard-deviation units produces a grade of 68, or 78 −2(5). I now know that approximately 68 percent of the grades were between 73 and 83 (+1 and −1 standard-deviation unit), 95 percent of the scores were between 68 and 88 (+2 and −2 standard-deviation units), and 99 percent of the scores were between 63 and 93 (+3 and −3 standard-deviation units). How did I know that? I looked at the table of areas under the normal curve shown in Appendix C.

The table of areas under the normal curve may be used on distributions approaching a normal curve. It gives the area between the mean and a selected standard-deviation unit. To use the table, add the first row and first column of the table together to obtain the selected standard-deviation unit. For example, a standard-deviation unit of 1.00 is located by matching the row labeled 1.0 with the column labeled 0.00. A standard-deviation unit of 1.36 is located by combining the row labeled 1.3 with the column labeled 0.06. A standard-deviation unit of 2.45 is located by linking the row labeled 2.4 to the column labeled 0.05.

In linking the appropriate row and column together, you find that they converge on a single number. That number is the area between the mean and the selected standard-deviation unit. For example, the area between the mean and a standard deviation of +1.00 is 0.3413. The area between the mean and a −1.00 standard-deviation unit is also 0.3413. Area is always positive, whether you look at scores above (plus units) or below (minus units) the mean.

Armed with that information, what's the area between the mean and a +2.58 standard-deviation unit? First, look for the row labeled 2.5 and match it to the column labeled 0.08. These numbers converge at the 0.4951 value. That tells us that 0.4951 of the area is between the mean and a +2.58 standard-deviation unit. Another interpretation is that 49.51 percent of the area or scores on the variable are between the mean and a +2.58 standard-deviation unit.

Returning to the exam example, I claimed that approximately 68 percent of the grades fell between 73 and 83. I made that claim on the basis of the table in Appendix C. I noted that the area between the mean and a +1.00 standard-deviation unit was 0.3413. Moving to the left and right of the mean by 1.00 standard-deviation unit, I covered twice that area, or approximately 68 percent of the cases. If your instructor decided to assign 68 percent of the students a C, students receiving grades between 73 and 83 would receive Cs.

Suppose your instructor decided to assign 50 percent of the students Cs; what grades would receive them? A figure of 50 percent means that 25 percent is on either side of the mean, or that 0.2500 of the area is between the mean and some standard-deviation unit. Looking in the body of the table for 0.2500, we find that it's not there. The values closest to 0.2500 are 0.2486 and 0.2517. Of the two, 0.2486 is closer to 0.2500, so let's use that area. It corresponds to a 0.67 standard-deviation unit. That means that students obtaining scores between 81 and 75— 78 + 0.67(5)—receive Cs.

The standard deviation indicates how, on the average, the scores depart from the mean. In addition, when we work with large samples, we assume that our variable is normally distributed. That assumption allows us to use the normal curve for additional interpretations.

C H E C K P O I N T

2. What areas correspond to the following standard-deviation units?
   a. +1.67
   b. +2.34
   c. −1.67
   d. −0.88

3. What standard-deviation units correspond to the following areas?
   a. 0.4834
   b. 0.0517
   c. 0.4100 .

4. In a sample of 2000 respondents, the mean age was 43 years and the standard deviation was 6 years.
   a. What ages correspond to a + and −1 standard-deviation unit?
   b. Between what ages do 68 percent of the cases fall?
   c. Between what ages do 80 percent of the cases fall?

Computer Calculations: Measures of Dispersion

To obtain measures of dispersion with SPSS^X, use the STATISTICS and FREQUENCIES commands. The following keywords calculate measures of dispersion:

1. RANGE subtracts the low from the high value.
2. MINIMUM and MAXIMUM select the low and high values in a distribution, respectively.
3. STDDEV calculates the standard deviation.
4. VARIANCE calculates variance.

What does the following command tell the computer?

```
FREQUENCIES VARIABLES = CHILDS SEX/
    STATISTICS = MEAN MEDIAN RANGE STDDEV/
```

It tells the computer to print frequency distributions for the CHILDS and SEX variables. In addition, it requests the calculation of two measures of central tendency (the mean and the median) and two measures of dispersion (the range and the standard deviation). The printout from this run is shown in table 7-1. Let's interpret the statistics.

The range for the CHILDS variable is 8, which tells us that there are 8 values between the high and the low values. If you decided that CHILDS is a ratio variable, you can examine the standard deviation. The standard deviation is 1.804. It indicates that, on the average, the number of children departs from 1.96 children, the mean, by 1.804 children. Assuming the CHILDS distribution approximates a normal curve, approximately 68 percent of the cases have between 3.76 and 0.16 children.

The range for SEX is 1.00 and the standard deviation is 0.498. How would you interpret these statistics? Did you decide that they are meaningless numbers? Good. You cannot interpret them. Since calculating a range means that the attributes must be ordered, such a calculation requires ordinal data, at a minimum. The standard deviation is a measure of variation around the mean. Since calculating the mean requires interval data, as discussed in chapter 6, the calculation of a standard deviation also requires data measured at least at the interval

Table 7-1 / Example Printout: Measures of Dispersion for CHILDS and SEX

```
CHILDS   CHILDREN EVER HAD
  MEAN       1.960    MEDIAN  2.000
  STD DEV    1.804    RANGE   8.000
VALID CASES  248      MISSING CASES  1


SEX
  MEAN       1.550    MEDIAN  2.000
  STD DEV     .498    RANGE   1.000
VALID CASES  249      MISSING CASES  0
```

NOTE: The request for measures of dispersion yields this information in addition to the information shown in table 5-1.

level. We have not described any measures of dispersion appropriate for nominal data. Measures of dispersion do exist for nominal data, but they are rarely used and therefore will not be discussed in this text.

Once again, it's your turn to write, run, and interpret programs that calculate measures of dispersion.

C H E C K P O I N T

5. Interpret the following SPSS[X] commands:

```
FREQUENCIES VARIABLES = AGE EDUC TRIAL/
  STATISTICS = MODE MEDIAN MEAN STDDEV MINIMUM MAXIMUM/
```

6. Write and execute an SPSS[X] program to obtain measures of central tendency and dispersion for the AGE and DEGREE variables in Appendix A.

7. Interpret the statistics obtained in checkpoint question 6, above.

chapter 8
An Introduction to Bivariate Analyses

You can now describe a single variable. Given two variables, salary (last year's net income) and sex (male, female), you can easily obtain and interpret their frequency distributions, measures of central tendency, and measures of dispersion. Although most data analyses begin with univariate analysis, research questions often require other types of analyses. For example, after examining the univariate distributions for salary and sex, you may want to know whether sex influences salary. An answer to that question requires bivariate analysis, the analysis of how two variables "go together."

Upon completion of this chapter, you should be able to do the following:

1. Define the term *bivariate analysis*
2. Give examples of bivariate analyses
3. Define the term *relationship*
4. Give examples of statements expressing a relationship between variables
5. Define the term *hypothesis*
6. Distinguish between and give examples of research hypotheses and null hypotheses
7. Describe covariational and causal relationships
8. Define positive and negative relationships
9. Explain the strategy for testing hypotheses

The Relationship

What does it mean to say that two variables are related? The answer to that question is similar to what we mean when we say two people have a relationship. We typically mean that the people or variables "go together." However, "going together" probably has a more precise definition for variables than for people!

Saying that there is a relationship or association between two variables means that certain attributes on one variable are linked to certain attributes on the other variable. For example, the following statements indicate relationships between two variables:

1. Women tend to earn less money than men.
2. Men are more likely to commit murder than women.
3. Higher educational levels tend to be related to higher income levels.

Let's look at each statement to determine the variables and the linkage between their attributes.

The first statement links the variables sex and income. The male attribute on sex tends to go with higher incomes than the female attribute on sex. If asked to predict a female's income, you would predict a lower income than if asked to predict a male's income.

The second statement links the variables sex and commission of murder (yes, no). The statement claims that the male attribute on sex is more likely to occur with the yes attribute on murder than is the female attribute on sex. If you were told a murder had been committed, you would be more likely to predict that a male had committed the murder than a female.

The third statement claims a relationship between education and income. Low attributes on education link to low attributes on income. Middle levels of education link to middle income levels. High educational levels link to high income levels. If, for example, you were told that someone had little education, you would be more likely to predict a low income than a high income.

Two variables are related when knowledge of an attribute on one variable tends to restrict the range of attributes on the second variable. Does the statement "Women always earn less money than men" assert a relationship between variables? Yes. It claims that the attribute female always links to lower incomes than the male attribute. Is that the same statement we looked at before? No! The difference between the two statements is important:

Women tend to earn less money than men.
Women always earn less money than men.

Do you see the difference? One statement uses the word *always* and the other uses the words *tend to*. These words dramatically alter the meaning of the statements.

Think about what it would take to disprove each statement. *One* woman who earned more money than a man would disprove the second statement. What would it take to disprove the first statement? Would one woman earning more money than a man disprove it? No. How about two women earning more than men? Three? You probably can't decide, because this statement involves a probability or significance level decision, which we will discuss shortly. For now, note that the first statement is a probability statement; women *tend* or are more likely to earn less money than men. The second statement is an absolute or lawlike statement; women *always* earn less than men. In social research, we work with probability statements. The probability statements that we actually test are called hypotheses.

Hypotheses

A **research hypothesis** is a tentative answer to a research question. Phrased in probability language, it states that there *is* a relationship between variables. The research hypothesis is empirically testable. The statement "Blacks are more likely than whites to receive long prison sentences" is a research hypothesis. It states, in probability form ("more likely"), a relationship between race and sentence length. An empirical test of the hypothesis requires the collection of data on race and length of prison sentence.

Examine the statement "Blacks and whites receive similar sentences." Is that a research hypothesis? Does it indicate a relationship between variables? No, not in the sense that certain attributes on one variable link to certain attributes on another. This statement claims that blacks and whites receive similar sentences; there are no differences in sentence by race. Knowledge of race does not help predict sentence length. A no-difference or equally likely statement is called a **null hypothesis**.

Hypotheses, therefore, are tentative answers to research questions that are phrased in terms of probability. The research hypothesis states that there *is* a relationship between variables, and the null hypothesis states that there is *no* relationship between variables.

C H E C K P O I N T

1. Given the following statements, put an L next to the laws, an R next to the research hypotheses, and an N next to the null hypotheses.

   a. Catholics are more likely to be against abortion than Protestants.

   b. Whether a lawyer is a public defender or a private counselor tends to have no impact on the case's outcome.

   c. In contrast to Democrats, Republicans tend to favor capital punishment.

   d. Elderly people have the same interest in sex that young people do.

   e. Highly educated people always earn more money than people with less education.

   f. Women are always more fearful of going out alone at night than men.

Types of Relationships

Covariational and Causal Relationships

Relationships and research hypotheses take two forms. They express either a **covariational** or a **causal** relationship between variables. A co-variational relationship means that the variables go together. Changes in one variable coincide with changes in the other variable; the variables change together. An example of a covariational hypothesis is "Prestige and power tend to vary together." This hypothesis states that as prestige increases, so too does power, and as power increases, so too does prestige.

Although covariational statements are interesting, we typically work with causal relationships. The preference for causal relationships is based on the types of questions and hypotheses social scientists study: What causes unemployment? What causes crime? What causes some children to do well in school? And so on.

Causal relationships have three characteristics: (1) they express a covariational relationship between variables; (2) there is a time order to the variables; and (3) they are not spurious relationships. The first characteristic, a covariational relationship, means that, to have causality, the variables must go together or change together. Changes in one variable must coincide with changes in the second variable. At a minimum, therefore, a causal relationship is a covariational relationship.

The second characteristic, time order, means that one variable must occur before the other in time; the cause must precede the effect. The variable that occurs first in time is called the **independent variable**. The variable that it is assumed to effect is called the **dependent variable**. Research typically focuses on the dependent variable. Researchers seek to explain the variation, spread, or differences on the dependent variable. Independent variables are examined to see if they help explain the changes or differences in the dependent variable.

For example, suppose you want to know what factors affect occupational choice. An examination of the univariate occupational distribution for the United States confirms that there is a variety of occupations. You want to know why people select particular occupations, what determines whether they become carpenters, or teachers, or accountants, and so on.

Do you think that sex might affect occupational choice? Do you think that certain occupations tend to be associated with men and others with women? If so, sex is an independent variable in your hypothesis, and occupation a dependent variable. Your research hypothesis states that sex tends to influence occupational choice. If there is a relationship, then knowing a person's sex allows you to predict occupation more accurately.

What about education? Do you think education influences occupation? Then we have identified another potential independent variable. Certain educational levels might link to particular occupations. If that's true, then knowledge of someone's educational level allows a more accurate prediction of his or her occupation. I suspect that you can think of even more potential independent variables that affect occupation.

The third characteristic of a causal relationship is that it is not spurious. A spurious relationship is a fake relationship; it appears to exist, and yet it does not! For example, empirically there is a relationship between the number of firefighters at a fire and the amount of damage. If you attended fires, counted the number of firefighters, and found out the extent of the damage, you would find that the more firefighters there are at a fire, the more fire damage. So empirically the variables exhibit a covariational relationship.

Furthermore, there is a time order to the variables. Firefighters tend to fires before damages are assessed. Therefore, the number of firefighters is the independent variable, and the amount of damage the dependent variable. Given the empirical relationship between the two variables, we could conclude that if you have a fire, you should not call the fire department. That's a pretty strange statement, but yet it follows from the data.

At this point, you're probably scratching your head and thinking that there's another factor that affects the number of firefighters at a fire, as well as the amount of damage—size of fire. You're right. If a third variable, size of fire, is taken into account, then there is no relationship between the number of firefighters and the amount of damage. The original relationship between number of firefighters and amount of damage was spurious. The size of the fire determines the number of firefighters called, and the size of the fire affects the amount of damage. So a supposedly causal relationship between number of firefighters and amount of damage is fake.

Notice that the determination of whether a relationship is spurious requires the examination of additional variables. Bringing additional variables into an analysis means doing multivariate analysis. Although we will not examine multivariate analyses until chapter 11, you can already see the need for doing that kind of analysis.

The three criteria for causality match the common concept of causality. For example, what do toothpaste advertisers tell us? They claim that toothpaste brands affect love lives. We're told that if we use a particular brand of toothpaste, others will be attracted to us, and the more we use the toothpaste, the more attractive we become. So we learn that the variables toothpaste brand and attractiveness go together; if we use a certain toothpaste brand, our attractiveness level increases. Second, we learn that there is a time order to the variables: we cannot be attractive until we use the toothpaste. Third, the advertisers claim that the relationship is not spurious. After all, it couldn't be a lively personality or a sense of humor that attracts people—it must be the toothpaste!

Positive and Negative Relationships

In addition to being either causal or covariational, some relationships, and therefore hypotheses, express either a **positive** or **negative** relationship. A positive relationship indicates that the values on the variables increase (or decrease) together. For example, "Prestige and power vary together" states a positive covariational relationship. The hypothesis claims that increases in prestige, or alternatively in power, accompany increases in the other variable. A positive causal statement is "Educational level tends to determine income level." This statement suggests that an increase in the attributes on the independent variable, educational level, causes an increase in the attributes on the dependent variable, income level.

Negative relationships state that increases in the attributes on one variable go along with declines in the attributes on the second variable. An example of a negative covariational relationship is "Occupational stress and amount of leisure time vary inversely." That hypothesis states that there is a negative relationship between stress and leisure time. As stress increases, leisure time declines, and as leisure time declines, stress increases.

An example of a negative causal hypothesis is "An offender's income tends to affect sentence length: the higher the income, the shorter the sentence." The hypothesis states that income, the independent variable, affects sentence length, the dependent variable, such that increases in income result in decreases in sentence length.

Do all hypotheses express either a positive or negative relationship? Remember that the null hypothesis is a statement of no relationship; it expresses neither a positive nor a negative relationship. Other than the null, do all hypotheses state either a positive or negative relationship? *No.* Think about the level at which variables are measured. Relationships between variables can be positive or negative only if the variables are measured at the ordinal, interval, or ratio levels. Hypotheses about nominal variables have no sign; there is no order to a nominal variable's attributes.

For example, the hypothesis "Women are more likely to be pro abortion than men" has no sign. What would it mean to increase in value on sex (male, female) or to decrease in attitude toward abortion (pro, con)? Nothing. These are nominal variables, and there is no order to the attributes. Therefore, hypotheses involving nominal variables have no sign.

C H E C K P O I N T

2. Given the following statements, put a COV next to those that state a covariational relationship and a C next to those that state a causal relationship. In addition, place a + next to the hypotheses that state a positive relationship and a − next to those that express a negative relationship.

   a. Father's educational level tends to determine son's educational level.

   b. The number of unplanned pregnancies in a society tends to decline as the average age of its women increases.

   c. People who were abused as children tend to abuse their own children.

   d. Fertility plans tend to vary with occupational plans.

Hypothesis Testing

Once the hypothesis is clearly stated, it can be tested. To test hypotheses, researchers use a hypothesis-testing strategy. Although there are several statistical techniques for doing hypothesis testing, the strategy remains the same for all.

The hypothesis to be tested is the null hypothesis. Recall that the null hypothesis states that there is no relationship between the variables. But why are we testing the null hypothesis and not the research hypothesis? That's a good question. The answer is based primarily on logic. We test the null hypothesis to avoid committing the fallacy of affirming the consequent.

The **fallacy of affirming the consequent** is committed when you claim to have proven something true. Logically, we can never prove anything true; we can simply fail to disprove it. So in the real world (which we will probably never know), there either is or isn't a relationship between the variables. We test the null hypothesis that states that there is no relationship between the variables. If we can reject the null hypothesis, it gives credibility to the idea that there is a relationship between the variables. It doesn't prove that there is a relationship, but it makes the idea that the variables are related more believable.

This seems like a devious and roundabout way to test a hypothesis, but remember that logically we never prove anything true—we simply fail to disprove it. This logic is similar to the logic used in American courtrooms. The accused is assumed innocent until the evidence indicates otherwise. Likewise, the null is assumed correct until the evidence indicates otherwise. How do we know when the evidence indicates otherwise?

Before testing the null hypothesis, we need to make a decision about when to reject and when to fail to reject ("accept") the null. As researchers, we have these two options. Remember, rejecting the null hypothesis gives us reason to believe that the variables are related. It does not, however, prove that the variables are related. A failure to reject the null hypothesis leads to the conclusion that the variables are not related. In reality, which we may never know, the variables either are or are not related.

Look at the model shown in table 8-1. In two cells of the table, all is well with the world. If you reject the null and in reality it's false, all is okay. Similarly, if you fail to reject the null and in reality it's true, you've done the right thing. However, in two cells you've committed an error. If you reject a true null, you've committed a **Type I error**. That is, you tell everyone the variables are related, and in reality they are not. If you fail to reject a false null, you've committed a **Type II error**. Now you tell everyone that the variables are unrelated, and in reality they do have a relationship. How does knowledge about errors help us to decide whether to reject or fail to reject the null?

The Type I error is also called the **significance level**, and we set

Table 8-1 / Hypothesis-Testing Decisions

		THE RESEARCHER'S DECISION	
		You Reject the Null	You Fail to Reject the Null
REALITY	The null is true	Type I error	Okay
	The null is false	Okay	Type II error

that value. The significance level represents the probability of rejecting a true null. Why set it at all? Why don't we always make the right decision, rejecting false nulls and failing to reject true nulls? Keep in mind that we usually work with samples. A sample often represents one out of probably hundreds that could have been drawn from the population. How sure are we of the sample results? Do you think we might get other results with another sample? Of course. So the best we can do is control the risk or probability with which we make errors.

In this book we focus on controlling the risk associated with the Type I error. Setting the significance level at a low value, say 0.05, means that we're willing to make the error of rejecting a true null 5 times in 100. Setting the Type I error at a higher value, say 0.3, means that we're willing to make the error of rejecting a true null 30 times in 100. The consequences of rejecting a true null should determine the significance level. If the consequences of making a Type I error are serious, we set the level at a small value, such as 0.01. If the consequences of making a Type I error are of little concern, we may set the value higher. In social science research the signficance level is usually set at 0.05 or 0.01.

Once the significance level is set, it can be used to determine the **critical region**. The critical region is a set of test statistic values that cause us to reject the null. By "test statistic" I mean the statistic we decide to use to assess the hypothesis (a topic we will discuss shortly). Once we decide on a particular statistical technique and a significance level, we can determine the critical region. The critical region is the region of rejection. If the data produce a statistic that falls in the critical region, we reject the null and conclude that the variables are related. In fact, if we reject the null, we conclude that there is a statistically significant relationship between the variables. If, however, the sample's statistic does not fall in the critical region, we usually fail to reject the null and conclude that the variables are not related.

We will apply the hypothesis-testing strategy in the next few chapters. The main ideas to keep in mind involve testing the null hypothesis. If the sample data could easily occur under the null, you fail to reject the null and assume the variables are not related. If, however, the sample data appear unusual under the null, you reject the null and assume the variables are related.

C H E C K P O I N T

3. Given the statement "Children who watch violence on television tend to be more violent than children who do not watch violence on television," answer the following questions:
   a. What is the research hypothesis?
   b. What is the null hypothesis?
   c. What would it mean to commit a Type I error?
   d. What would it mean to commit a Type II error?
   e. If you set the significance level at 0.01, what does that mean? At 0.4?

Perhaps you're wondering why we're spending so much time discussing types of relationships and hypotheses. The truth is that the form of a relationship, and therefore of a hypothesis, tends to determine the kinds of analyses that are appropriate. When hypotheses are clearly stated, they suggest the appropriate analyses and statistics. For example, some statistics are designed for causal ordinal statements, and other statistics are used when working with covariational ordinal statements. In the remaining chapters we will look at the analyses and statistics intended for the different kinds of relationships.

chapter 9

Bivariate Analyses: The Construction of Crosstabulation Tables and Tests of Significance

In the last chapter we examined the concept of a relationship. We also looked at the notion of a hypothesis, the various forms hypotheses take, and the logic of hypothesis testing. In this chapter and chapter 10 we focus on the bivariate analyses of nominal and ordinal data. We seek to determine whether two variables are related and, if so, to examine the form and strength of that relationship. In this chapter we examine the construction of crosstabulation tables and tests of significance. In the next chapter we will look at statistics that summarize the strength of the bivariate relationship, measures of association.

Upon completion of this chapter, you should be able to do the following:

1. Describe a crosstabulation table
2. Construct crosstabulation tables
3. Interpret percentages
4. Explain the basis for a chi square calculation
5. Interpret chi square
6. Write SPSS^X commands to construct crosstabulation tables

Newspapers often print tables showing the percentage of males and females who approve, disapprove, and have no opinion on government policies and practices. These tables are called either **crosstabulation**, **contingency**, or **joint frequency tables**. The tables are constructed by counting how many females in the sample said they approved of the policies, how many females said they disapproved, and how many females said they had no opinion. The same tallies are then made on the males in the sample. A table constructed from these counts portrays the bivariate relationship between sex and opinion. Table 9-1 shows a crosstabulation table for sex and opinion.

All crosstabulation or contingency tables are described as $r \times c$ tables, where r represents the number of rows in the table and c the number of columns. In table 9-1 there are three rows and two columns. It is, therefore, a 3×2 table. Notice that the totals (also called marginals) are not included in that count. Totals are considered external (marginal) to the table. Multiplying the number of rows in a table by the number of columns gives the number of cells in the table. For example, a 3×2 table has six cells. Looking at table 9-1, we find six cells: males who approve, males who disapprove, males who are undecided, females who approve, females who disapprove, and females who are undecided.

Well-constructed tables have titles. Titles describe the information contained in the table. For example, titles often name the variables, describe the data set, indicate the year the data were collected, and state whether the numbers appearing in the cells are frequencies or percentages. The title of table 9-1 includes all these elements: 1984 data on Attitude Toward the U.S. Invasion of Grenada by Sex, $N = 265$, and Frequencies and (Percentages).

The cells in table 9-1 contain both frequencies and percentages. Cell frequencies are joint frequencies, the frequency with which *both* attributes occur together. For example, the joint frequency for females who approve is 70; that is, there were 70 respondents who were female *and* approved. Similarly, we learn that 80 males approved. Should we conclude, from looking at these frequencies, that males are more likely to support government policies than females? No! True, more males (80) support government policies than females (70), but does that indicate a relationship between the variables? Compare the number of males in the sample to the number of females. There are 160 males versus 105 females. To control for differing totals, frequencies must be converted to percentages.

Percentages

What are percentages? "Percent" means per 100. To calculate a percentage, divide a frequency by a total and multiply the resulting number by 100. What does that do? Percentages standardize on the basis of 100 cases. In table 9-1, for example, the percentages indicate the number of cases in each category, assuming 100 males and 100 females; that is, the table was percentaged within categories of sex. For example, the 50 percent statistic for males who approve was obtained by dividing 80, the number of males who approved, by 160, the number of males in the sample. The result, 0.5, was multiplied by 100 to get 50 percent.

Why wasn't the table percentaged within categories of attitude? For example, why wasn't 80, the number of males who approved, di-

Table 9-1 / Attitude Toward the U.S. Invasion of Grenada by Sex, Hypothetical
Data, 1984, $N = 265$, Frequencies & (Percentages)

| | | SEX | | |
		Male	Female	Total
	Approve	80 (50%)	70 (66.66%)	150
OPINION	Undecided	10 (6.25%)	5 (4.76%)	15
	Disapprove	70 (43.75%)	30 (28.57%)	100
	TOTAL	160 (100%)	105 (99.99%)	265

vided by 150, the total number who approved? Or, why wasn't the table
percentaged using the total sample size as the denominator? For example, why wasn't each cell divided by 265 and then multiplied by 100?

Think about the variables in the table. What question or hypothesis do you think is being asked? The interesting question here seems
to me to be whether a person's sex affects his or her attitude toward
government policies. The research hypothesis states, therefore, that men
and women have different attitudes toward government policies. The
null hypothesis states that sex does not affect attitude toward government policies. Given these hypotheses, sex is the independent variable
and attitude the dependent variable.

A *rule of thumb*, then, is to percentage within categories of the
independent variable. This method of percentaging enables us to begin
to see the effect of the independent on the dependent variable. Thus,
if you percentage down, you should compare across, and if you percentage across, you should compare down. In this case, percentages
were calculated within categories of sex, the independent variable, allowing us to see the effect of sex on attitude.

These percentages indicate that women were more likely than men,
66.66 percent versus 50 percent, to have approved of the government's
action. Notice that if we had looked only at the frequencies, we would
have made the erroneous conclusion that men are more likely than
women to have approved of the government's action! Remember, it's
percentages, *not* frequencies, that we compare.

Percentages enable us to "get a feel" for whether there is a relationship between two variables by standardizing on the basis of 100
within each category of the independent variable. But how do percentages indicate whether the variables are related? In chapter 8 it was stated
that a relationship existed between two variables if knowledge of the
attributes on one variable restricted the range of the attributes on the
second variable. Working with contingency tables and percentages, let's
examine that idea.

Suppose you believe that religion is related to attitude toward abortion such that religion determines attitude toward abortion. Religion is therefore the independent variable, and attitude is the dependent variable. Suppose data produced the joint frequencies and percentages shown in table 9-2. Are the variables related? If you were told a repondent was Catholic, would that help you to predict his or her attitude toward abortion? If you knew the respondent was Protestant or Jewish, would that help to predict attitude? Is the attribute range on attitude toward abortion restricted when the attribute on religion is known?

The answer to all these questions is no. Table 9-2 indicates absolutely no relationship between the variables. Knowledge of the attributes on one variable tells you nothing about the attributes on the other variable. If you knew a respondent's religion, you would do equally well to predict that they were against, for, or neutral toward abortion.

Now let's look at table 9-3. Are the variables related? If you were told a respondent was Catholic, would that help you to predict his or her attitude toward abortion? Is the attribute range on attitude toward abortion restricted when you know the respondent's religion? Did you answer those questions with a yes? Good. Table 9-3 shows a perfect relationship between variables—knowledge of the attributes on one variable allows perfect prediction of the attributes on the other variable. For example, if you knew someone was Catholic, you would predict that he or she was against abortion, and if told someone was Jewish, you would predict that he or she was neutral on abortion. Both predictions would be correct.

In reality, contingency tables rarely resemble either table 9-2 or table 9-3. Rather, the relationships exhibited in real data tend to fall somewhere between these two extremes. The question then becomes whether the data more closely resemble table 9-2 or table 9-3. Before turning to that question, let's check what we've just discussed and see how to use the computer to generate contingency tables.

C H E C K P O I N T

1. Make up variables and attributes for a 4 × 3 table. Draw the table.

2. How many cells are there in a 6 × 2, a 2 × 2, a 4 × 3, and a 3 × 4 table?

3. Use table 9-4 to answer the following questions.
   a. How many rows are there?
   b. How many columns are there?
   c. What do the row percentages indicate?
   d. What do the column percentages indicate?
   e. Which percentages, column or row, are more interesting? Why?

Table 9-2 / Attitude Toward Abortion by Religion, Hypothetical Data, N = 270, Frequencies & (Percentages)

		RELIGION			Total
		Catholic	Protestant	Jewish	
	Against	30 (33.33%)	30 (33.33%)	30 (33.33%)	90
ATTITUDE	Neutral	30 (33.33%)	30 (33.33%)	30 (33.33%)	90
	For	30 (33.33%)	30 (33.33%)	30 (33.33%)	90
	TOTAL	90 (99.99%)	90 (99.99%)	90 (99.99%)	270

Table 9-3 / Attitude Toward Abortion by Religion, Hypothetical Data, N = 270, Frequencies & (Percentages)

		RELIGION			Total
		Catholic	Protestant	Jewish	
	Against	90 (100%)	0 (0%)	0 (0%)	90
ATTITUDE	Neutral	0 (0%)	0 (0%)	90 (100%)	90
	For	0 (0%)	90 (100%)	0 (0%)	90
	TOTAL	90 (100%)	90 (100%)	90 (100%)	270

Table 9-4 / Fun by Hair Color, N = 75, Frequencies

		HAIR COLOR			Total
		Blonde	Brown	Red	
	Lots	10	25	5	40
FUN	Some	5	10	5	20
	None	5	5	5	15
	TOTAL	20	40	15	75

Crosstabulation Tables: Computer Calculations

Let's look at contingency tables based on data in Appendix A. To obtain a joint frequency table, we use the SPSS[X] CROSSTABS command:

```
CROSSTABS TABLES = SEX BY ABDEFECT
```

What have we told the computer? We told it to generate the crosstabulation table for SEX and ABDEFECT. The placement of the variable names indicates the row and column variable. Remember, tables are expressed as $r \times c$ tables. Therefore, the variable named before $\times$ is the row variable, and the variable named after $\times$ is the column variable. In this case, SEX is the row variable, and ABDEFECT is the column variable.

If additional tables are needed, place a slash (/) between tables. For example, what do you think the following CROSSTABS command does?

```
CROSSTABS TABLES = SEX BY ABDEFECT/SEX BY ABNOMORE/
  RELIG BY ABDEFECT
```

It tells the computer to produce three different crosstabulation tables, one for SEX and ABDEFECT, one for SEX and ABNOMORE, and one for RELIG and ABDEFECT. SEX is the row variable in the first two tables, and RELIG is the row variable in the third table.

If several crosstabulation tables are needed for variables that are consecutively coded, use the TO specification. For example, the following two CROSSTABS commands produce identical printouts:

```
CROSSTABS TABLES = SEX BY ABDEFECT/SEX BY ABNOMORE/
  SEX BY ABHLTH/SEX BY ABPOOR/SEX BY ABRAPE/
  SEX BY ABSINGLE

CROSSTABS TABLES = SEX BY ABDEFECT TO ABSINGLE
```

In both cases the command produces six tables. Since the abortion items are consecutive items, the use of the TO specification shortens the command.

When used alone, the CROSSTABS procedure produces a table with cell frequencies. For reasons previously discussed, we usually want to examine percentages. To obtain percentages, we add an OPTIONS command. OPTIONS 3 calculates row percentages, OPTIONS 4 calculates column percentages, and OPTIONS 5 calculates each cell's percentage of the total. OPTIONS 18 calculates the row, column, and total percentages. In addition, OPTIONS 18 prints expected cell frequencies and residuals information. We'll discuss this additional information shortly. Try the following program, and then let's examine the printout.

```
TITLE "CROSSTABS FOR SEX AND ABORTION ITEMS"
DATA LIST RECORDS=1/
 SEX 17 ABDEFECT 57 ABNOMORE 58 ABHLTH 59 ABPOOR 60
 ABRAPE 61 ABSINGLE 62
COMMENT THIS DATA IS FROM APPENDIX A
 RESEARCH HYPOTHESIS: THERE IS A RELATIONSHIP BETWEEN
 SEX AND ATTITUDE TOWARD ABORTION; SEX AFFECTS ATTITUDE
 NULL HYPOTHESIS: THERE IS NO RELATIONSHIP BETWEEN SEX
 AND ATTITUDE TOWARD ABORTION; MALES AND FEMALES FEEL
 THE SAME ABOUT ABORTION
MISSING VALUES ABDEFECT TO ABSINGLE(8,9)
VALUE LABELS SEX 1 'MALE' 2 'FEMALE'/
 ABDEFECT TO ABSINGLE 1 'YES' 2 'NO'
CROSSTABS TABLES=SEX BY ABDEFECT TO ABSINGLE
OPTIONS 18
BEGIN DATA

    . (data cards)
    .
END DATA
```

Table 9-5 shows the printout for one of the tables generated from the above program, SEX by ABDEFECT. What do we learn about the relationship between these two variables? The frequencies indicate that 95 males said an abortion should be legal if there was a strong chance of a defect in the baby, and 108 females responded similarly. Ten males said an abortion under this condition should not be legal, and 26 females felt the same. The univariate distribution for SEX is 105 males and 134 females. The univariate distribution on ABDEFECT includes 203 yes and 36 no responses. The total sample size was 239. Notice that the cell frequencies are the first number in each cell and correspond to the upper left cell's COUNT label.

Because totals differ for each attribute, we know that frequencies should be converted to percentages. Should we use row, column, or total percentages? According to the upper left cell, these correspond to the third, fourth, and fifth numbers in each cell, respectively. Which should we examine and interpret?

Row percentages are obtained by percentaging within categories of SEX. For example, 95 was divided by 105 and the result was multiplied by 100 to yield 90.5 percent. These percentages tell us that of the males, 90.5 percent said yes and 9.5 percent said no. Of the females, 80.6 percent said yes and 19.4 percent said no. So 90.5 percent of the males said that abortion should be legal in this case, whereas 80.6 percent of the females said that abortion should be legal.

Column percentages are obtained by percentaging within categories of ABDEFECT. For example, 95 was divided by 203 and that result was multiplied by 100 to yield 46.8 percent. These statistics tell us that of the yes responses, 46.8 percent were male and 53.2 percent

Table 9-5 / SPSS^X Printout: SEX by ABDEFECT, N = 239

	ABDEFECT		
COUNT EXP VAL ROW PCT COL PCT TOT PCT RESIDUAL STD RES ADJ RES	YES	NO	ROW TOTAL
SEX MALE 1	95 89.2 90.5% 46.8% 39.7% 5.8 .6 2.1	10 15.8 9.5% 27.8% 4.2% −5.8 −1.5 −2.1	105 43.9%
FEMALE 2	108 113.8 80.6% 53.2% 45.2% −5.8 −.5 −2.1	26 20.2 19.4% 72.2% 10.9% 5.8 1.3 2.1	134 56.1%
COLUMN TOTAL	203 84.9%	36 15.1%	239 100.0%

were female. Of the no responses, 27.8 percent were male and 72.2 percent were female. So 46.8 percent of the yes responses were male, whereas only 27.8 percent of the no responses were male.

The total percentages are calculated by dividing each cell frequency by 239 and multiplying that result by 100. From these percentages we learn that 39.7 percent of the sample were males saying yes, 45.2 percent of the sample were females saying yes, and so on.

Of the three percentages, which do you want to examine? Each method gives different information and therefore answers a different question. The issue here is whether sex affects attitude toward abortion. Do men and women feel different about the legality of abortion under varying circumstances? Phrased in those terms, which percentage is of interest? Think about the hypothesis and the rule of thumb. Saying that sex affects attitude means that sex is the independent variable and attitude the dependent variable. Following the rule of thumb, we would percentage within categories of sex (row percentages). Returning to the row percentages, we find that 90.5 percent of the males said yes as compared to 80.6 percent of the females. There is a difference of almost 10 percentage points between males and females.

Does this mean that sex affects attitude? Yes and no. It appears that there is a difference between men and women in their attitude toward abortion, but is it a fluke, a quirk of the sampling procedure? Is a difference of 10 percentage points a likely or unlikely event under the null hypothesis? Is there a statistically significant relationship between SEX and ABDEFECT? To answer these questions, we need to discuss the chi square statistic. Before doing that, however, see if you can interpret and write some CROSSTABS commands.

CHECKPOINT

4. Examine your printout for the five remaining tables. Which percentages (row, column, or total) are the most interesting? What do the percentages indicate?

5. What does the following command tell the computer to do? Draw the dummy tables. (Dummy tables are tables without numbers in cells.)

```
MISSING VALUES DEGREE(8,9) SPKATH TO SPKHOMO(8,9)
  SMOKE(9)
CROSSTABS TABLES=DEGREE BY SPKATH TO SPKHOMO/
  SEX BY SMOKE
OPTIONS 18
```

6. Finish writing the SPSS^X program for checkpoint question 5, above. Run the program and interpret the results.

Is the Relationship Statistically Significant?

If percentages indicate the possibility of a relationship, researchers often go on to ask, "Is the relationship statistically significant?" **Statistical significance** refers to the idea that a relationship is not due simply to chance. For example, we found a difference of 10 percentage points between men and women in their attitude toward legal abortions if there was a chance of a defect in the baby. Sex affected attitude such that men were more likely than women to say the abortion should be legal.

This leads to the question of whether the result obtained from this sample was a likely or unlikely event under the null hypothesis. Phrased slightly differently, we're asking the question, Is is likely that the sample was drawn from a population in which the variables were unrelated? How do we decide that? As discussed in chapter 8, we do hypothesis testing. When we are working with nominal or ordinal data, chi square is the statistic we use to determine whether a relationship is statistically significant.

Before turning to a description of chi square, we need to make a distinction between inferential and descriptive statistics. Chi square is an inferential statistic. **Inferential statistics** allow us to make statements about the properties of a population based upon sample results. In previous chapters we focused on descriptive statistics. **Descriptive statistics** enable us to describe our sample.

Researchers often move from descriptive to inferential statistics. After a researcher describes a particular sample, it is not at all unusual for the researcher to attempt to draw generalizations about the population from which the sample was drawn. The appropriateness of these generalizations depends, however, upon the sampling scheme. It is beyond the scope of this book to describe sampling schemes. Check with your instructor about sampling procedures.

Chi Square

Chi square is an inferential statistic used with crosstabulation tables to assess whether a relationship is statistically significant. It *does not* indicate whether a relationship is weak, strong, or perfect. Chi square simply answers the question, Is it a statistically significant relationship? Phrased slightly differently, chi square answers the question, Is it likely that the sample was drawn from a population in which the variables were unrelated?

The logic of chi square is simple. It compares two sets of data, the data you collected (the observed data) to a hypothetical data set (the expected data). The hypothetical data illustrates a true null hypothesis. The hypothetical data shows, therefore, no relationship between the variables. A crosstabulation table based on the hypothetical data illustrates the table you would expect to find if the variables were unrelated.

Suppose your observed data match the hypothetical data. What does that tell you? It tells you that there is no relationship between your variables. It tells you that the data you observed are what you would expect to find if the variables were unrelated. Under this condition you fail to reject the null. Suppose, however, that your observed data set is "very different" from the hypothetical data set. What does that tell you? Under this condition you reject the null hypothesis and conclude that there is a statistically significant relationship between your variables.

Calculating Chi Square

How do we obtain the hypothetical data set? Fortunately, it's calculated as part of the SPSS^X program. It's called the EXP VAL, the second number in each cell. EXP VAL stands for expected values or frequencies,

Table 9-6 / A Table Supporting the Null Hypothesis: SEX by ABDEFECT

		ABDEFECT		
		Yes	No	Total
SEX	Male	84.9%	15.1%	105 (100.0%)
	Female	84.9%	15.1%	134 (100.0%)
	TOTAL	203	36	239

the frequencies you would expect to find under the null hypothesis. The logic behind the EXP VAL calculation is easy and allows us to understand better the idea of no relationship. Let's examine the logic.

As you know, the expected data are calculated on the basis of the assumption that the null hypothesis is true. In addition, they are calculated using the observed marginals. That means that we know the univariate distributions on both variables. If the only information we have is the univariate distributions, what would a no-relationship table look like?

Let's return to the SEX-ABDEFECT relationship. Remember, when percentaging a table, we percentage within categories of the independent variable. In the SEX-ABDEFECT case, SEX is the independent variable. Looking at the dependent variable, ABDEFECT, we know that 84.9 percent of the sample said yes and 15.1 percent said no. Suppose we replicated those percentages within each category of sex; that is, we assume 84.9 percent of the males said yes and 84.9 percent of the females said yes. Similarly, let's assume that 15.1 percent of the males said no and 15.1 percent of the females said no. The resulting table is shown in table 9-6. What does this table indicate? It shows no relationship between SEX and ABDEFECT. There is no difference between men and women in their attitude toward abortion. The same percentage of both sexes—84.9—said that abortion should be legal, and therefore sex does not affect attitude.

Notice that we constructed this table by replicating the dependent variable's univariate percentage distribution within each category of the independent variable. Once we know percentages, frequencies can easily be calculated. For example, for males the 105 total multiplied by 0.849 yields the EXP VAL of 89.2, and for females the 134 total multiplied by 0.849 yields the EXP VAL for yes of 113.8.

Basically, chi square compares the observed frequency distribution with the expected frequency distribution. See Appendix B for the complete formula. In this case, chi square is 4.49091 (before Yates' correction). Is that statistically significant? To decide that, we need additional information. (I know, it always seems like we need additional information!). Recall from chapter 8 that we need to decide on a significance level, and the significance level in turn helps to construct a critical region.

Suppose we select the traditional 0.05 significance level. Again, recall from chapter 8 that the 0.05 level means that 5 times out of 100 we're willing to run the risk of rejecting a true null. Then what would the critical region be? When working with chi square, we need to look at degrees of freedom. **Degrees of freedom** (df) refers to the number of nonredundant cells that need to be completed so that the rest of the table can be completed, given the constraints of the marginals. What does that mean?

Look at the 2×2 table in table 9-7 and the dummy table beneath it. Given the marginals, fill in the marginals in the dummy table. If you fill in the upper left-hand cell of the dummy table, could you replicate the original table? Yes. Is the upper left-hand cell a magical cell? No. By filling in only one of the four cells you could correctly replicate the frequencies in the other three cells for the 2×2 table. How many degrees of freedom are there in a 2×2 table? One.

We don't really sit around filling in cells to see how many we need to fill in to determine the degrees of freedom. There is a formula, given in Appendix B, to calculate degrees of freedom. However, note that the printout of SEX BY ABDEFECT TO ABSINGLE gives the degrees of freedom. Is the relationship statistically significant? We still need to know the critical region. This time, we have all the information needed to determine the critical region. We simply need to put it all together.

Look at the chi square table in Appendix D. Notice that the columns represent significance levels and the rows represent degrees of freedom. Go to a significance level of 0.05 and 1 degree of freedom. At what value do the row and column coincide? Did you find 3.84? Good. The critical region is all values greater than or equal to 3.84. Is the result in the critical region? Yes, the calculated chi square of 4.49091 is certainly greater than 3.84. Therefore, it is a result that falls in the critical region. As we said in the last chapter, when a result falls in the critical region, it's an unlikely event under the null hypothesis. In fact, it's so unlikely that we reject the null. In this case, therefore, we reject the null hypothesis and conclude that, at the 0.05 level, there is a statistically significant relationship between sex and attitude toward abortion.

Look at the SEX BY ABDEFECT printout again. Notice that there is a value labeled significance, and in this case it equals 0.0341. What do you think that value represents? It is the probability level at which there is a statistically significant relationship between the variables. Since this value is provided in the printout, you really don't need to examine the chi square table in Appendix D. When testing at the 0.05 level, you can simply look at the printout significance. If it's smaller than or equal to 0.05, as is true in this case, the relationship is statistically significant at the 0.05 level. If, however, the significance level is larger than the one you wish to test—for example, 0.12, then the relationship is not statistically significant at the level you are testing.

To obtain chi square from SPSS^X, simply add a STATISTICS com-

Table 9-7 / Illustration of Degrees of Freedom for Chi Square

		Variable A		
		(a)	(b)	Total
VARIABLE B	(a)	3	4	7
	(b)	2	10	12
	TOTAL	5	14	19

		Variable A		
		(a)	(b)	Total
VARIABLE B	(a)	3		7
	(b)			12
	TOTAL	5	14	19

NOTE: Cell values are frequencies.

mand to the CROSSTABS command. For example, to obtain chi square for the SEX by abortion items, use the following commands:

```
CROSSTABS TABLES = SEX BY ABDEFECT TO ABSINGLE
STATISTICS ALL
OPTIONS 18
```

We will discuss the STATISTICS command in more depth in chapter 10. Before turning to the next chapter, however, add that STATISTICS command to your program and run it. Then do the next checkpoint.

C H E C K P O I N T

7. Interpret chi square for the remaining five SEX by attitude toward abortion tables. Test for significance at the 0.05 and the 0.1 levels. Are the relationships statistically significant at those levels?

In this chapter we examined the construction of crosstabulation tables. We discussed how to percentage these tables and thereby begin to understand the variables relationship. In addition, we learned how to decide, using chi square, whether the relationship between the variables is statistically significant. There is, however, another question that we have not yet answered: How strong is the relationship? Supposing that the percentages indicate a difference, or supposing that chi square is statistically significant, we would then want to know the strength of the variables' relationship. We will learn how to assess the strength of a relationship in the next chapter.

chapter 10

Bivariate Analysis: Measures of Association

A question researchers often ask if the percentage distributions differ in a table is, How strong is the relationship between the variables? Researchers often ask the same question if a relationship is statistically significant. **Measures of association** help answer questions about the strength of a relationship for nominal and ordinal variables. **Measures of correlation** indicate the strength of a relationship for interval and ratio variables.

In this chapter we will focus on measures of association. Upon completion of this chapter, you should be able to do the following:

1. Explain when to use a measure of association
2. Describe criteria for selecting a measure of association
3. Interpret selected measures of association
4. Calculate measures of association using SPSS^X

Measures of association answer the question, How strong is the relationship? For example, in a checkpoint question in the last chapter, we examined the SEX BY ABRAPE contingency table. The percentage distributions within SEX indicated a difference by sex; that is, 90.7 percent of the males said an abortion should be legal if a woman became pregnant as a result of a rape, whereas 80.6 percent of the females said it should be legal under this circumstance. There is a difference of 10.1 percentage points between the sexes. It appears, therefore, that there is a relationship between SEX and ABRAPE. How strong is the relationship?

In the last chapter we found a statistically significant relationship between SEX and ABDEFECT at the 0.05 level. How strong is the relationship? Are these relationships very strong? Are they moderate? Are they weak? How much information have we gained in predicting either ABRAPE or ABDEFECT from SEX? To answer these questions, we calculate measures of association.

There are dozens of measures of association. Several criteria aid in selecting an appropriate measure of association: the level at which variables are measured, the form of the relationship and hypothesis, the desired interpretation, and the quirks of particular measures. Let's examine each criterion.

Criteria for Selecting a Measure of Association

Level of Measurement

You know from previous chapters that variables are measured at different levels and that measurement influences the choice of statistical technique. The level at which you have measured variables affects the choice of measure of association. Some measures of association require only nominal data, and others require ordinal data. If you were examining the relationship between two nominal variables, a nominal-based measure of association would be appropriate. If you were working with two ordinal variables, you could use either a nominal- or an ordinal-based measure of association. However, only the ordinal-based measures take the rankings on the variables into account; that is, using a nominal-based measure of association on ordinal data ignores the ordinal feature of the variables.

What type of measure do you use if you're examining the relationship between a nominal and an ordinal variable? For example, suppose you were examining the relationship between religion (Catholic, Protestant, Jewish, other) and family size (small, medium, and large). Since religion is a nominal variable and family size an ordinal variable, do you report a nominal- or an ordinal-based measure of association? Although this point is debated, statistical and methodological purists believe that an ordinal-based measure of association would be inappropriate in this situation. A *rule of thumb*, then, is to select a statistic appropriate for the variable measured at the lowest level. In this case, therefore, a nominal-based measure of association would be selected.

Type of Relationship

The second criterion to consider in selecting a measure of association is the form of the relationship expressed in the hypothesis. Does the hypothesis state a covariational or a causal relationship? Recall from chapter 8 that a covariational relationship claims the variables "go together." There is no independent or dependent variable specified in such a relationship. Statistics corresponding to covariational hypotheses are termed **symmetric** measures of association. Symmetric measures do not require the specification of an independent or dependent variable.

For example, the relationship between women's fertility plans and occupational plans has been called covariational; that is, the two plans go together, but it's unclear whether occupational plans determine fertility plans or whether fertility plans determine occupational plans. Since the relationship is covariational, a symmetric measure of association is appropriate.

If, however, the specified relationship is causal, not only do the variables go together, but there is a sequence to the variables. The independent variable, the cause, occurs prior to the dependent variable, the effect. Measures of association that utilize this information are termed **asymmetric** measures. Two asymmetric measures can be calculated for one table. One measure treats the row variable as dependent, and the other measure treats the column variable as dependent. In actual use, however, only one of these measures is meaningful. The asymmetric measure that utilizes the dependent variable as the dependent variable is the only asymmetric measure to examine.

For example, the relationship between education and occupation has been treated as causal. Since educational level has been thought to influence occupational level, educational level is the independent variable and occupation the dependent variable. When the relationship is phrased as a causal one, an asymmetric measure treating occupation as the dependent variable would be appropriate for detecting the strength of the relationship.

You could—and canned computer programs like SPSS[x] often do—calculate not only the asymmetric measure with occupation as the dependent variable, but also the asymmetric measure with education as the dependent variable. Although it can be calculated, the asymmetric measure with education as the dependent variable makes no theoretical sense and should not be interpreted.

Before we go on, try the following checkpoint.

C H E C K P O I N T

1. What type of measure of association (nominal or ordinal, and symmetric or asymmetric) would you use to study the following hypotheses?
    a. Father's occupational level (low, middle, high) tends to determine son's occupational level (low, middle, high).
    b. Race (white, nonwhite) tends to affect the likelihood of arrest (yes, no).
    c. Feelings of political power (strong, moderate, low) and voting behavior (voted, did not vote) are related.
    d. Subjective reports of one's health (excellent, good, fair, and poor) are related to subjective reports of happiness (very happy, pretty happy, not too happy).

Chi Square Versus Proportionate Reduction in Error Measures

The third criterion, the desired interpretation, raises the issue of whether to select a chi square–based measure or a proportionate reduction in error (PRE) measure of association. Before discussing these two types of measures, let's talk a bit more about measures of association in general.

How does a measure of association indicate the strength of a relationship between two variables? If a measure of association equals 23, what does that indicate about the strength? What about 0.5, or 0.9? The truth is that none of these figures is meaningful unless the range for the measure is known (recall from chapter 6 that range is a statement of the high and the low value). We prefer to work with standardized ranges for the various measures. Measures of association are normed from 0 to 1. This isn't an unusual procedure; recall from chapter 9 that percentages standardize on the basis of 0 to 100.

Standardizing on the basis of 1 means that some measures of association range from 0 to 1, while others range from -1 through 0 to $+1$. To understand the difference in range, think back to the level of measurement issue. Nominal-based measures of association range from 0 to 1 in value. No relationship is indicated by 0, and a perfect relationship is indicated by 1. Tables 9-2 and 9-3 in chapter 9 illustrate no relationship and a perfect relationship, respectively, for nominal variables.

Ordinal-based measures of association range from -1 through 0 to $+1$. No relationship is still indicated by 0. However, why a $+1$ and a -1? The $+1$ indicates a perfect positive relationship—as the values on one variable increase, so too do the values on the other variable. Table 10-1*a* illustrates a perfect positive relationship. The low attribute on the column variable goes with the low attribute on the row variable. If the value on the column variable increases from low to middle, the value on the row variable also increases from low to middle. Furthermore, if the attributes on the column variable increase from middle to high, the attributes on the row variable also increase from middle to high.

A measure of association equal to -1 indicates a perfect negative relationship—as the values on one variable increase, the values on the other decline. Table 10-1*c* illustrates the perfect negative relationship. As the values on the row variable increase from low to middle, the values on the column variable decrease from high to middle. Similarly, as the values on the row variable increase from middle to high, the values on the column variable decrease from middle to low.

Table 10-1*b* illustrates no relationship. Focusing on the column variable's low attribute tells us nothing about the value on the row variable. Similarly, focusing on the column variable's high attribute does not help predict the row variable's value.

The -1 to $+1$ range means that, at the ordinal level, the magni-

Table 10-1*a* / Hypothetical Data Illustrating a Perfect Positive Relationship between Two Variables

		COLUMN VARIABLE			
		Low	Middle	High	Total
ROW VARIABLE	Low	60	0	0	60
	Middle	0	60	0	60
	High	0	0	60	60
	TOTAL	60	60	60	180

Table 10-1*b* / Hypothetical Data Illustrating No Relationship between Two Variables

		COLUMN VARIABLE			
		Low	Middle	High	Total
ROW VARIABLE	Low	20	20	20	60
	Middle	20	20	20	60
	High	20	20	20	60
	TOTAL	60	60	60	180

Table 10-1*c* / Hypothetical Data Illustrating a Perfect Negative Relationship between Two Variables

		COLUMN VARIABLE			
		Low	Middle	High	Total
ROW VARIABLE	Low	0	0	60	60
	Middle	0	60	0	60
	High	60	0	0	60
	TOTAL	60	60	60	180

tude *and* the sign of the relationship must be interpreted. For example, although a +0.6 measure of association is equal in strength to a −0.6 measure of association, they are two very different relationships. The +0.6 relationship is positive, and the −0.6 relationship is negative. Now, let's return to the issue of chi square–based measures of association versus PRE measures.

Chi square–based measures, as you probably anticipate, use chi square in their formula. Remember, chi square itself is *not* a measure of association. Tables 10-2*a* and 10-2*b* illustrate this idea. When we percentage both tables within categories of the column variable, we find identical percentage distributions. The two variables, therefore,

Table 10-2a / Hypothetical Data on Subjective Assessment of Health by
Smoking, 300 Respondents

		SMOKE		
		Yes	No	Total
HEALTH	Excellent	5	40	45
	Good	20	100	120
	Fair	25	40	65
	Poor	50	20	70
	TOTAL	100	200	300

Table 10-2b / Hypothetical Data on Subjective Assessment of Health by
Smoking, 600 Respondents

		SMOKE		
		Yes	No	Total
HEALTH	Excellent	10	80	90
	Good	40	200	240
	Fair	50	80	130
	Poor	100	40	140
	TOTAL	200	400	600

have identical relationships in both tables. However, table 10-2b has
twice as many cases in each cell as table 10-2a. Drawing on the discussion in chapter 9, let's calculate each table's chi square.

The chi square for table 10-2a is 71.6, and the chi square for table
10-2b is 143.2. Notice that the chi square for table 10-2b is twice that
for table 10-2a. Does that mean that the relationship shown in table
10-2b is twice as strong as that shown in table 10-2a? No. Chi square
is *not* a measure of association. Its value, as we just saw, is affected by
sample size. However, chi square can be used to calculate measures
that describe the relationship between nominal variables. In fact, phi
and the contingency coefficient are two popular chi square–based measures of association calculated by SPSS^X. Their formulas are given in
Appendix B.

How would you interpret a phi or a contingency coefficient of 0.3?
You could be correct whether you called it weak, moderate, or strong.
Chi square–based measures of association do not have a strict interpretation. Their interpretation tends to be linked to previous research. For
example, suppose prior research indicated a 0.15 relationship between
the two variables. The 0.3 relationship may now seem quite strong. If,
however, previous researchers found a 0.7 or higher relationship be-

tween the two variables, the 0.3 seems quite weak. Although guidelines have been written for interpreting chi square–based measures as weak, moderate, or strong, there is no strict interpretation for chi square–based measures. Their best interpretation lies in the context of prior research.

PRE measures, on the other hand, have very strict interpretations. Their name—**proportionate reduction in error** measures of association—suggests how they are interpreted. Their coefficients indicate how much we reduce error in predicting one variable's values from knowledge of the other variable's values. For example, a PRE coefficient of 0.3 indicates a 30 percent reduction in error in predicting one variable's values from the other variable. Or, phrased slightly differently, a 0.3 PRE coefficient indicates that 30 percent of the differences in one variable can be explained by knowledge about the other variable.

A PRE measure equal to 0 indicates no reduction in error; that is, one variable does not help to predict or explain the other variable. Similarly, a PRE measure equal to 1 indicates 100 percent reduction in error; that is, knowledge of one variable allows the other variable to be perfectly described or predicted. Popular PRE measures calculated by SPSS[x] include lambda, gamma, and Somer's d.

Quirks of Measures

Many measures of association have an oddity that makes them useful under certain circumstances and of little use under others. We already noted, for example, an oddity of all chi square–based measures—they lack a strict interpretation. In addition, both phi and the contingency coefficient have their own quirks.

Phi: Phi requires only nominal variables. Given our previous discussion on range standardization, we expect phi to range from 0 to 1, where 0 indicates no relationship and 1 indicates a perfect relationship. When either the row or column variable has only two categories, phi does in fact range from 0 to 1. However, the range of phi exceeds the upper limit of 1 in tables that do not have a dichotomous variable. Therefore, although phi may be useful, for example, on 2×2, 2×4, 3×2, or 6×2 tables, its interpretation becomes problematic on 4×3, 3×3, or 5×4 tables. For tables that are not $2 \times k$ or $k \times 2$ in size (where k is any value greater than 1), the contingency coefficient might prove more useful.

Contingency Coefficient: The contingency coefficient requires only nominal variables and should therefore range from 0 to 1. However, the contingency coefficient has a range from 0 to something less than 1. The actual upper limit depends on the table's size. For example, the range for the contingency coefficient in a 2×2 table is 0 to 0.707. Thus, the interpretation of the contingency coefficient is not straightforward. One must determine the coefficient's upper limit for the particular table and interpret it accordingly.

The upper limit is easily calculated on square tables. Divide $r - 1$ by r and then take the square root (r equals the number of rows in the table). For example, the upper limit in a 3×3 table is 0.816: 2 divided by 3 equals 0.666, and the square root of 0.666 is 0.816. Statistics books often given the upper limit for nonsquare tables. The interpretational problems associated with chi square–based measures lead researchers to use PRE measures of association.

PRE measures of association tend to avoid many of the problems related to the chi square–based measures. First, as previously noted, PRE measures have a strict interpretation. Second, all PRE measures range from 0 to 1, where 0 means no relationship and 1 means a perfect relationship. Third, neither table size nor sample size interferes with the PRE interpretation. Still, there are some problems associated with particular PRE measures, which I'll illustrate with lambda and gamma.

Lambda: Lambda, a PRE measure, requires nominal data. Its range is from 0 to 1, where 0 indicates no relationship and 1 indicates a perfect relationship. Lambda is typically used as an asymmetric measure. There is a symmetric lambda that "averages" together the two asymmetric lambdas, but it is the asymmetric lambda that tends to be reported. Although we are focusing on the interpretation of statistics rather than their calculation, let's calculate lambda to learn more about PRE measures in general and lambda specifically.

The general formula for PRE measures is

$$\frac{E_1 - E_2}{E_1}$$

What's an E_1 and what's an E_2? E_1 represents the number of errors made knowing only one variable's univariate distribution. E_2 represents the number of errors made knowing the bivariate distribution for the variables. The rules for calculating an error differentiate the various PRE measures.

Table 10-3 presents hypothetical data relating respondents' sex (male, female) to their fear of walking alone at night within a mile of their home (yes, no). The hypothesis states that males are less likely than females to express fear. Sex is therefore the independent variable and fear the dependent variable. Lambda seems a likely choice for examining the strength of the relationship between sex and fear. Why? First, both variables are nominal, and second, the hypothesis clearly calls for an asymmetric statistic. Let's calculate lambda.

The guiding rule for calculating lambda is the assignment of cases to the modal category. Recall from chapter 5 that the mode is the most frequently occurring category and the only measure of central tendency used on nominal data. To calculate lambda's E_1 we know only the univariate distribution on the dependent variable, and we assign all cases to that distribution's modal category. In this case we assign all 1150 cases to the no fear category. But only 1092 cases actually belong there. Therefore, we misassigned 58 cases (1150 − 1092). E_1 equals 58.

To calculate lambda's E_2, we know the bivariate distribution. We now work within each category of the independent variable, assigning

Table 10-3 / Hypothetical Data on Fear of Walking Alone at Night by Sex,
1150 Respondents

		SEX		Total
		Male	Female	
FEAR	Yes	20	38	58
	No	380	712	1092
	TOTAL	400	750	1150

cases to the modal category on the dependent variable. For example, if
we look only at the males and assign all 400 males to the modal category on the dependent variable (no fear), we misassign 20 males
(400 − 380).

Looking at females, we assign all 750 females to the modal category on the dependent variable (no fear), but only 712 actually belong
there. Therefore we made 38 errors (750 − 712). To find E_2, simply sum
the errors within each category of the independent variable. In this
case E_2 equals 20 + 38, or 58. If we plug these values into the formula
$(E_1 − E_2)/E_1$, lambda equals 0.

The interpretation of lambda is that there is no relationship between the variables. There is a 0 percent reduction in error in predicting fear, the dependent variable, from sex, the independent variable.
Another way of saying this is that knowledge of sex tells us nothing
about fear. Notice that if we had examined the percentages first, we
would not have bothered to calculate lambda! The percentage distributions indicate no difference between males and females: approximately 5 percent of the males and 5 percent of the females said yes on
fear. So the lambda coefficient of 0 confirms what we should have known
from the percentages.

Proceeding in the suggested manner, let's calculate lambda for table
10-4. The percentage distributions clearly differ by sex. Whereas only
5 percent of the males express fear, 49.3 percent of the females express
fear. It seems clear that sex is related to fear. How strong is the relationship? Try calculating lambda yourself. You should find E_1 equal to
390 and E_2 equal to 20 + 370, or 390. If you plug these values into the
formula, lambda equals 0. But that means that there's no relationship
between sex and fear. How can that be, when the percentages indicate
a big difference between male and female reports of fear?

If you check your calculation again, you will still get a lambda of
0. You have just found lambda's quirk. Look at the calculation very
carefully. Although lambda may equal 0, it doesn't automatically mean
no relationship. It may be, as was true here, that the mode for all categories on the independent variable is the same. Thus, a lambda of 0
really means no reduction in error when the mode is used as the prediction rule, rather than no relationship! In a table like this, lambda is
an inappropriate measure of association. You might use phi or the contingency coefficient instead.

Table 10-4 / Hypothetical Data on Fear of Walking Alone at Night by Sex,
1150 Respondents

		SEX		
		Male	Female	Total
	Yes	20	370	390
FEAR	No	380	380	760
	TOTAL	400	750	1150

Gamma: Gamma, an ordinal-based measure of association, has quirks produced by its calculation. Like many other ordinal-based measures, gamma looks at cases in pairs; that is, it makes use of the fact that contingency tables tend to examine grouped data. "Grouped data" refers to the idea that many cases share the same classification. Table 10-5 contains examples of grouped data. Sixty cases share the classification very satisfied with life and excellent health. Twenty cases share the classification somewhat satisfied with life and fair health. The strategy underlying gamma is the assessment of the way in which pairs of cases are related.

In any table there are $[N(N-1)]/2$ pairs, where N represents the number of cases. In table 10-5 there are, therefore, $[255(254)]/2$ pairs, or 32,385 pairs. The total number of pairs can be subdivided into five categories: like-ordered pairs, different-ordered pairs, pairs tied on X, pairs tied on Y, and pairs tied on X and Y.

To find out what that means, let's go back to table 10-5. Look at cell (a). Sixty respondents indicated that they were very satisfied and in excellent health. Compare these 60 respondents to the 50 respondents in cell (e). In comparison to cell (a) respondents, cell (e) respondents are less satisfied with life and in poorer health. Cell (e) respondents therefore declined in value on both variables relative to cell (a) respondents. Cells (a) and (e) are in like order because the attributes on both variables move in the same direction.

Can you find any other like-ordered cells? How about (a) and (f)? In comparison to cell (a), the attributes for cell (f)'s variables decline on both satisfaction and health. How about cells (b) and (d)? In comparison to cell (b) respondents, cell (d) respondents increase in life satisfaction and decline in health. This is not a like-ordered pair but a different-ordered pair; that is, the values increased on one variable and declined on the other. What about cells (f) and (h)? These too are different ordered. Whereas cell (h) increases relative to cell (f) in life satisfaction, it declines in terms of health.

Cells (f) and (i) illustrate a third kind of ordered pair. Although cell (i) declines relative to cell (f) on health, the two cells share the same value on life satisfaction, not satisfied. This is called a tie on X, where X simply represents the life satisfaction variable. Cells (g) and (h) are tied on Y, where Y represents the health variable; that is, in compari-

Table 10-5 / Hypothetical Data on Life Satisfaction by Health Condition, 255 Respondents

		LIFE SATISFACTION			
		Very Satisfied	Somewhat Satisfied	Not Satisfied	Total
	Excellent	(a) 60	(b) 20	(c) 10	90
HEALTH	Good	(d) 25	(e) 50	(f) 15	90
	Fair	(g) 5	(h) 20	(i) 50	75
	TOTAL	90	90	75	255

son to cell (g), cell (h) declines in life satisfaction. However, the two cells share the fair value on health. If we compare the five people in cell (g) to each other, we find the fifth type of pair, a pair tied on X and Y; that is, all five cell (g) respondents share the same health and life satisfaction values.

Try categorizing some pairs yourself. Try cells (d) and (b); cells (c) and (e); cells (b) and (e); cells (d) and (h); cells (e) and (e). You should get different-ordered, different-ordered, tied on X, like-ordered, and tied on X and Y. How does this help? Many ordinal-based measures of association assess the strength of a relationship by examining the types of pairs in a contingency table. As already noted, gamma is one such measure.

Gamma looks only at the like- and different-ordered pairs in a table and compares their numbers. Gamma ignores all ties. Although gamma can be described in terms of the general PRE formula presented earlier, a common computing formula for gamma is

$$\gamma = \frac{L - D}{L + D}$$

L and D represent the number of like-ordered and different-ordered pairs, respectively. When the number of like-ordered pairs exceeds the number of different-ordered pairs, gamma is positive and the relationship between the variables is positive. When the number of different-ordered pairs exceeds the number of like-ordered pairs, both gamma and the relationship between the variables are negative. The magnitude of gamma indicates the extent to which either the like-ordered or different-ordered pairs dominate. Let's calculate gamma for table 10-5.

To calculate like-ordered pairs, start by comparing all cells to cell (a). We can ignore cells (b) and (c) because they are tied with cell (a) on Y. We can also ignore cells (d) and (g)—they are tied with cell (a) on X. Cells (e), (f), (h), and (i), however, are in the same order as cell (a). Therefore, the number of pairs in like order with cell (a) is 60 (50 + 15 + 20 + 50), or 8100.

Now move to cell (b). In reference to cell (b) we ignore cells (a) and (c), which are tied on Y, and cells (e) and (h), which are tied on X. Cells (d) and (g) are in different order. Therefore, only cells (f) and (i) are in like order with cell (b). So 20 (15 + 50), or 1300, is the number of like-ordered pairs in reference to cell (b).

To calculate the number of like-ordered pairs in a table, you must follow this procedure for every cell in the table. In reference to cell (c) there are no like-ordered cells. Cell (d) is in like order with cells (h) and (i). So 25 (20 + 50), or 1750, represents the number of like-ordered pairs in reference to cell (d). Cells (e) and (i) are like-ordered and have 50 (50), or 2500, like-ordered pairs. Adding these numbers together yields the number of like-ordered pairs for this table, 13,650.

Now try to calculate the different-ordered pairs on your own. Start with cell (c), and look at cells below and to the left. Did you come up with 2225? Good. Plugging that into the formula, you will find that gamma equals 0.719. The interpretation of this figure is that there is a 71.9 percent reduction in error in predicting either life satisfaction from health or health from life satisfaction. The positive sign indicates a positive relationship—as health increases in value, so too does life satisfaction.

Calculate gamma for tables 10-6a, b, and c. (See p. 104.) You should find that gamma for all three tables equals 1. Yet the patterns illustrated in these tables look entirely different. In fact, the configuration shown in table 10-6c is the one we previously referred to as perfect. Knowledge of social class allows perfect prediction of life satisfaction. In table 10-6b, however, knowledge that a case is high on the social class variable means that it might be either middle or high on life satisfaction, and in table 10-6a any value on life satisfaction is possible.

Therein lies a quirk of gamma. Although there is only one gamma per table, a particular value of gamma may correspond to several different configurations. Note too that the patterns illustrated in the three tables entail ties; that is, cases tend to be concentrated in a few categories. Gamma does not take ties into account. Except for the diagonal tied-on X and Y pattern in table 10-6c, the calculation of gamma may be inappropriate when a table contains many ties. In situations like those shown in tables 10-6a and 10-6b, ordinal-based measures that use ties may be more appropriate.

SPSS[x] calculates several other measures of association. Table 10-7 reviews these measures, pointing out their characteristics in terms of level of measurement, type of relationship, range, and quirks.

C H E C K P O I N T

2. The following contingency tables are based on variables in Appendix A. Without looking at the data, decide what measures of association would be most appropriate and explain why.

   a. CLASS BY HEALTH   **c.** CAPPUN BY GRASS

   b. MARITAL BY AGED

Table 10-6a / Hypothetical Data on Life Satisfaction by Social Class, 120 Respondents

		SOCIAL CLASS			
		Low	Middle	High	Total
LIFE SATISFACTION	Low	30	20	40	90
	Middle	0	0	20	20
	High	0	0	10	10
	TOTAL	30	20	70	120

Table 10-6b / Hypothetical Data on Life Satisfaction by Social Class, 120 Respondents

		SOCIAL CLASS			
		Low	Middle	High	Total
LIFE SATISFACTION	Low	30	20	0	50
	Middle	0	20	10	30
	High	0	0	40	40
	TOTAL	30	40	50	120

Table 10-6c / Hypothetical Data on Life Satisfaction by Social Class, 120 Respondents

		SOCIAL CLASS			
		Low	Middle	High	Total
LIFE SATISFACTION	Low	40	0	0	40
	Middle	0	40	0	40
	High	0	0	40	40
	TOTAL	40	40	40	120

Calculating Measures of Association with SPSS[x]

Obtaining measures of association with SPSS[x] is easy. It requires the addition of a STATISTICS command after the CROSSTABS procedure. The statistics that you can request are as follows:

- STATISTICS 1 calculates chi square.
- STATISTICS 2 calculates phi for 2 × 2 tables, Cramer's *V* for larger tables.
- STATISTICS 3 calculates the contingency coefficient.

Table 10-7 / Measures of Association: Summary Table

Measure	Level of Measurement	Hypothesis	Range	PRE?	Quirks
Phi	Nominal	Symmetric		No	In 2 by k or k by 2 tables, phi ranges from 0 to 1. In other tables, phi's range may exceed 1. Phi squared has a PRE interpretation.
Contingency Coefficient	Nominal	Symmetric	0 to less than 1	No	The upper value depends on table size.
Cramer's V	Nominal	Symmetric	0 to 1	No	
Lambda	Nominal	Asymmetric	0 to 1	Yes	Lambda may equal 0 when modes are in same column or row.
Gamma	Ordinal	Symmetric	$+1$ to -1	Yes	A variety of patterns may equal 1.
Somer's d	Ordinal	Asymmetric	$+1$ to -1	Yes	
Kendall's Tau-b	Ordinal	Asymmetric	$+1$ to -1	Yes	Use only for $r = c$ tables.
Kendall's tau-c	Ordinal	Asymmetric	$+1$ to -1	Yes	
Eta	Nominal & Ordinal	Asymmetric	0 to 1	Yes	Use for nominal independent variable & interval dependent variable.
Pearson's r	Interval	Symmetric	$+1$ to -1	No	r square has a PRE interpretation.

- STATISTICS 4 calculates lambda, symmetric and asymmetric.
- STATISTICS 5 calculates the uncertainty coefficient, symmetric and asymmetric.
- STATISTICS 6 calculates Kendall's tau-b.
- STATISTICS 7 calculates Kendall's tau-c.
- STATISTICS 8 calculates gamma.
- STATISTICS 9 calculates Somer's d, symmetric and asymmetric.
- STATISTICS 10 calculates eta.
- STATISTICS 11 calculates Pearson's r.

For example, if you want to examine lambda for the SEX BY ABDE-FECT table, use the following command:

```
CROSSTABS TABLES=SEX BY ABDEFECT
STATISTICS 4
```

If, however, you want to see all the measures of association calculated for a table, use the keyword ALL. To obtain these measures for SEX BY ABDEFECT, use this command:

```
CROSSTABS TABLES=SEX BY ABDEFECT
STATISTICS ALL
```

Remember, although the keyword ALL results in the calculation of all SPSS^X's measures of association, not all the measures will be of interest. Some measures will utilize an inappropriate level of measurement, others will be geared for a different type of hypothesis, and still others will have quirks that reduce their utility. Eventually you will find one or two measures that make sense.

C H E C K P O I N T

3. Write and run an SPSS[X] program to examine the contingency tables and measures of association from checkpoint question 2. Combine the widowed, divorced, and separated categories on MARITAL. Be sure to exclude don't knows and no answers from the analysis. What measures of association are appropriate for each table? Why? Interpret the measures you selected.

4. Tables 10-2 and 10-3 presented hypothetical data for HEALTH BY SMOKE and FEAR BY SEX. Write a program to replicate these tables using data from Appendix A. What did you find? Interpret the appropriate measures of association.

At this point we've learned quite a bit about the bivariate analysis of nominal and ordinal variables. In the next chapter we turn to the bivariate analysis of interval and ratio variables.

chapter 11

Bivariate Analysis: Correlation and Regression

In chapters 9 and 10 we discussed bivariate analysis techniques for nominal and ordinal variables. In this chapter we will examine the bivariate analysis of interval and ratio variables. The form of the bivariate relationship is **linear regression**, and **measures of correlation** indicate the relationship's strength. Upon completion of this chapter, you should be able to do the following:

1. Explain when to use linear regression and correlation techinques
2. Explain the logic underlying linear regression analysis
3. Interpret regression coefficients
4. Explain the logic underlying measures of correlation
5. Interpret correlation coefficients
6. Use SPSS^X to do bivariate correlation and regression analysis

Plotting the Relationship: Scattergrams

Variables measured at the interval or ratio level have many attributes. For example, age at last birthday may range from 0 to 120 years, or income measured in dollars may range from 0 to 5 billion. The resulting 5 billion × 120 contingency table would be incredibly unwieldy! Therefore, interval or ratio variables tend to be plotted on **Cartesian coordinates**.

Thinking back to your algebra days, you may recall plotting graphs on Cartesian coordinates. The horizontal axis, the **abscissa**, and the vertical axis, the **ordinate**, were divided into units. The two axes crossed at the **origin**, the point with a zero value on both axes. A typical graph on Cartesian coordinates is shown in figure 11-1. The graph contains

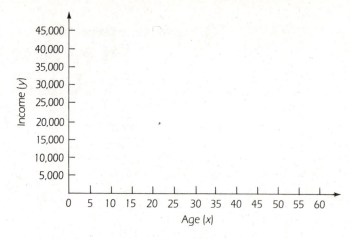

Figure 11-1 Plot of age and income on Cartesian coordinates.

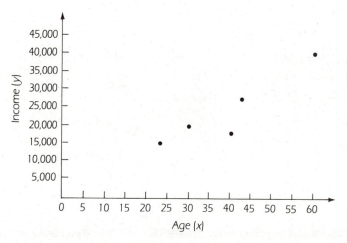

Figure 11-2 Plot of five age and income data points.

two variables: age, measured in years (0 to 65) and income, measured in dollars (0 to 45,000). The age grid marks are in five-year intervals, and the income grid marks are in $5000 units. The age variable is plotted on the abscissa, the x-axis, and the income variable is plotted on the ordinate, the y-axis.

Suppose we had the following data on five respondents:

1. 24 years old, $15,000
2. 30 years old, $20,000
3. 60 years old, $40,000
4. 40 years old, $19,850
5. 42 years old, $26,325

Let's plot the information on figure 11-1. Place a pencil mark for the first person at the point where 24 years on age converges with 15,000 on income. Try plotting the remaining data points. Your graph should match the one in figure 11-2. These plots or graphs are often referred to as **scattergrams**.

Scattergrams show bivariate distributions in graphic form. They give you a first look at the relationship between interval or ratio variables. Recall from chapter 8 that when there is a relationship between variables, the attribute on one variable limits the range for the attributes on the second variable. (See figures 11-3a–d on pp. 110 & 111.)

The scattergram in figure 11-3a shows a relationship between age and income. For example, at age 20, income fluctuates between $5,000 and $8,000, and at age 35, income ranges from $20,000 to $30,000. Nobody at age 20 earns more than $8,000 or less than $5,000. Similarly, no 35-year-old respondent earned more than $30,000 or less than $20,000. Respondents' age clearly limits the range in income. Furthermore, the direction or sign of the bivariate relationship is positive: as age increases, income tends to increase.

The scattergram in figure 11-3b shows a very different relationship, a relationship between ideal family size and respondents' educational level. For example, completion of the eighth grade corresponds to an ideal family size of eight to ten, whereas completion of the twelfth grade reduces the ideal family size range to four to six. This scattergram illustrates a negative relationship: as educational level increases, the ideal family size tends to decline.

The scattergram in figure 11-3c indicates no relationship. Knowing a respondent's age does not limit the range on the amount of time spent watching TV. People of all ages spend entirely different amounts of time watching TV.

The scattergram in figure 11-3d changes its shape in the middle. Up until about the age of 50, the relationship between age and number of hours spent at work is positive: as age increases, so does the number of hours spent at work. After age 50, the relationship is negative: as age increases, the number of hours spent at work declines. A relationship that changes sign is called a **curvilinear** relationship.

Thus, a simple plot of the bivariate distribution on Cartesian coordinates gives us a sense of whether variables are related and indicates the direction or sign of the relationship and its form. Figures 11-3a, 11-3b, and 11-3d show relationships. Figure 11-3a illustrates a positive relationship, and figure 11-3b indicates a negative relationship. The form or shape of the relationship is linear in figures 11-3a and 11-3b. The form or shape in figure 11-3d resembles an inverted U and is curvilinear.

The correlation and regression techniques discussed in this text assume a linear bivariate relationship, as shown in figures 11-3a and 11-3b; that is, we focus on linear regression and linear correlation. If you have a scattergram that looks curvilinear, you should not do linear regression and correlation. Why draw a straight line through figure

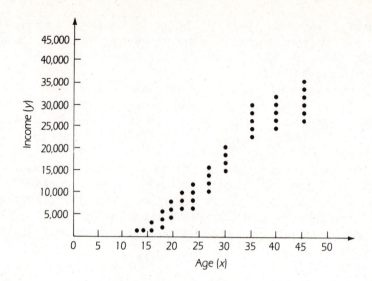

Figure 11-3a Scattergram: age and income.

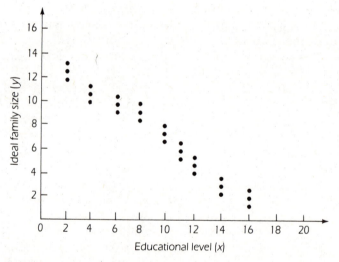

Figure 11-3b Scattergram: ideal family size and educational level.

11-3*d* when a parabola clearly fits the data? You will have to refer to other texts to do curvilinear regression, since it is beyond the scope of this book.

Scattergrams with SPSS[x]

Fortunately we don't hand-plot bivariate distributions; SPSS[x] performs that task quite efficiently. To obtain a scattergram, you simply use the SCATTERGRAM command. For example, to plot MEMNUM and TVHOURS, you would use the following command:

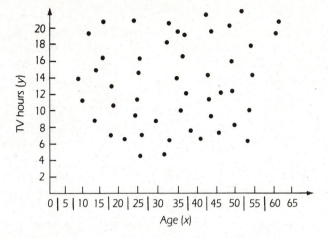

Figure 11-3c *Scattergram: age and hours watched TV.*

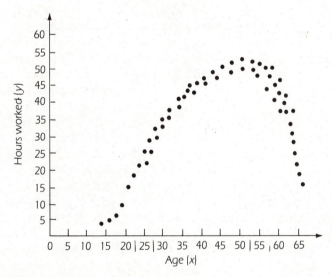

Figure 11-3d *Scattergram: age and hours worked.*

    SCATTERGRAM MEMNUM WITH TVHOURS

The variable name first, MEMNUM, is treated as the *y*-axis variable,
and the variable following WITH is plotted on the *x*-axis. The variable
named first is assumed to be the dependent variable, and the variable
named after WITH is treated as the independent variable. In the MEM-
NUM WITH TVHOURS scattergram, MEMNUM is the dependent
variable, and TVHOURS is the independent variable.

To do additional plots, you add a slash after the last variable named
and continue to list variables. For example, what do you think the following SCATTERGRAM command would produce?

SCATTERGRAM TVHOURS WITH AGE/MEMNUM WITH AGE

Your printout would contain two scattergrams. One scattergram treats TVHOURS as the dependent variable, plotted on the y-axis, and AGE as the independent variable, plotted on the x-axis. The second scattergram plots MEMNUM on the y-axis, as the dependent variable, and AGE on the x-axis, as the independent variable.

Do the scattergram run for MEMNUM WITH TVHOURS. Declare the don't know and no answer responses as missing on both variables. Your printout should resemble the one in figure 11-4. Let's examine it together.

Stars or numbers represent data points. Stars represent single data points. For example, there was only one respondent who belonged to no organizations and watched about 17.9 hours of TV. The numbers 2, 3, 4, and so on represent the number of cases tied in value on both variables. For example, two people watched about 6.3 hours of TV and belonged to one organization. The number 9 is printed if nine or more cases share a value.

Look at the two axes. The default in SPSS^x is a y-axis split into 51 units and an x-axis split into 101 units. By default the low and the high values on the variable are used to scale the scatterplot. The range is then divided by the number of units contained in the axis. For example, the variable TVHOURS has a high value of 18 and a low of 0. The range is 19 $[(18 - 0) + 1]$. The range was then divided by 101, the number of units along the x-axis, yielding a result of 0.188. Each dash on the x-axis therefore represents an additional 0.188 hours of TV.

Two OPTIONS to consider when doing scattergrams are 4 and 7. OPTIONS 4 constructs integer grids; that is, instead of being in decimals, the grid units are whole numbers. For example, the TVHOURS grid mark of 1.8 would be rounded to 2, or the MEMNUM 3.6 grid mark would be rounded to 4. The OPTIONS 7 command deletes the grid marks that run through the scattergram's plot. If OPTIONS 7 is used, only data points appear within grid coordinates. To use one or more of these commands, simply add an OPTIONS command after the SCATTERGRAM command. For example, try the following:

```
SCATTERGRAM MEMNUM WITH TVHOURS
OPTIONS 4 7
```

What, by the way, did you learn about the relationship between MEMNUM and TVHOURS? The scattergram indicates that there is neither a strong positive relationship nor a strong negative relationship between MEMNUM and TVHOURS. The scattergram indicates that there's very little relationship between MEMNUM and TVHOURS.

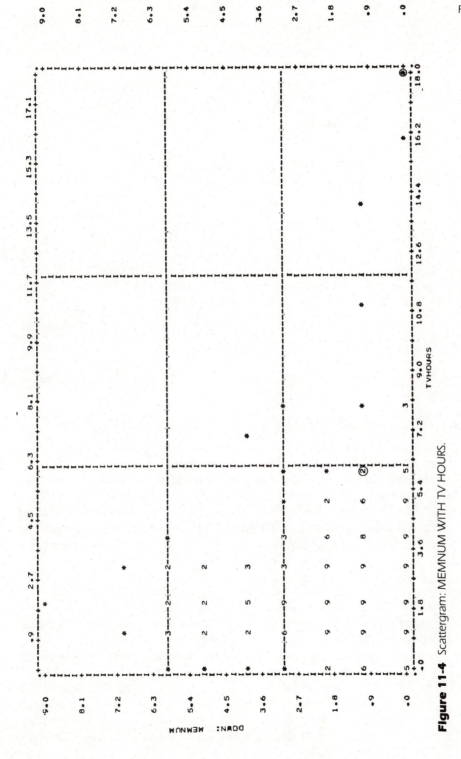

Figure 11-4 Scattergram: MEMNUM WITH TV HOURS.

C H E C K P O I N T

1. Draw and interpret the scattergram for the following data set:

Number of Hours Studied Per Week	Number of Dates Per Week
2	0
4	3
10	6
6	5
25	8
1	0
14	7
14	6
12	5
5	2

2. Write and run a program to examine the scattergrams for MEMNUM and AGE, and TVHOURS and MEMNUM. Be sure to exclude the don't know and no answer responses as MISSING VALUES.

3. What do the scattergrams from checkpoint question 2 indicate about the relationships between the variables?

The Regression Line

Our ability to visualize shapes and forms allowed us to describe figures 11-3a and 11-3b as linear. Typically, however, we want to describe the bivariate relationship mathematically. If the bivariate scattergram relationship looks linear, we perform linear regression analysis. The objective of regression analysis is to state a mathematical description of the bivariate relationship. Working with linear relationships only, we know that the mathematical function that best describes the data is a line. The general equation for a line is

$$Y = b_0 + b_1 X$$

where Y is the dependent variable, X the independent variable, b_0 the intercept, and b_1 the slope of the line. You already know what variables are, so let's discuss intercepts and slopes.

The **intercept** is the point at which the regression line crosses the y-axis. In the above equation it is the point where $X = 0$. The **slope** is the tilt of the line. It indicates how much Y changes for each unit change in X. The meaning of slope in linear equations is similar to the meaning of the term for downhill skiers! Expert skiers ski steep mountains, mountains with large slopes. Bunny hills or novice slopes are

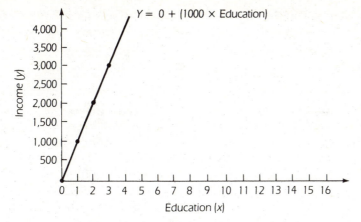

Figure 11-5a *Regression equation and graph: education and income.*

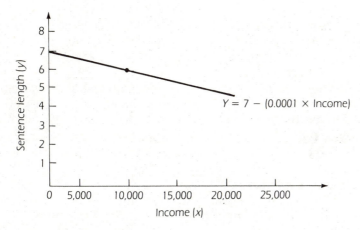

Figure 11-5b *Regression equation and graph: sentence length and income.*

less steep and therefore have little slope. A positive slope indicates that, for each increase in X, Y increases by b_1 units. A negative slope indicates that, for each increase in X, Y declines by b_1 units. Figures 11-5a and 11-5b present the graphs of a line with a positive slope and a line with a negative slope, respectively.

Now that you're familiar with the idea of a line, we need to alter the equation! The Y in a regression equation does not represent the variable Y but rather the predicted value of the variable Y, symbolized as $\hat{Y}$. The regression equation is actually

$$\hat{Y} = b_0 + b_1 X$$

Using this equation we predict values on Y for given values on X. The predicted Y can then be compared to the actually obtained Y.

For example, suppose we examined a scattergram for income (measured in dollars) and education (measured as last year in school completed) and concluded that the relationship looked linear. Given a linear relationship, we then draw the best-fitting line through the data points. Mathematically, let's suppose the best-fitting line had the following equation:

Income = 2,300 + (500 × Education)

What does this equation tell us? It indicates that we expect respondents with no formal schooling—education = 0—to earn $2,300. Notice that when education = 0 the predicted value of income is the intercept, $2,300. The positive slope indicates that for each additional year in school completed, earnings increase by $500. Therefore, someone with a twelfth-grade education can expect to earn $8,300, and someone with a college degree (16 years) can expect to earn an additional $2,000, or $10,300. Notice that the equation is used to predict income given a specific level of education.

We can then compare respondents' predicted incomes ($\hat{Y}$) with their actual incomes (Y). It may be, for example, that some respondents with 16 years of education earned $10,300, that others earned $15,000, and that still others earned $9,500. Comparing the predicted value on Y with the actually obtained value begins to tell us about the strength of the bivariate relationship.

Before we turn to the strength of the relationship, however, some additional comments on the regression line are in order. Slopes are often referred to as **unstandardized regression coefficients**. The regression coefficients indicate how much and in what direction the predicted variable changes given a unit change in the predictor variable. Provided that variables were measured in the same way, regression coefficients can be compared across equations or across samples. For example, if we looked at the relationship between number of hours studied and exam grade in two different classes, we might find the following:

Class 1: Grade = 30 + (5 × Hours)
Class 2: Grade = 25 + (10 × Hours)

A comparison of the two equations indicates that if you don't plan to study—hours = 0—it's better (in terms of your grade) to attend class 1. If, however, you plan to study, class 2 gives greater rewards, ten points per hour as compared to five.

Before we explain how SPSS^X calculates the regression equation, we need to discuss correlation. But first, try the following checkpoint.

C H E C K P O I N T

4. Interpret the following regression lines:

    a. Desired family size = 9 − (0.5 × Education)

    b. Sentence length = 1 + (1 × Age)

5. Given respondents with a twelfth-grade, an eighth-grade, and a fourth-grade education, what predictions would you make about their desired family size, based on the equation in the previous checkpoint question?

Correlation

Correlation coefficients indicate the strength of relationships. Two popular measures of correlation are the **Pearson product-moment correlation coefficient**, often referred to either as **Pearson's r** or as the **correlation coefficient**, and **Pearson's r squared.** The range of Pearson's r is from -1 through 0 to $+1$. At this point you know that a -1 coefficient indicates a perfect negative relationship: as the values on one variable increase, the values on the second decline. A $+1$ coefficient indicates a perfect positive relationship: as the values on one variable increase, the values on the other increase. A 0 coefficient indicates no linear relationship. Pearson's r does not have a PRE interpretation. However, r squared is a PRE measure.

The range for r squared is from 0 to 1, where 0 indicates no reduction in error in predicting one variable from the other, and 1 indicates a 100 percent reduction in error in predicting one variable from the other. Let's examine how these coefficients relate to the regression line.

Suppose a plot of exam grade and the number of hours studied produced the scattergram shown in figure 11-6. A glance at the scattergram indicates that a line easily describes the data. In fact, the data are arranged in a straight line. The equation for the line is

$$\text{Grade} = 15 + (2.5 \times \text{Hours})$$

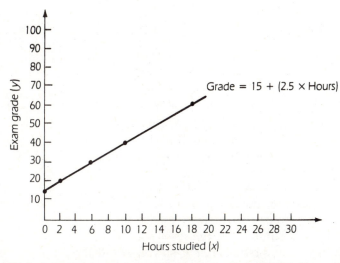

Figure 11-6 Scattergram and regression equation: exam grade and hours studied.

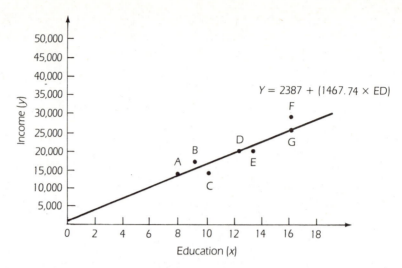

Figure 11-7 Scattergram and regression line: education and income.

Furthermore, since all data points fall on the line, each respondent's predicted grade matches the grade he or she actually obtained. This illustrates a perfect relationship, and the correlation coefficient equals 1. Knowledge of hours studied allows perfect prediction of grade. Knowledge of hours studied reduces the errors in predicting grade by 100 percent: r squared is also 1.

Suppose, however, that some data points were not on the line. Figure 11-7 illustrates a situation in which there are discrepancies between the predicted value and the actually observed value of income. The relationship is no longer perfect; the line no longer perfectly describes the data. However, a relationship still exists: education reduces the range in income. The question is, How much? or How strong is the relationship? The correlation coefficient and r squared answer these questions.

The logic underlying r squared, also called the **coefficient of determination,** is the PRE logic. The formula for r squared can be thought of in the E_1 and E_2 terms described in chapter 10. E_1 represents the number of errors made in predicting Y when all that is known is the distribution on Y. E_2 represents the number of errors in predicting Y when the variables' joint distribution is known. In the case of r squared, E_1 represents the total variation of the data around the mean, and E_2 represents the error variation around the predicted value of Y.

Figure 11-7 shows the scattergram for education and income. Income is the dependent variable and education the independent variable. Suppose, for a moment, that the only information you had was the distribution on the dependent variable; that is, you only knew respondents' incomes. If you were forced to pick only one number to represent the income of all the respondents, what number would you choose? Income is a ratio variable, so you would choose the mean. Let's draw a line representing the mean, as shown in figure 11-8a.

Figure (graph):

Income (y) vs Education (x)

Calculation of E_1

Point	Y Value	$(Y - \bar{Y})$ (Value – 20,000)	$(Y - \bar{Y})^2$ (Value – 20,000)²
A	15,000	−5,000	25,000,000
B	17,000	−3,000	9,000,000
C	15,000	−5,000	25,000,000
D	20,000	0	0
E	20,000	0	0
F	30,000	10,000	100,000,000
G	23,000	3,000	9,000,000
	140,000	0	$E_1 = 168,000,000$
Mean =	20,000		

Figure 11-8a Total variation: E_1—sum of the deviations from the mean squared.

Comparing the mean line to the data points, you find that some data points fall on the line (D and E), and others do not (A, B, C, F, and G). The differences between incomes that are less than the mean and the mean are negative numbers. For example, point A falls below the mean by − $5,000. Points above the mean are a positive distance from the mean. For example, point F is + $10,000 above the mean. Differences between a point and the mean $(Y - \bar{Y})$ are called **deviations from the mean**. If we square each point's deviation from the mean—$(Y - \bar{Y})^2$—and add them all together, the resulting number is E_1. Another name for E_1 is the **total variation in variable Y.**

Suppose we know the bivariate distribution, and we draw the best-fitting line through the data points, as shown in figure 11-8b. We can now look at the difference between each respondent's actual income and the income predicted by the regression line $(Y - \hat{Y})$. These differences are called **residuals**. For example, the observed income (Y) for respondent A is $15,000. Based on the regression equation, the pre-

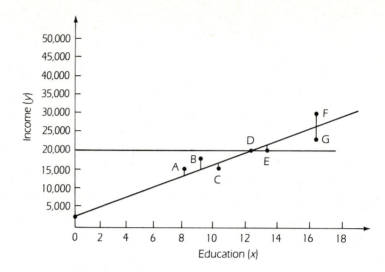

Calculation of E_2

Point	Y Observed	$\hat{Y}$ Predicted From Equation	$Y - \hat{Y}$ Residual	$(Y - \hat{Y})^2$ (Residual)^2
A	15,000	14,129	871	758,641
B	17,000	15,597	1,403	1,968,409
C	15,000	17,064	−2,064	4,260,096
D	20,000	20,000	0	0
E	20,000	21,468	−1,468	2,155,024
F	30,000	25,871	4,129	17,048,641
G	23,000	25,871	−2,871	8,242,641
				$E_2 = 34,433,452$

Figure 11-8b Error variation: E_2—residuals.

dicted income $(\hat{Y})$ for respondent A is \$14,129. That is, respondents with an eighth-grade education are expected to earn \$14,129. The expected income for A is \$14,129, and the actual income is \$15,000. Therefore, the regression equation is off in the prediction by \$871. The residual is \$871.

If we take each residual, square that value—$(Y - \hat{Y})^2$—and add all the residuals together, we have calculated E_2. E_2 is also referred to as **error variation** or **unexplained variation**. In essence, it indicates how much information the regression equation could not explain. When the error variation is smaller than the total variation, it means that there is a relationship between the variables. In fact, a comparison of the errors via the E_1 and E_2 formula indicates how strong the relationship is between the variables.

If we plug these values into the PRE formula—$(E_1 - E_2)/E_1$—we find that r squared equals 0.795. Since r squared has a PRE interpretation, this means that 79.5 percent of the variation in income is explained by education. Although r squared has a PRE interpretation and the correlation coefficient does not, you will want to examine both coefficients. Why? They provide you with different pieces of information. The correlation coefficient indicates the sign of the relationship, which is lost in the squaring process. However, r squared gives you the strict PRE interpretation that the correlation coefficient lacks.

    We're now ready to let the computer do all the computations. Before doing that, however, try the following checkpoint.

C H E C K P O I N T

6. Interpret the following statistics:

   a. r squared = 0.4

   b. correlation coefficient = 0.52

7. Which is stronger, a correlation coefficient equal to 0.5 or a correlation coefficient equal to −0.5? Explain.

Using SPSS^x to do Linear Regression and Correlation

SPSS^x has two procedures for calculating correlation coefficients. One of these procedures will also produce the information needed to write a regression equation. Adding a STATISTICS command to the SCATTERGRAM command will result in the calculation of the intercept, slope, correlation coefficient (R), and r squared. For example, the following commands will give you all the information needed to write the regression equation predicting MEMNUM from TVHOURS. In addition, measures to assess the relationship's strength are printed.

```
SCATTERGRAM MEMNUM WITH TVHOURS
OPTIONS 4 7
STATISTICS ALL
```

The above combination of commands produces a scattergram with integer axes. In addition, the grid lines will be omitted from the diagram. Furthermore, the regression line and the correlation coefficients will be calculated.

    A command for obtaining only the correlation coefficient is the PEARSON CORR command. Try the following command:

```
PEARSON CORR AGE TVHOURS
STATISTICS ALL
```

Your printout will contain the correlation coefficient for AGE and TVHOURS. In addition, the mean, the standard deviation, and the number of cases used for each variable will be provided. Put SPSS^X to work in the following checkpoint.

C H E C K P O I N T

8. Write and run a program that allows you to write the regression equation and determine the strength of the relationship between MEMNUM and AGE, and AGE and TVHOURS. Remember to exclude the don't know and no answer responses as MISSING VALUES.

In this chapter we examined bivariate linear regression and correlation. At this point, however, you know that bivariate explanations tend to be simplistic. To add another variable to the equation, let's look at the next chapter on multivariate analysis.

chapter 12

Multivariate Analysis: Nominal and Ordinal Variables

I n the last three chapters we have discussed bivariate analysis, the analysis of how two variables go together. For example, we looked at whether education influenced income and whether sex affected attitude toward abortion. Of course, sex is not the only variable that influences attitude toward abortion, nor is education the only determinant of income. We also have to consider, for example, the impact of religion or education on people's attitudes toward abortion and the impact of occupation or aspirations on income. Bivariate explanations tend to be very simplistic. In social research, one variable alone rarely explains or predicts another variable. Researchers often do bivariate analysis to get "a feel for the data." Most research, however, focuses on the relationship among three or more variables.

Adding a third (fourth, fifth, and so on) variable to a contingency table or regression equation results in **multivariate analysis**. Multivariate analysis refers to the examination of the relationship among three or more variables. In this chapter we will focus on the multivariate analysis of nominal and ordinal variables. We will examine the **elaboration method**, a technique for adding a third (fourth, fifth, and so on) variable to a contingency table. We will also discuss how to interpret the resulting tables. In the next chapter we will examine multivariate correlation and regression. Upon completion of this chapter, you should be able to do the following:

1. Describe why researchers do multivariate analysis
2. Explain the logic underlying the elaboration technique
3. Interpret contingency tables involving three or more variables
4. Use SPSS^X to do multivariate contingency analysis

Did you know that storks bring babies? It's true! In Sweden there is a high association between the number of storks and the number of births. Did you know that hospitals cause death? After all, there's a very high association between hospitalization and death rates. These two relationships are empirically observable, and yet they seem absurd. In fact, they seem remarkably like the relationship between the number of firefighters and the amount of fire damage discussed in chapter 8, and that was a spurious relationship. Are you thinking that these are too? You're absolutely right. When additional variables are examined, we find that these relationships are spurious and absurd.

In Sweden there is a high association between the number of storks and the number of babies. However, both variables are influenced by a third variable, region of the country. Rural areas happen to have more storks than urban areas. People living in rural areas tend to have higher birth rates than urban dwellers. So much for the theory that storks bring babies!

Let's turn to the idea that hospitalization causes death. Empirically, these two variables are related, but there is a third variable producing that relationship. What variable affects both the likelihood of hospitalization and the likelihood of death? As you might guess, the seriousness of the illness affects both the likelihood of hospitalization and the likelihood of death. So much for the idea that hospitals cause death!

These two examples illustrate the importance of multivariate analysis. In both examples the original bivariate relationship disappeared after a third variable was introduced. To understand a bivariate relationship fully, it is important to examine the impact of additional variables on the original bivariate relationship. Both examples illustrate, therefore, the importance of the elaboration technique.

The Elaboration Technique

The **elaboration technique** refers to the introduction of a third variable, often called a **test factor** or a **control variable**, into a two-variable relationship. The third variable is introduced so that the original two-variable relationship can be examined in more detail, under the conditions of the third variable. When this is done, there are essentially three possible outcomes: the original relationship holds for all attributes of the third variable; the original relationship holds under some attributes of the third variable and disappears under others; the original relationship disappears under all conditions of the third variable.

For example, suppose we pursued our interest in the SEX-ABDEFECT relationship. In chapter 9 we found a bivariate relationship between the two variables: men were more likely than women to favor abortion if there was a strong chance that the baby had a serious defect. In considering the SEX-ABDEFECT relationship, religion looms as an important variable that needs to be controlled; that is, maybe it's not sex but religion that influences people's attitudes toward abortion. Or maybe a relationship exists between SEX and ABDEFECT for Catholics but not for Protestants. Or maybe the relationship between SEX and ABDEFECT holds across all religions. We'll never know the impact of religion on the SEX-ABDEFECT relationship unless we control for RELIG. Now that we've overviewed the elaboration method, let's examine the process in more detail.

Test Factors

Why do we select a particular variable as a test factor? Why for example when we are looking at the relationship between offender's social class and type of sentence (fine, suspended, jail, prison) do we add the third variable type of legal representation (private attorney, court-appointed attorney)? Or why did we decide that the third variable religion might be important in examining the relationship between sex and abortion attitudes?

Particular variables are selected as test factors because they are thought to be related to the independent and dependent variables. Some test factors are thought to influence the dependent *and* the independent variable. These are called **antecedent** test factors. Antecedent test factors occur prior in time to both the independent and dependent variables and therefore are able to influence them.

Other test factors are thought to occur between the independent and dependent variables; these are called **intervening** test factors. They are believed to be affected by the independent variable, and they in turn affect the dependent variable. The difference between an antecedent and intervening test factor is the theoretical or time-order relationship to the original variables. Figure 12-1 illustrates relationships between test factors and independent and dependent variables.

Let's reexamine the theoretical relationship among sentence type, offender's social class, and type of legal representation. The original relationship focused on offender's social class as the independent variable and sentence type as the dependent variable. Researchers believe

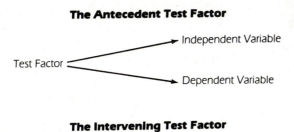

The Antecedent Test Factor

Test Factor → Independent Variable
Test Factor → Dependent Variable

The Intervening Test Factor

Independent Variable → Test Factor → Dependent Variable

Figure 12-1 Models of test factors.

that social class influences sentence type. However, many researchers believe that this relationship is mediated by the type of legal representation; that is, social class affects the type of legal representation, and that in turn influences sentence type. What kind of test factor is legal representation? Antecedent? Nobody claims that the type of lawyer affects offender's social class, so it cannot be an antecedent variable. Legal representation is therefore an intervening test factor.

In the relationship between the number of firefighters and the amount of damage caused by a fire, the size of the fire is an antecedent test factor. The size of the fire affects how many firefighters are called to a fire, and the size of the fire affects the amount of damage. Let's examine in more detail what may happen after a test factor is introduced into a contingency table. But first, try the following checkpoint.

C H E C K P O I N T

1. Place an A next to the test factors that are probably antecedent variables and an I next to the test factors that are probably intervening variables.

   a. Original relationship: Life satisfaction and health
      Possible test factors: Age
                             Race
                             Income

   b. Original relationship: education and occupation
      Possible test factors: Skills
                             Aspirations
                             Parents' income

   c. Original relationship: Birthrate and industrialization level
      Possible test factor: Sex ratio

After the Test Factor is Controlled

Partials

Introducing a test factor into a bivariate relationship produces additional contingency tables. These tables are called **partial tables**. One partial is constructed for each attribute of the test factor. The partials show the crosstabulation of the two original variables under conditions of the test factor. They are called partials because adding the corresponding cell frequencies in all partials produces the original frequency table.

For example, table 12-1a shows the original HAPPY BY HEALTH contingency table. Tables 12-1b and 12-1c are the partial tables controlling for SEX. Table 12-1b is the partial for women, and table 12-1c is the partial for men. If we add the frequency for women's excellent health and very happy responses ($N = 20$) with the corresponding frequencies for men ($N = 14$), the result is 34. In table 12-1a, the fre-

Table 12-1 a / HAPPY BY HEALTH

		HEALTH				
COUNT EXP VAL ROW PCT COL PCT TOT PCT RESIDUAL STD RES ADJ RES		EXC 1	GOOD 2	FAIR 3	POOR 4	ROW TOTAL
HAPPY VERY	1	34 27.4 41.5% 41.0% 13.7% 6.6 1.3 1.9	33 33.1 40.2% 33.0% 13.3% -.1 .0 .0	14 17.5 17.1% 26.4% 5.6% -3.5 -.8 -1.2	1 4.0 1.2% 8.3% .4% -3.0 -1.5 -1.9	82 33.1%
PRETTY	2	41 44.5 30.8% 49.4% 16.5% -3.5 -.5 -.9	55 53.6 41.4% 55.0% 22.2% 1.4 .2 .4	30 28.4 22.6% 56.6% 12.1% 1.6 .3 .5	7 6.4 5.3% 58.3% 2.8% .6 .2 .3	133 53.6%
NOT TOO	3	8 11.0 24.2% 9.6% 3.2% -3.0 -.9 -1.2	12 13.3 36.4% 12.0% 4.8% -1.3 -.4 -.5	9 7.1 27.3% 17.0% 3.6% 1.9 .7 .9	4 1.6 12.1% 33.3% 1.6% 2.4 1.9 2.1	33 13.3%
COLUMN TOTAL		83 33.5%	100 40.3%	53 21.4%	12 4.8%	248 100.0%

CHI-SQUARE	D.F.	SIGNIFICANCE	MIN E.F.	CELLS WITH E.F.< 5
10.06640	6	0.1219	1.597	2 OF 12 (16.7%)

STATISTIC	SYMMETRIC	WITH HAPPY DEPENDENT	WITH HEALTH DEPENDENT
LAMBDA	0.00380	0.0	0.00676
UNCERTAINTY COEFFICIENT	0.01842	0.02070	0.01659
SOMERS' D	0.15467	0.14416	0.16682
ETA		0.19718	0.18553

STATISTIC	VALUE	SIGNIFICANCE
CRAMER'S V	0.14246	
CONTINGENCY COEFFICIENT	0.19750	
KENDALL'S TAU B	0.15508	0.0033
KENDALL'S TAU C	0.14648	0.0033
PEARSON'S R	0.18551	0.0017
GAMMA	0.24452	

NUMBER OF MISSING OBSERVATIONS =   1

Table 12-1b / HAPPY BY HEALTH, WOMEN

		HEALTH				
COUNT EXP VAL ROW PCT COL PCT TOT PCT RESIDUAL STD RES ADJ RES		EXC 1	GOOD 2	FAIR 3	POOR 4	ROW TOTAL
HAPPY	1	20	17	9	1	47
VERY		12.4 42.6% 55.6% 14.7% 7.6 2.1 3.1	20.7 36.2% 28.3% 12.5% -3.7 -.8 -1.4	11.8 19.1% 26.5% 6.6% -2.8 -.8 -1.1	2.1 2.1% 16.7% .7% -1.1 -.7 -.9	34.6%
PRETTY	2	13 19.3 17.8% 36.1% 9.6% -6.3 -1.4 -2.5	36 32.2 49.3% 60.0% 26.5% 3.8 .7 1.3	20 18.3 27.4% 58.8% 14.7% 1.8 .4 .7	4 3.2 5.5% 66.7% 2.9% .8 .4 .7	73 53.7%
NOT TOO	3	3 4.2 18.8% 8.3% 2.2% -1.2 -.6 -.7	7 7.1 43.8% 11.7% 5.1% -.1 .0 .0	5 4.0 31.3% 14.7% 3.7% 1.0 .5 .6	1 .7 6.3% 16.7% .7% .3 .4 .4	16 11.8%
COLUMN TOTAL		36 26.5%	60 44.1%	34 25.0%	6 4.4%	136 100.0%

CHI-SQUARE	D.F.	SIGNIFICANCE	MIN E.F.	CELLS WITH E.F.< 5
10.07086	6	0.1217	0.706	2 OF 12 (41.7%)

STATISTIC	SYMMETRIC	WITH HAPPY DEPENDENT	WITH HEALTH DEPENDENT
LAMBDA	0.07194	0.11111	0.03947
UNCERTAINTY COEFFICIENT	0.03361	0.03792	0.03019
SOMERS' D	0.20164	0.18778	0.21772
ETA		0.23538	0.23316

STATISTIC	VALUE	SIGNIFICANCE
CRAMER'S V	0.19242	
CONTINGENCY COEFFICIENT	0.26257	
KENDALL'S TAU B	0.20220	0.0045
KENDALL'S TAU C	0.18896	0.0045
PEARSON'S R	0.21155	0.0067
GAMMA	0.31701	

NUMBER OF MISSING OBSERVATIONS = 1

Table 12-1c / HAPPY BY HEALTH, MEN

		HEALTH				
COUNT EXP VAL ROW PCT COL PCT TOT PCT RESIDUAL STD RES ADJ RES		EXC 1	GOOD 2	FAIR 3	POOR 4	ROW TOTAL
HAPPY VERY	1	14 14.7 40.0% 29.8% 12.5% −.7 −.2 −.3	16 12.5 45.7% 40.0% 14.3% 3.5 1.0 1.5	5 5.9 14.3% 26.3% 4.5% −.9 −.4 −.5	0 1.9 .0% .0% .0% −1.9 −1.4 −1.7	35 31.3%
PRETTY	2	28 25.2 46.7% 59.6% 25.0% 2.8 .6 1.1	19 21.4 31.7% 47.5% 17.0% −2.4 −.5 −1.0	10 10.2 16.7% 52.6% 8.9% −.2 −.1 −.1	3 3.2 5.0% 50.0% 2.7% −.2 −.1 −.2	60 53.6%
NOT TOO	3	5 7.1 29.4% 10.6% 4.5% −2.1 −.8 −1.1	5 6.1 29.4% 12.5% 4.5% −1.1 −.4 −.6	4 2.9 23.5% 21.1% 3.6% 1.1 .7 .8	3 .9 17.6% 50.0% 2.7% 2.1 2.2 2.4	17 15.2%
COLUMN TOTAL		47 42.0%	40 35.7%	19 17.0%	6 5.4%	112 100.0%

CHI−SQUARE	D.F.	SIGNIFICANCE	MIN E.F.	CELLS WITH E.F.< 5
9.69639	6	0.1380	0.911	2 OF 12 (33.3%)

STATISTIC	SYMMETRIC	WITH HAPPY DEPENDENT	WITH HEALTH DEPENDENT
LAMBDA	0.01709	0.0	0.03077
UNCERTAINTY COEFFICIENT	0.03993	0.04411	0.03648
SOMERS' D	0.10528	0.09954	0.11171
ETA		0.26344	0.21084

STATISTIC	VALUE	SIGNIFICANCE
CRAMER'S V	0.20806	
CONTINGENCY COEFFICIENT	0.28277	
KENDALL'S TAU B	0.10545	0.1075
KENDALL'S TAU C	0.09926	0.1075
PEARSON'S R	0.17413	0.0331
GAMMA	0.16501	

NUMBER OF MISSING OBSERVATIONS =   1

quency for very happy and excellent health is also 34. Ignoring the control variable sex, we find that 34 respondents indicated that they were very happy and in excellent health. Thus, combining corresponding cells in all partials produces the original table.

We analyze a partial as we would analyze any other contingency table. As described in chapter 9, we percentage each partial to see if a bivariate relationship is indicated within that partial. If that looks promising, we calculate a measure of association for each partial. If we are interested in generalizing to the population from which the sample was drawn, we calculate each partial's chi square. All these procedures for examining and interpreting contingency tables were described in chapters 9 and 10. Thus far, elaboration follows the same pattern. Now let's add some procedures and use the elaboration technique.

Replication, Specification, Interpretation, Explanation

After examining each partial, we compare its relationship to the relationship expressed in the original table. As already stated, one of three situations may be evident. We may find that the relationships expressed in the partials resemble the relationship found in the original bivariate table. This is called **replication**: the partials replicate the original relationship.

Researchers are often pleased by replication because it means that under all conditions of the third (or fourth, or fifth, and so on) variable, the original relationship still holds. Replication increases the researcher's faith in the original relationship, because it continues to exist under varied conditions.

For example, let's examine the data in table 12-2a. This table shows the original relationship between SEX and ABDEFECT found in chapter 9. Now let's look at the hypothetical partials controlling for education shown in tables 12-2b, 12-2c, and 12-2d. The partials for less than high school, high school, and more than high school show a relationship between SEX and ABDEFECT. In fact, the relationship expressed in each partial resembles the relationship expressed in the original table, table 12-1a. This means that education does *not* influence the SEX-ABDEFECT relationship. Regardless of educational level, there is a relationship between SEX and ABDEFECT.

Now let's examine the hypothetical partials shown in tables 12-3a, 12-3b, and 12-3c. The partial for less than high school, table 12-3a, replicates the original SEX-ABDEFECT relationship. However, tables 12-3b and 12-3c, the partials for high school and more than high school, do not show any relationship between SEX and ABDEFECT. A situation in which one or more partials show no relationship *and* one or more partials show a relationship is called **specification**. Specification allows us to specify the conditions under which the original relationship holds. In this instance, we've learned that there is a relationship between SEX and ABDEFECT for people with less than a high school education, but not for people with a high school or more than a high school education.

Table 12-2a / SPSS[x] Printout: SEX by ABDEFECT, *N* = 239

ABDEFECT

COUNT EXP VAL ROW PCT COL PCT TOT PCT RESIDUAL STD RES ADJ RES	YES	NO	ROW TOTAL
SEX MALE 1	95 89.2 90.5% 46.8% 39.7% 5.8 .6 2.1	10 15.8 9.5% 27.8% 4.2% −5.8 −1.5 −2.1	105 43.9%
FEMALE 2	108 113.8 80.6% 53.2% 45.2% −5.8 −.5 −2.1	26 20.2 19.4% 72.2% 10.9% 5.8 1.3 2.1	134 56.1%
COLUMN TOTAL	203 84.9%	36 15.1%	239 100.0%

Table 12-2b / SEX by ABDEFECT, Less Than High School, Percentages

		ABDEFECT		
		Yes	No	Total
SEX	Male	90%	10%	100%
	Female	80%	20%	100%

Table 12-2c / SEX by ABDEFECT, High School, Percentages

		ABDEFECT		Total
		Yes	No	
SEX	Male	89%	11%	100%
	Female	81%	19%	100%

Table 12-2d / SEX by ABDEFECT, More Than High School, Percentages

		ABDEFECT		Total
		Yes	No	
SEX	Male	91%	9%	100%
	Female	79%	21%	100%

Table 12-3a / SEX by ABDEFECT, Less Than High School, Percentages

		ABDEFECT		Total
		Yes	No	
SEX	Male	90%	10%	100%
	Female	80%	20%	100%

Table 12-3b / SEX by ABDEFECT, High School, Percentages

		ABDEFECT		Total
		Yes	No	
SEX	Male	90%	10%	100%
	Female	90%	10%	100%

Table 12-3c / SEX by ABDEFECT, More Than High School, Percentages

		ABDEFECT		Total
		Yes	No	
SEX	Male	88%	12%	100%
	Female	88%	12%	100%

Now let's look at tables 12-4*a*, 12-4*b*, and 12-4*c*. These tables show no relationship between SEX and ABDEFECT. Although the original bivariate table (table 12-2*a*) indicated a relationship between SEX and ABDEFECT, it "vanished" in all the partials. The situation of "vanishing partials" is called either explanation or interpretation, depending on the theoretical placement of the test factor.

If the test factor is an antecedent variable, the situation of vanishing partials or partials that are severely reduced relative to the original relationship is called **explanation**. Explanation also refers to the situation that we've previously called **spurious**. A relationship is spurious when an antecedent control variable explains the empirical bivariate relationship. If, however, the test factor is an intervening variable, a situation in which partials vanish or are reduced relative to the original relationship, it is called **interpretation**. This is an important point, so let me reiterate it here: *The difference between explanation and interpretation is theoretical, not statistical.*

Are we dealing with explanation or interpretation in tables 12-4*a*, 12-4*b*, and 12-4*c*? One way to decide is to model the two possibilities, as shown in figure 12-2. Does it make sense to say that educational level influences sex, and educational level influences abortion attitudes (explanation)? Or doe it make more sense to say that sex influences educational level, and educational level in turn influences abortion attitudes (interpretation)? The latter is obviously more sensible. Education operates as an intervening variable. SEX affects EDUC, and EDUC in turn affects ABDEFECT.

Examine tables 12-4*a*, 12-4*b*, and 12-4*c*, and decide whether they illustrate replication, specification, explanation, or interpretation. Oh, you probably are wondering how much a relationship has to be reduced before it is considered a vanishing or severely reduced relationship. Unfortunately there are no clearcut rules to follow. The assessment of whether a partial's relationship differs from the original table's rela-

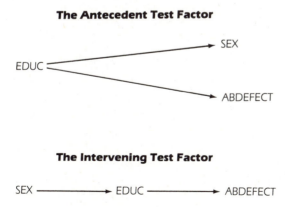

Figure 12-2 *Antecedent or intervening?*

Table 12-4a / SEX by ABDEFECT, Less Than High School, Percentages

		ABDEFECT		Total
		Yes	No	
SEX	Male	95%	5%	100%
	Female	95%	5%	100%

Table 12-4b / SEX by ABDEFECT, High School, Percentages

		ABDEFECT		Total
		Yes	No	
SEX	Male	75%	25%	100%
	Female	77%	23%	100%

Table 12-4c / SEX by ABDEFECT, More Than High School, Percentages

		ABDEFECT		Total
		Yes	No	
SEX	Male	89%	11%	100%
	Female	91%	9%	100%

Table 12-5a / Auto Accident Rate by Sex, Percentages

		SEX	
		Male	Female
ACCIDENT RATE	None	70%	90%
	At least one	30%	10%
	TOTAL	100%	100%

Table 12-5b / Auto Accident Rate by Sex, Drive Less Than 5,000 Miles per Year, Percentages

		SEX	
		Male	Female
ACCIDENT RATE	None	80%	80%
	At least one	20%	20%
	TOTAL	100%	100%

Table 12-5c / Auto Accident Rate by Sex, Drive 5,000 Miles or More per Year, Percentages

		SEX	
		Male	Female
ACCIDENT RATE	None	45%	45%
	At least one	55%	55%
	TOTAL	100%	100%

tionship is a judgment, and the only way to gain skill at making judgments is to gain experience. Do the following checkpoint, and then we'll use SPSS[x] to construct partial tables.

C H E C K P O I N T

2. Examine tables 12-5a, 12-5b, and 12-5c. Which is (are) the original table(s), and which is (are) the partial(s)?

3. Do tables 12-5a, 12-5b, and 12-5c illustrate replication, interpretation, specification, or explanation? Explain your answer.

Multivariate Contingency Tables via SPSS[x]

Obtaining contingency tables for three (four, five, and so on) variables is easy with SPSS[x]. In fact, all you do is add the name of the test factor(s) to the CROSSTABS command. For example, the following command produces two tables:

CROSSTABS TABLES = HAPPY BY HEALTH BY UNEMP

One table illustrates the relationship between HAPPY and HEALTH for the unemployed, those who answer yes to UNEMP. The second table presents the relationship between HAPPY and HEALTH for those who have not been unemployed, no to UNEMP.

Actually, the above CROSSTABS command may produce two, three, or four tables, depending on how many values are declared as missing. Two tables are produced if the don't know and no answer codes on UNEMP are declared as MISSING VALUES. If these are not declared as missing, four tables would be produced. In addition to the two tables already described, the command would produce a table showing the HAPPY-HEALTH relationship for the don't know respondents and a HAPPY-HEALTH table for the no answer respondents. Three tables would be produced if only one value was declared as missing.

The third variable listed on the CROSSTABS command is considered the test factor or control variable. It is within conditions of this variable that the original bivariate relationship is examined. More variables can be added. For example, what do you think the following CROSSTABS command does?

CROSSTABS HEALTH BY HAPPY BY UNEMP BY SEX

You now have two test factors, UNEMP and SEX. Your printout should contain four tables. The four tables include one showing the HAPPY-HEALTH relationship for employed females, a second table showing the HAPPY-HEALTH relationship for unemployed females, a third table showing the HAPPY-HEALTH relationship for employed males, and a fourth table showing the HAPPY-HEALTH relationship for unemployed males. These are the four tables that would be produced if the don't know and no answer codes are excluded.

Suppose you wanted to examine the HAPPY-HEALTH relationship controlling for UNEMP and the HAPPY-HEALTH relationship controlling for SEX. In this situation you do not want to control for UNEMP and SEX simultaneously. What do you do? Try the following command:

CROSSTABS HEALTH BY HAPPY BY UNEMP,SEX

This command produces four tables; HAPPY-HEALTH for the unemployed, HAPPY-HEALTH for the employed, HAPPY-HEALTH for males, and HAPPY-HEALTH for females. In two tables UNEMP is the only control variable, and in the other two tables SEX is the only control variable.

All the guidelines on STATISTICS and OPTIONS described in chapters 9 and 10 still pertain to the running of a multivariate CROSS-

TABS procedure. The following list provides a quick review of the frequently used OPTIONS described in chapter 9:

- OPTIONS 3 calculates row percentages.
- OPTIONS 4 calculates column percentages.
- OPTIONS 5 calculates cell percentage of total.
- OPTIONS 18 calculates cell count; row, column, and total percentages; expected values; and residual information.

Statistics are calculated and interpreted on partials in the same fashion as described in chapter 10. The following list provides a quick review of the STATISTICS more completely described in chapter 10:

- STATISTICS 1 calculates chi square.
- STATISTICS 2 calculates phi for 2×2 tables, Cramer's V for larger tables.
- STATISTICS 3 calculates the contingency coefficient.
- STATISTICS 4 calculates lambda, symmetric and asymmetric.
- STATISTICS 5 calculates the uncertainty coefficient, symmetric and asymmetric.
- STATISTICS 6 calculates Kendall's tau-b.
- STATISTICS 7 calculates Kendall's tau-c.
- STATISTICS 8 calculates gamma.
- STATISTICS 9 calculates Somer's d, symmetric and asymmetric.
- STATISTICS 10 calculates eta.
- STATISTICS 11 calculates Pearson's r.
- STATISTICS ALL calculates all statistics (1 through 11) on the table(s).

Remember, the interpretation of partials is the same as the interpretation of a bivariate contingency table. The unique aspects of the multivariate elaboration method come into play when you compare partial relationships to the original relationship. The four most common situations that result from that comparison are replication, specification, interpretation, and explanation.

C H E C K P O I N T

4. Draw the tables produced by the following set of SPSS[x] commands. Be sure to label which table is the original and which tables are the partials.

```
MISSING VALUES HEALTH(8,9) SMOKE(9)
CROSSTABS TABLES=HEALTH BY SMOKE/HEALTH BY SMOKE BY SEX
OPTIONS 18
STATISTICS ALL
```

5. Write the commands to obtain the tables shown in tables 12-1*a*, 12-1*b*, and 12-1*c*. Assume that a researcher believes that HAPPY influences HEALTH. Interpret these tables using the elaboration technique.

Now let's turn to multivariate analysis using interval and ratio data.

chapter 13
Multivariate Analysis: Multiple Correlation and Regression

In the last chapter we discussed the analysis of three or more nominal or ordinal variables. We focused on contingency table analysis using the elaboration technique. In this chapter we will analyze the relationship among three or more interval or ratio variables using correlation and regression techniques. We will assume that a second (or third, or fourth, and so on) interval- or ratio-level independent variable is being added to the regression equation.

The bivariate correlation and regression explanation may be too simplistic for a particular problem. For example, consider the correlation coefficient and *r* squared for AGE and TVHOURS. When we looked at this bivariate relationship in chapter 11, we found that Pearson's *r* equaled 0.05026 and that *r* squared equaled 0.00253. These statistics indicate that the relationship between AGE and TVHOURS is positive—as age increases, so too does the number of hours spent watching TV.

However, the relationship is extremely weak. The PRE interpretation for *r* squared indicates that age explains only 0.25 percent of the variance in TVHOURS! That means that 99.75 percent of the variance in TVHOURS is unexplained. Additional independent variables may be entered into the model to help explain the remaining variance in TVHOURS.

Upon completion of this chapter, you should be able to do the following:

1. Explain when to use multiple correlation and regression
2. Interpret the coefficients in a multiple regression equation
3. Interpret a multiple correlation coefficient and the squared multiple correlation coefficient
4. Perform and interpret a significance test for the regression equation

5. Perform and interpret significance tests on the individual regression coefficients

6. Use SPSS^X to obtain a multiple correlation and regression analysis

What influences the number of organizations people join? Do you think that people join more organizations as their educational level increases? If so, is educational level the only determinant of organizational membership? Probably not; most likely, income, age, and family size influence organizational membership as well. That is, as incomes increase, people are more likely to join organizations; as people grow older, they join more organizations; and as family size increases, the number of organizations joined declines. Once again, so much for the bivariate explanation! As stated in chapter 12, research often focuses on the relationships among three or more variables. So now let's add a second independent variable to the regression equation.

Multiple Regression

Incorporating a third variable into a regression analysis is easy. For example, instead of saying that the number of organizations is a function of education only, as shown in equation 1, we might say that the number of organizations is a function of education and income as shown in equation 2.

Equation 1: Number of memberships = $b_o + (b_1 \times \text{Education})$

Equation 2: Number of memberships = $b_o + (b_1 \times \text{Education}) + (b_2 \times \text{Income})$

Equation 1 represents the bivariate regression of number of memberships on education. Equation 2 is the multiple regression equation. It states that number of memberships is dependent on both education and income. Number of memberships is, therefore, regressed on both education and income. Equations 1 and 2 are similar. Both equations contain intercept and slope coefficients, and the interpretation of these coefficients is similar for both equations. Let's examine these coefficients in greater detail.

Intercepts

The intercept in equation 1 is our prediction of the number of organizations people join when they have no formal education (education = 0). For example, if the intercept in equation 1 were 2, we would predict that people with no education join approximately two organizations. The intercept is interpreted similarly in equation 2. It tells us how many organizational memberships we would predict for people with no formal schooling (education = 0) *and* no income (income = 0). For example, if the intercept in equation 2 were 1, we would predict that people with no education and no income join approximately one organization.

Suppose we included a third variable, age, in equation 2. The intercept now indicates the predicted number of memberships when education, income, and age all equal zero. But how can anyone have no age (age = 0)? Theoretically it's possible (remember, age is a ratio variable and could be measured as age at last birthday). But in reality it's unlikely. Unless your sample contains infants, people in your sample have an age that exceeds zero. The intercept, however, is calculated on the basis of the mathematical possibility of zero values on the independent variable(s).

Regression Coefficients

Equations 1 and 2 contain unstandardized regression coefficients, or slopes. Equation 1 contains only one independent variable, education, and therefore only one regression coefficient (b_1). The slope in equation 1 indicates that, for each unit change in education, there is an expected b_1 change in number of memberships. For example, a regression coefficient of 2 indicates that, for each additional year of schooling, the number of organizations joined is expected to increase by two. If the slope for education were -0.5, it would indicate that, for each additional year of schooling, the number of organizations joined is expected to decline by one-half.

Equation 2 contains two independent variables and, therefore, two unstandardized regression coefficients (b_1 and b_2). In a multiple regression equation, regression coefficients are often called **partial regression coefficients**, because each coefficient indicates only the effect of its independent variable on the dependent variable. The effects of all other independent variables in the equation are controlled. Therefore, the slope for education, b_1, indicates the expected change in number of memberships for each unit change in education when income is held constant. Similarly, the regression coefficient for income, b_2, indicates the expected change in number of memberships for each unit change in income when education is controlled.

There are other ways of phrasing the interpretation of partial regression coefficients. For example, if we assumed that all respondents had the same income, the coefficient for education would indicate the expected effect of education on number of memberships. Similarly, if we assumed that all respondents had the same education, the coefficient for income would indicate the effect of income on number of memberships.

Now let's interpret the intercept and regression coefficients for equation 3:

Equation 3: Number of memberships $= -3 + (1 \times$ Education$) + (0.0002 \times$ Income$)$

The intercept is -3. For respondents having no formal schooling and no income, we predict that they join minus three organizations! That obviously does not sound plausible, and yet neither did an age of zero. The regression coefficient for education is 1. This means that net of income (that is, controlling for income), a one-year increase in formal schooling is expected to increase organizational membership by one. If educational level were held constant, the 0.0002 income regression coefficient indicates that, for each additional dollar earned, organizational membership is expected to increase by 0.0002.

Suppose a respondent completed the eighth grade and earned $12,000. How many organizations would you predict he or she belonged to? Plugging these values into equation 3 results in an estimate of 7.4 organizations. Note that in the equation

Number of memberships $= -3 + 1(8) + 0.0002(12000)$

the unstandardized education regression coefficient (1) is larger than the unstandardized income regression coefficient (0.0002). That does not mean that education is the more important explanatory variable. To determine the relative importance of the independent variables, we must examine the standardized regression coefficients.

Standardized Regression Coefficients

To interpret the relative importance of the independent variables on the dependent variable, we need to look at another statistic, the **standardized regression coefficient**, also called a **beta weight**. The metrics of independent variables often differ. For example, in equation 3 educational level was measured in years, and income was measured in dollars. The coefficient for education indicates the predicted change in organizational membership for a one-year change in education, and the coefficient for income indicates the predicted change in organizational membership for a one-dollar change in income. The two coefficients are not directly comparable. A one-year change in education does not equal a one-dollar change in income. Since the metrics differ, it is difficult to determine the relative importance of each independent variable by looking at the unstandardized regression coefficient. We need to examine a statistic that ignores the original metric.

Standardized regression coefficients standardize each independent variable on the basis of that variable's standard deviation and of the dependent variable's standard deviation. The formula for the standardized regression coefficient appears in Appendix B. The standardized regression coefficient indicates how much a one-unit change in the independent variable changes the dependent variable. That sounds just like the interpretation of the unstandardized regression coefficient. The difference is that the unit change in the standardized regression coefficient is not in the original metric. It is in standard-deviation units.

For example, if the standard deviations were 1.00, 0.408, and $2245 for organizational membership, education, and income, respectively, the standardized regression coefficients for equation 3 would be 0.408 and 0.449 for education and income, respectively. This indicates that income contributes more to explaining organizational membership than does education. A one-unit change in education increases organizational membership by 0.408 units, whereas a one-unit change in income increases membership by 0.449 units. The influence of income is 10 percent greater than the influence of education on organizational membership—$(0.449 - 0.408)/0.408 = 0.100$.

Regression equations can be written with standardized coefficients. Equation 4 shows the standardized regression equation for the regression of education and income on organizational membership.

Equation 4: **Number of memberships** = (0.408 × Education) + (0.449 × Income)

Notice that a standardized regression equation has no intercept. Since the variables are standardized with means of zero, the intercept is 0.

Remember never to judge the relative importance of an independent variable on the basis of the unstandardized regression coefficients. Now try the following checkpoint.

C H E C K P O I N T

1. Interpret the intercept and unstandardized regression coefficients in the following equations:

   a. Income = 1500 + (250 × Education) + (35 × Age)

   where income is measured in dollars, education is last year in school completed, and age is age in years at last birthday

   b. Marital Happiness = 15 + (2 × #Years married) − (1 × #Childs)

   where marital happiness is a scale from 0 to 100

2. Using the equations from checkpoint question 1 and the following information, calculate the respondents' predicted value on the dependent variable.

   a. What is the predicted income for a 25-year-old respondent who has completed college (16 years of education)?

   b. What is the predicted marital happiness of a respondent who has been married 20 years and has two children?

3. Interpret the following standardized regression coefficients:

   a. Income = (3 × Education) + (0.5 × Age)

   b. Marital Happiness = (4 × #Years married) − (2.5 × #Childs)

Multiple Correlation

The **multiple correlation coefficient** (R) is analogous to the bivariate correlation coefficient (r). Both statistics indicate how well the regression equation fits the data. The larger the correlation coefficient, the better the fit between the regression equation and the data points. However, whereas r varies between -1 and $+1$, R ranges from 0 to 1.

As was true in the bivariate case, a PRE interpretation for R is obtained by squaring the multiple correlation coefficient (R squared). R squared, also called the **coefficient of determination**, is the more useful multiple correlation statistic. R squared ranges from 0 to 1, as does r squared. R squared indicates the proportion of the variance in the dependent variable that is explained by all the independent variables acting together.

For example, an R squared of 0.42 for equation 3 means that 42 percent of the variance in number of memberships is explained by the joint operation of income and education. Of course, this also means that 58 percent of the variance in number of memberships is left unexplained by these two variables. To try to explain more of the dependent variable's variance, researchers often add additional independent variables. Adding more independent variables to a regression equation often increases R squared. Although R squared may not increase dramatically, the inclusion of additional independent variables will never cause it to decline.

C H E C K P O I N T

4. Interpret the following statistics:

    a. $R = 0.38$, R squared $= 0.144$

    b. $R = 0.82$, R squared $= 0.672$

Drawing Inferences

Up to this point, multiple regression and correlation analysis has been presented as a descriptive device, a set of statistical procedures that allow researchers to describe their sample. Sometimes, however, they wish to generalize their results to the population from which the sample was drawn. In drawing inferences about the population, researchers test hypotheses about the population's parameters. We are turning, therefore, from descriptive statistics to inferential statistics. We will examine two hypotheses, the overall goodness-of-fit test for the regression equation and significance tests for specific regression coefficients.

The Overall Goodness-of-Fit Test

The null hypothesis in the overall goodness-of-fit test states that the population's squared multiple correlation coefficient (R squared) is equal to zero. Phrased slightly differently, the null hypothesis states that there is no relationship among the variables in the population from which the sample was drawn. Think about the implications of testing that null hypothesis! Rejecting the null hypothesis increases our faith that the variables are related in the population. A failure to reject the null hypothesis indicates that the variables may not be related in the population from which the sample was drawn.

The statistic used to test the null hypothesis is the **F ratio**. The F ratio is a ratio of the explained (R squared) to the unexplained ($1 - R$ squared) variance. The F ratio is distributed with k and $N - k - 1$ degrees of freedom, where k equals the number of independent variables in the equation and N equals sample size. Equation 5 shows the formula for the F ratio.

$$\textit{Equation 5: } F = \frac{R \text{ squared}/k}{(1 - R \text{ squared})/N - k - 1}$$

To determine whether to reject or fail to reject the null hypothesis on the basis of the calculated F ratio, it is necessary to look at tables showing the F ratio's distribution. Appendix E shows the F ratio's distribution for significance levels of 0.05 and 0.01.

For example, suppose you are working with a regression equation that has four independent variables and a sample size of 125. Testing whether the population's squared multiple correlation coefficient equals zero means the calculation of an F ratio with 4 and 120 ($125 - 4 - 1$) degrees of freedom. At the 0.05 level, the table's critical value for the F distribution with 4 and 120 degrees of freedom is approximately 2.44. If the F ratio calculated on your data is larger than the table's F value, you reject the null hypothesis. A rejection of the null hypothesis indicates that the squared multiple correlation coefficient is statistically significant at the 0.05 level.

You may also conclude that the relationship expressed in your data was not due solely to chance. In fact, the likelihood of obtaining an F ratio equal to or greater than the calculated F ratio is less than 0.05. If, however, the F ratio calculated on your data is smaller than the table's F ratio, you fail to reject the null hypothesis. In failing to reject the null hypothesis you may conclude that the relationship expressed in your data could be due to sampling error. That is, the likelihood of obtaining the calculated F ratio is more than 0.05.

Let's work through an example together. Suppose we obtained an R squared of 0.42 for equation 3. Is it likely that this sample was drawn from a population in which R squared equaled zero? Equation 3 contained two independent variables (education and income). If we assume that $N = 350$, the calculated F ratio is 125.74 with 2 and 347 degrees of freedom.

$$F = \frac{0.42/2}{0.58/350 - 2 - 1} = \frac{0.21}{0.00167} = 125.74$$

Testing at the 0.05 level, we look in Appendix E for the table's F value corresponding to 2 and 347 degrees of freedom. It's not there, but we find table values for 2 and 200 and 2 and 400 degrees of freedom. Since 347 is closer to 400 than to 200, let's use the critical value at 2 and 400 degrees of freedom. The critical value for F is 3.02. The calculated F ratio, 125.74, clearly exceeds the critical value, 3.02, and therefore we reject the null hypothesis. We conclude that it is unlikely that our sample was drawn from a population in which R squared was zero. Furthermore, education and income account for about 42 percent of the variance in number of memberships, and this finding is statistically significant at the 0.05 level.

Testing a regression equation's overall goodness-of-fit is similar to testing the null hypothesis that all the population's regression coefficients equal zero. If you reject a null hypothesis that states that R squared is zero, you tend to reject a null that states that all the population's regression coefficients equal zero. If, however, there are several independent variables in the equation, the overall goodness-of-fit test does not indicate which regression coefficients have values greater than zero. To determine which regression coefficients are larger than zero in the population, you need to test the individual regression coefficients.

Tests of Significance: Individual Regression Coefficients

The null hypothesis states that the regression coefficient being tested is equal to zero in the population. Remember, a test of a particular regression coefficient assumes that all the other variables in the equation are controlled. If the null is rejected, the researcher concludes that, for the particular variable, the population's regression coefficient is greater than zero. If the researcher fails to reject the null hypothesis, he or she concludes that the population's regression coefficient may equal zero for that variable.

Either the F ratio or the t distribution is used as the test statistic. SPSS[x] prints either of these statistics, although the t test is the default. F and t are highly related, since $t = \sqrt{F}$ at 1 and $N - k - 1$ degrees of freedom. The test of a regression coefficient is at 1 and $N - k - 1$ degrees of freedom, so whether you work with F or t is simply a matter of preference. The calculation and interpretation of a regression coefficient's significance will be illustrated here using the F ratio.

A standard method for testing for significance treats each variable as if it had been added to the regression equation after all other variables had been included. The increment to R squared is taken as that variable's contribution to the equation. As before, the explained variance constitutes the F ratio's numerator, and the unexplained the dominator. For example, supposed we found that by itself education explained 22 percent of the variance in number of memberships. The F ratio for education's regression coefficient would be 100.

$$F = \frac{0.22/1}{(1-0.22)/350-2-1} = \frac{0.22}{0.78/347} = 100$$

Testing at the 0.01 level, the table's F values at 1 and 347 degrees of freedom is approximately 6.70. The probability of getting an F ratio equal to or greater than the calculated F ratio of 100 is less than 0.01. Therefore, we reject the null hypothesis, and we conclude that the regression coefficient for education is statistically significant and greater than zero in the population.

Fortunately, we do not need to calculate regression coefficients, R squared, F ratios, and so on. These statistics are calculated by the SPSS^X program. Before we go on to multiple regression and correlation with SPSS^X, try the following checkpoint.

C H E C K P O I N T

5. Given the following F ratios for the overall goodness-of-fit test, what conclusions do you draw?

   a. Calculated F ratio = 34.56, sample size = 4200, number of independent variables = eight, and you test at the 0.05 level.

   b. Calculated F ratio = 2.18, sample size = 220, number of independent variables = four, and you test at the 0.01 level.

6. Given the following information, which, if any, of the following regression coefficients are statistically significant at the 0.05 level?

   a. N = 225, age explained 15 percent of the variance in sentence length, and there are three independent variables.

   b. N = 475, number of hours studied explained 65 percent of the variance in exam grade, and there are six independent variables.

Using SPSS^X to do Multiple Regression and Correlation

The commands used in a typical regression run are illustrated below. Try it, and be sure to declare don't know and no answer as MISSING VALUES.

```
REGRESSION VARIABLES=MEMNUM,CHILDS,TVHOURS/
   STATISTICS=ALL/
   DEPENDENT=TVHOURS/STEPWISE
```

What do these commands tell the computer? The first command, REGRESSION, tells the computer to do a multiple regression analysis.

The subcommand VARIABLES= tells the computer the names of all the variables to use in the regression analysis.

The STATISTICS subcommand tells the computer which statistics to print. The STATISTICS subcommand must appear before the DEPENDENT= subcommand. SPSS^x provides the researcher with several statistics. In this case the computer was instructed to print ALL the statistics. You may, however, wish to be more selective in the statistics you want printed. The following keywords specify particular statistics:

- R prints multiple R, R squared, and the standard error of the estimate.
- CHA prints the change in R squared at each step, the F value, and the significance level of F.
- COEFF prints the unstandardized (B) and the standardized (beta) regression coefficients, the standard error of B, the t value for B, and the two-tailed significance level of t for each variable in the equation.
- OUTS prints the standardized regression coefficient, the t value for B, and the significance level of t for variables not yet entered in the equation. These statistics are calculated as if the variable were the next variable to be entered.
- F prints the F value for the unstandardized regression coefficient and its significance level. Remember, $t = \sqrt{F}$, and at 1 and $N-k-1$ degrees of freedom, the significance levels are identical for the two statistics.

There are several other statistics that SPSS^x calculates and therefore prints, but the five keywords listed above are basic to a multiple regression analysis. For a discussion of additional statistics, see the SPSS^x manual. If you do not specify any statistics, SPSS^x prints R, COEFF, and OUTS by default.

The subcommand DEPENDENT= names the dependent variable or variables to be used in the analysis. If two or more variables are listed as dependent, SPSS^x enters the same independent variables into each regression equation. A variable named as a dependent variable is not treated as an independent variable in another regression equation. For example, what do the following commands tell the computer?

```
REGRESSION VARIABLES=EDUC,INCOME,OCCUP,AGE/
  STATISTICS=R COEFF/
  DEPENDENT=INCOME,OCCUP/STEPWISE
```

The DEPENDENT= command tells the computer to construct two regression equations. One equation regresses education and age on education, and the other regresses education and age on occupation. We want the multiple correlation coefficients and the regression coefficients printed for each equation.

The keyword STEPWISE is one of six subcommands that could be selected to specify the method for entering variables into the regression equation. Among the more typical methods for building a multiple regression equation are the following:

Enter: All variables are included in the equation that satisfy a statistical criterion. The criterion is the tolerance level. A **tolerance level** is a variable's proportion of variance not accounted for by the other independent variables in the equation. SPSS^X's default tolerance is 0.01. That means that a variable is entered into the equation if it accounts for at least 1 percent of the variance in the dependent variable.

Forward: Variables are entered one at a time into the equation according to their contribution to the variance explained. After each entry the variables not yet included in the equation are examined for entry. The variable with the smallest F value probability is entered next, provided it meets the tolerance level. If defaults are used, SPSS^X does not enter a variable whose significance level is greater than 0.05 and whose tolerance is less than 0.01.

Stepwise: Variables are entered according to statistical criteria. The variables' entry order is determined by the contribution each variable makes to explaining the dependent variable's variance. Using this procedure, variables are also removed from the equation if they no longer meet the preestablished statistical criteria once another variable has been added.

To decide on a method of variable entry, you need to look at your theoretical problem. For example, if you want to look at the impact of family background on occupational choice, and then at the impact of education on occupational choice, the FORWARD method would be appropriate. If, however, you want to examine the impact of family background and education on occupational choice, and you don't care about the order of entry, the ENTER method is appropriate.

One other major decision that has to be made when you are doing multiple regression relates to SPSS^X's treatment of missing values. The REGRESSION procedure handles missing values primarily in three ways. By default, cases are excluded from the regression analysis that have a missing value on any variable named in the VARIABLES subcommand. Therefore, only cases with no missing values are used in the analysis. This is referred to as the **listwise** treatment of missing values. For example, if in the above regression analysis, respondent 4 refused to answer the TVHOURS question but did answer MEMNUM and CHILDS, case 4 would be excluded from the regression analysis.

There are, however, two other ways of handling cases with missing values. One way is to select to replace the missing values with the variable's mean. All cases are therefore used in the analysis, and those that had missing values receive the variable's mean as their value. This is called the **mean substitution** treatment of missing values, and to use it, you specify MEANSUBSTITUTION on a MISSING subcommand. For example, in the above analysis, any case that had a missing value on TVHOURS would be treated as if its value on TVHOURS had actually been 2.854, the mean for TVHOURS.

A third way of working with missing values is to delete cases with missing values in a **pairwise** fashion. Pairwise deletion means that each correlation coefficient is calculated using cases that have complete information on the two variables. Whether a case has missing values on any other variable is irrelevant for the pairwise treatment. For example, if a case had a missing value on TVHOURS, it would be deleted from the calculation of the correlation coefficient for TVHOURS-CHILDS and TVHOURS-MEMNUM. However, the case would be included in the calculation of the correlation coefficient for CHILDS-MEMNUM.

Whichever method you select, the MISSING treatment must be specified before the VARIABLES= subcommand. Suppose we decided to use the mean substitution technique in the example cited earlier. We would need the following commands:

```
REGRESSION MISSING=MEANS/
 VARIABLES=EDUC INCOME OCCUP AGE/
 STATISTICS=R COEFF/
 DEPENDENT=INCOME,OCCUP/STEPWISE
```

What are the pros and cons of these various treatments? The listwise deletion may produce a drastic reduction in sample size. The pairwise deletion may produce some peculiar statistics, such as multiple correlation coefficents that exceed 1.0. If only a few cases have missing values, and you are really dealing with a ratio variable, the mean substitution may be a useful techinque.

Overall, however, the most conservative treatment of missing values is probably the listwise deletion. It ensures that you are working with the same sample for each correlation. Although listwise deletion reduces sample size, it is more difficult to obtain statistical significance with a small sample than it is with a large sample. Thus, a listwise deletion produces the most conservative estimate of significance.

The SPSS[x] Printout in Review

Let's look at the REGRESSION printout from the commands that were presented earlier in this section. We told the computer to regress MEMNUM and CHILDS on TVHOURS. The two independent variables were to be entered in a STEPWISE fashion, using a listwise deletion of cases with missing values. All statistics were to be printed. Table 13-1 presents information from the resulting printout. What does it tell us?

The regression equation is as follows:

Equation 6: TVHOURS = 3.65 − (0.29 × MEMNUM) − (0.17 × CHILDS)

The intercept, referred to in the SPSS^x printout as the constant, equals 3.65. The interpretation of the constant is that people without any children or organizational memberships watch approximately 3.65 hours of television a day. The unstandardized regression coefficients for number of organizations and number of children are approximately −0.29 and −0.17, respectively.

The interpretation given to the unstandardized regression coefficient for MEMNUM is that increasing organizational membership by one decreases TVHOURS by 0.29 hours. The interpretation given to the unstandardized regression coefficient for CHILDS is that, as the number of children in the family increases by one, the number of hours spent watching TV declines by 0.17 hours. Which is the more important predictor of TVHOURS?

To answer that question, we need to look at standardized regression coefficients, beta. The beta for MEMNUM is −0.215, and for CHILDS it is −0.134. Therefore, MEMNUM is the better predictor of TVHOURS. Together, MEMNUM and CHILDS explain 6.24 percent of the variance in TVHOURS. This means that 93.76 percent of the variance in TVHOURS is left unexplained. Could multiple R be zero in the population?

Testing at the 0.05 level, it is unlikely that this sample could be drawn from a population with a multiple R equal to zero. With 2 and 243 degrees of freedom, the calculated F ratio for the equation is approximately 8.09. The significance level associated with that F ratio is 0.0004. The individual regression coefficients are statistically significant at the 0.05 level. At the 0.01 level, only MEMNUM is statistically significant.

Table 13-1 / Selected Information from an SPSS^x Printout: TVHOURS Regressed on MEMNUM and CHILDS

```
MULTIPLE R  .24986           ANALYSIS OF VARIANCE
R SQUARE    .06243           OF SUM OF SQUARES MEAN SQUARE
                REGRESSION  2      82.12570     41.06285
                RESIDUAL  243     1233.30926      5.07535
                  F =    8.09065   SIGNIF F =  .0004
```

VARIABLE	B	SE B	BETA	T	SIG T
MEMNUM	−.28982	.08349	−.21578	−3.472	.0006
CHILDS	−.17161	.07977	−.13372	−2.151	.0324
(CONSTANT)	3.65080	.25397		14.375	.0000

Although other statistics appear in the printout, we have focused on the statistics that are basic to a multiple regression analysis. To be sure that you can use SPSS^X and interpret the statistics, do the following checkpoint.

C H E C K P O I N T

7. You think that the number of organizations (MEMNUM) is dependent on AGE, TVHOURS, and CHILDS. Write and run an SPSS^X multiple regression program. When writing the program, keep the following issues in mind:

   a. Your analysis should be limited to cases with complete information on all variables. Do not include the don't know, no answer, or refused to answer respondents in the analysis.

   b. Your model should enter variables that meet statistical criteria and remove them if they fail to meet the criteria.

   c. The printout should contain R squared, the standarized and unstandardized regression coefficients, and the F values associated with the unstandardized regression coefficients.

We have discussed how to analyze nominal and ordinal variables and how to analyze interval and ratio variables. What do you do when you want to analyze a nominal and an interval variable? The next two chapters explain analytical techniques for working with "mixed" levels of measurement.

chapter 14

The t Test: Differences Between Means

We discussed measures of central tendency in chapter 6. Recall that the mean is a measure of central tendency designed for interval- or ratio-level data. Based on that information, you can calculate and interpret a sample's mean educational level (measured as last year in school completed) or its mean income (measured in dollars). Sometimes, however, you may want to examine the difference between two means. For example, you may want to know whether the men and women in your sample receive, on the average, the same income. Or you may wish to know whether the blacks and whites in your sample attain, on the average, the same educational level. The **t test** is used to answer these questions.

The t test is an inferential statistic used to determine whether a difference between means could be expected by chance. Phrased slightly differently, the t test answers the question of whether the samples could have been drawn from a population in which the means for the two groups were identical. The t test enables us to test whether there is a statistically significant difference between two means.

Upon completion of this chapter, you should be able to do the following:

1. Describe situations in which t tests would be appropriate
2. Explain the logic underlying t tests
3. Select the appropriate t test version
4. Use SPSS^X to run t tests
5. Interpret an SPSS^X t test printout

Assume that we're interested in comparing the number of hours males and females spend watching television. We draw a random sample of males and females. We examine the number of hours 111 males watch TV and the number of hours 136 females watch TV. Next, we calculate the mean number of TV hours for males and the mean number of TV hours for females. Suppose we learn that the means are 2.59 and 3.06 hours for males and females, respectively. Is it likely that these two samples, males and females, were drawn from a population in which the means on TV differed? Is there a statistically significant difference in the average number of TV hours watched by men and women? Is the 0.47 difference (3.06 − 2.59) in the mean number of TV hours statistically significant? Or is the 0.47 difference in the means for women and men one that we expect to occur by chance? These questions can be answered by t tests.

Issues in Selecting a t test

There are several versions of the t test. The appropriate t test version depends upon the sampling scheme and assumptions regarding the data.

Sampling Issues

The first consideration, sampling scheme, refers to whether groups were drawn independently. **Independent sampling** means that the selection of elements for one group does not influence the selection of elements for the other group. In our example that means that the selection of the females for the sample did not influence the selection of the males for the sample. If we drew a sample of husbands and then used their wives for the sample, we would *not* have independent samples. The latter sampling technique produces **correlated** or **matched** or **paired samples**. All these names indicate that the samples were not selected independently. To determine whith t test version to use, we must first decide whether we have independent or related groups.

Variance Issues

The second criterion for selecting a t test pertains to the population's variance. All t tests assume that the population's variance(s) is(are) unknown. However, t tests differ on whether the unknown variances are assumed to be equal or unequal.

Variance, as you'll recall from chapter 7, is a measure of dispersion. It measures how scores are spread around the mean. The larger the variance, the more score spread around the mean. Assume that the average number of hours spent watching television was three for men and three for women. The fact that the means are identical would probably lead you to conclude that men and women watch TV, on the average, the same number of hours.

But suppose we learned that the variance in TV hours was 0 for men and 5 for women. The mean is therefore representative of men's TV watching. In fact, all men watch three hours of TV per day—there is no variance. The mean is not as representative a statistic for women. A variance of 5 indicates that some women may watch half an hour and others seven hours. Among women there is a good deal of spread around the mean. t tests take both a measure of central tendency and a measure of spread into account by looking at both the means and the variances of the two groups.

Deciding whether variances are equal is not an arbitrary decision. We test a null hypothesis that states that the variances are equal. To test the null, we use an F ratio with $N_1 - 1$ and $N_2 - 1$ degrees of freedom, where N_1 represents the group with the larger variance, and N_2 represents the group with the smaller variance. As shown in equation 1, the F ratio is simply a ratio of group 1 variance to group 2 variance:

Equation 1: $F = \dfrac{\text{larger variance}}{\text{smaller variance}}$

For example, suppose the mean number of TV hours for 111 men is 2.59, and the mean for 136 women is 3.07. Assume that the standard deviations are 1.62 and 2.74 for men and women, respectively. Were these groups drawn from populations in which the variances are equal? Do we reject or fail to reject the null hypothesis? A failure to reject the null hypothesis leads to the conclusion that the variances are probably the same for the two groups. Rejecting the null hypothesis leads to the conclusion that the variances differ for the two groups.

To determine whether the variances are equal, we use the F ratio. Testing at the 0.05 level, we look in the F table at 135, 110 degrees of freedom. We don't find those specific values, so we use the values closest to 135, 110—the critical value of F associated with 100, 100 degrees of freedom. The critical value of F is 1.39. The calculated F ratio is 2.861. Remember from chapter 7 that variance is the standard deviation squared. To calculate the F ratio, we square the two standard deviations and then divide the larger (7.508) by the smaller variance (2.624). The calculated F ratio (2.861) exceeds the critical value (1.39). We reject the null hypothesis and conclude that the variances in the population are probably unequal. This conclusion means that we use a t test in which the variances for the two groups are assumed unequal. If, however, we conclude that two variances were probably the same in the population, we would use a t test that assumed equal variances.

In this chapter we'll look at two versions of the t test, the one intended for independent samples and unequal variances, and the one designed for independent samples and equal variances. If you are interested in working with paired samples, check a statistics book for the computations and logic. Before we look at the specific t tests, however, try the following checkpoint.

C H E C K P O I N T

1. Given the following sampling plans, would you use a *t* test designed for independent or matched samples? Place an I next to the independent samples and an M next to the matched samples.

   a. You are doing research on the doctor-patient relationship. You interview patients and gain their permission to interview their doctors. You plan to examine whether doctors and patients differ in their perception of the average amount of time spent in consultation.

   b. You are doing research on family size. You ask some women about the ideal family size, and then you ask some men about the ideal family size. You plan to compare whether men and women differ, on the average, in stated ideal family size.

2. You're doing a test for equality of variances. Given the following information, do you reject or fail to reject the null hypothesis?

   a. Testing at the 0.05 level, the calculated *F* ratio is 45.23, and you have 400, 100 degrees of freedom.

   b. Testing at the 0.01 level, the calculated *F* ratio is 2.78, and you have 130, 80 degrees of freedom.

Independent Samples: Unequal Variances

The null hypothesis used in this *t* test states that there is no difference between the means of the two groups. In our example, the null hypothesis states that there is no difference in the average number of hours that men and women spend watching TV. A failure to reject the null indicates that the means for the two groups are not statistically different; the averages for men and women are the same. Rejecting the null hypothesis indicates that the means for the two groups are significantly different; that is, on the average, men and women spend different amounts of time watching TV.

The formula for the *t* statistic is easily used and is shown in Appendix B. Suppose we calculated a *t* equal to -1.68. To find out what that means, we look in the *t* table. Uh, oh, we find that there are two 0.05 levels! Which do we use? Notice that there are two headings in the *t* table, one labeled "Level of significance for one-tailed test" and the other labeled "Level of significance for two-tailed test." What do these headings mean?

Your research hypothesis determines whether you use a **one-tailed** or a **two-tailed** test. A one-tailed test refers to a directional research hypothesis. When you use a one-tailed test, you claim that the population parameter differs from the hypothesized one, *and* you indicate the direction of the difference. For example, a one-tailed research hypothesis may state that males and females spend, on the average, different amounts of time watching TV, *and* that women watch significantly more TV than men.

A two-tailed test, often called a nondirectional research hypothesis, does not indicate the direction of difference. A two-tailed test works with a hypothesis that says that the population's parameters differ from the hypothesized one. In our case, a two-tailed research hypothesis may state that males and females spend, on the average, different amounts of time watching TV. No claims are made in this hypothesis about which group watches more TV.

Let's assume our research hypothesis states that men and women differ in the average number of hours they spend watching TV. We do not make any predictions as to whether men or women watch more TV. We therefore use a two-tailed t test. At the 0.05 level the critical value of t for a two-tailed test with 245 degrees of freedom, $(N - 2) + (N - 1)$ is 1.96. The absolute value of our calculated t value (-1.68) is 1.68. (Absolute values ignore the signs on numbers.)

The absolute value of the calculated t statistic (1.68) does not exceed the critical value (1.96). Therefore, we fail to reject the null. We conclude that the difference in the average number of TV hours watched by males and females is not statistically significant. Males and females spend, on the average, similar amounts of time watching TV. It is unlikely that our samples were drawn from populations in which the mean number of television hours differed.

Independent Samples: Equal Variances

Suppose we failed to reject the null hypothesis in an equal variance test. This would indicate that the variances of the groups were probably equal. We would then use a t test for independent samples and equal variances.

Whether you use a t test for equal or unequal variances, the procedure is the same. The difference between the two techniques is the t test formula. If you look at the formulas in Appendix B, you will find only one variance in the denominator of the equal variance t test, but two variances specified in the unequal variance t test. The difference is due to the fact that variances may be combined or pooled when the variances for the two groups are assumed to be identical. Pooling is done after you have concluded that the two variances are not significantly different.

Suppose we want to examine whether men and women receive different salaries, on the average. Assume that the variances for the two groups are found to be approximately the same, and that the means are $13,000 and $9,500 for 250 men and 350 women, respectively. Suppose the research hypothesis states that the difference between men's and women's incomes is statistically significant and that men earn more than women. The t test you would use is an equal variance, independent sample, one-tailed t test. Suppose the calculated t equals 4.56. What would you conclude?

Testing at the 0.05 level, we look in the t table at a one-tailed test and find that the critical value for t with 598 degrees of freedom ($N_1 + N_2 - 2$) is 1.645. The calculated t (4.56) exceeds the critical value (1.645), and therefore we reject the null hypothesis. We conclude that the difference between the means is statistically significant and that men earn, on the average, more than women. Furthermore, we conclude that it is unlikely that these two samples were drawn from populations in which the means were equal.

Don't worry about all the calculations—SPSS^X handles that work. All we need to do is interpret the printout! Before turning to SPSS^X and its t test program, try the following checkpoint.

C H E C K P O I N T

3. Indicate which of the following hypotheses require a one-tailed test and which require a two-tailed test:

   a. Blondes average more dates than redheads.

   b. Men and women differ, on the average, in the number of times they go to the doctor.

   c. People over the age of 60 know more words, on the average, than people aged 60 or below.

   d. The experimental group will perform differently than the control group.

Using SPSS^X to Calculate t Tests

The following command is a typical t test command:

```
T-TEST GROUPS=SEX/VARIABLES=TVHOURS,MEMNUM
```

Run the command. What have we told the computer?

The T-TEST command tells the computer to calculate a t test. The GROUPS= keyword tells SPSS^X to use a t test formula that assumes independent samples. (If you're working with matched samples, a PAIRS= subcommand replaces the GROUPS= subcommand. Check the SPSS^X manual for additional details.) Only one variable is named after the GROUPS= subcommand, and it indicates the two groups you want compared. SPSS^X automatically labels these as group 1 and group 2. The variable SEX easily subdivides into two groups.

Suppose you want to compare the incomes of people who have three or more children with those who have fewer than three children.

The following command would tell the computer to do this comparison:

```
T-TEST GROUPS=CHILDS(3)/VARIABLES=INCOME
```

The (3) after CHILDS tells SPSSˣ to create two groups differentiated by whether they have more or fewer than three children. One group consists of all values on the specified variable greater than and equal to the value in the parentheses. The other group is composed of all values on the variable less than the value specified in the parentheses. In this case, therefore, group 1 consists of all cases with a value greater than and equal to 3 on CHILDS. Group 2 consists of all cases with a value less than 3 on CHILDS.

Suppose you want to compare the INCOME of Protestants and Catholics. What do you do? Neither one of the above commands will work. Try the following command:

```
T-TEST GROUPS=RELIG(1,2)/VARIABLES=INCOME
```

The two values specified in the parentheses tell SPSSˣ that you want to construct two groups from the RELIG variable, using only the 1 and 2 codes on RELIG and ignoring all others. In this case 1 and 2 correspond to Protestant and Catholic.

The VARIABLES= subcommand follows a slash. The variable(s) named is(are) the interval or ratio variable(s) whose means you want compared. In the first t test command we told the computer that we wanted t tests calculated comparing the average organizational memberships and average TV hours for two independently sampled groups, males and females. Let's look at the printout for that run together. If your printout does not resemble table 14-1, did you declare the 99 code on MEMNUM as missing and the 98 and 99 codes on TVHOURS as missing? If you forgot, do it again.

The printout tells us that group 1 is composed of cases where SEX equals 1, and group 2 is composed of cases where SEX equals 2. In our data, groups 1 and 2 correspond to males and females, respectively. Next, SPSSˣ prints the group name, the number of cases in the group, and the group's mean and standard deviation. Remember, t test formulas work with variance rather than standard deviations, and therefore the standard deviations are squared for the formulas.

The two blocks headed F-VALUE and 2-TAIL PROB are used for the equal variance test. Remember, the null hypothesis states that the variances for the two groups are equal. The F ratio for TVHOURS equals 2.86, and the probability associated with that ratio is 0.000. Testing at the 0.05 level, we reject the null hypothesis of equal variance. It is unlikely that these two groups were drawn from populations in which the variances were equal. We now know that we need to work with a t test that assumes unequal variance.

The next major block, entitled POOLED VARIANCE EST, is the t test assuming equal variances. The last major block, SEPARATE VAR-

Table 14-1 / *t* Tests, Comparing TVHOURS and MEMNUM by SEX

```
GROUP 1   SEX   EQ   1
GROUP 2   SEX   EQ   2
```

VARIABLE	NUMBER OF CASES	MEAN	STANDARD DEVIATION	STANDARD ERROR
TVHOURS				
GROUP 1	111	2.5946	1.620	.154
GROUP 2	136	3.0662	2.741	.235
MEMNUM				
GROUP 1	112	1.7500	1.753	.166
GROUP 2	137	1.4818	1.715	.147

	F VALUE	2-TAIL PROB	POOLED VARIANCE EST T VALUE	DEGREES OF FREEDOM	2-TAIL PROB	SEPARATE VARIANCE EST T VALUE	DEGREES OF FREEDOM	2-TAIL PROB.
TVHOURS	2.86	.000	−1.60	245	.111	−1.68	224.76	.095
MEMNUM	1.04	.807	1.22	247	.225	1.21	235.20	.226

IANCE EST, is the *t* test assuming unequal variances. In the TVHOURS case we look at the *t* test for the separate variance estimate. Notice that SPSS[x] prints the two-tailed test. This means that it is assumed that we are testing a nondirectional research hypothesis. The probability associated with a *t* value of − 1.68 is 0.095. If we were testing at the 0.05 level, we would fail to reject the null. We conclude that the difference in mean TV hours is not statistically significant. The two samples could have been drawn from populations in which the means were identical.

Suppose you want to do a one-tailed *t* test. SPSS[x] prints only the two-tailed probability. What do you do? You simply divide the two-tailed probability in half. For example, working with the TVHOURS variable, simply divide 0.095 in half. The result is 0.0475. Testing at the 0.05 level, we reject the null of equal means using a one-tail test. Now it's your turn to interpret some printouts in the following checkpoint.

C H E C K P O I N T

4. What do the following T-TEST commands tell the computer?

    a. T−TEST GROUPS−MARITAL(1,5)/VARIABLES=MEMNUM

    b. T−TEST GROUPS=DEGREE(4)/VARIABLES=PRESTIGE

5. Write an SPSS^X T-TEST command to compare Protestants and Catholics on occupational prestige.

6. Part of the SPSS^X program we already ran includes a *t* test for SEX and MEMNUM. Interpret that part of the printout. Assume that your research hypothesis states that men and women join, on the average, different numbers of organizations.

In this chapter we examined how to compare the means for two groups. In the next chapter we will examine the analysis of variance when there are more than two groups.

chapter 15

Analysis of Variance

In chapters 9, 10, and 12 we discussed analytical techniques designed for nominal and ordinal variables. In chapters 11 and 13 we discussed analytical techniques designed for interval and ratio variables. Which of these techniques allows us to analyze an interval or ratio dependent variable with a nominal or ordinal independent variable? Which technique, for example, allows us to examine the impact of sex (male, female) on income (measured in dollars)?

Bivariate correlation and regression will not work, because the regression analysis that we discussed requires that all variables, dependent and independent, be measured at the interval or ratio level. Contingency tables analysis will work, but with the drawback that we will have to collapse the interval or ratio variable into an ordinal or nominal variable. Reducing a higher-level variable to a lower-level variable entails a loss of information about the variable. The technique we should use is called **analysis of variance**.

Analysis of variance (ANOVA) is an inferential technique used to test for differences among the means of two or more groups. ANOVA requires a dependent variable measured at the interval or ratio level and independent variables measured at the nominal level or higher. In this chapter we will discuss **one-way** and **two-way ANOVA**. One-way ANOVA refers to the use of one nominal- or ordinal- level independent variable to explain one interval- or ratio-level dependent variable. Two-way ANOVA refers to the use of two nominal- or ordinal-level independent variables to explain one interval- or ratio-level dependent variable. By the way, an ANOVA that has an interval or ratio dependent variable and an interval or ratio independent variable is called bivariate correlation and regression. As we shall see, the two techniques are interrelated.

Upon completion of this chapter, you should be able to do the following:

1. Describe research problems requiring the use of ANOVA
2. Explain and interpret the *F* ratio used in ANOVA
3. Explain and interpret eta squared
4. Write SPSS^X programs to do ANOVA
5. Interpret an SPSS^X ANOVA printout

One-Way ANOVA

Suppose you're interested in the impact of offenders' socioeconomic status (low, middle, high) on sentence length (measured in months). You want to know whether the three groups of offenders (low, middle, and high socioeconomic status) differ significantly in their average sentence length. The technique you use is ANOVA.

ANOVA indicates whether or not the mean sentence length is identical for the three offender groups. In fact, the null hypothesis used in ANOVA states that the means for the three groups (populations) are identical. In this case the null states that the means for low, middle, and high socioeconomic groups are equal.

A failure to reject the null hypothesis indicates that the three groups do not differ significantly in their means. Rejecting the null hypothesis leads to the conclusion that the three groups differ in their means. ANOVA does not, however, indicate which means differ. It may be, for example, that the means for the low and high socioeconomic groups are statistically different, while the means for the low and middle or the middle and high groups do not differ. Remember, ANOVA does not indicate which means differ. We have discussed one technique that may help to determine which means differ—the *t* test. Wait a minute, if we can use *t* tests to determine which means differ, why use ANOVA?

ANOVA gives a single test of whether the means for two or more samples differ. *t* tests require pair-by-pair comparisons. In our example involving the three offender groups we performed one ANOVA. The same problem requires three *t* tests. If we had five groups on the independent variable, then ten *t* tests would be required, and still only one ANOVA. If three of the ten *t* tests were significant, it isn't clear what we would conclude. Herein lies the advantage of ANOVA: it offers a single test of whether the means for two or more samples differ.

There is one additional point to be made about ANOVA and *t* tests.

In chapter 13 we noted that F and t distributions are related such that $t = \sqrt{F}$ at 1 and $N - k$ degrees of freedom. This means that ANOVA is really an extension of the t test presented in chapter 14. When the independent variable contains only two groups, the t test and the ANOVA analyses are identical.

The Decomposition of Variation

The null hypothesis used in ANOVA focuses on means. However, as its name implies, ANOVA actually works with variances. I know that sounds odd, so let's examine this idea in more detail. ANOVA divides the variation in the dependent variable into two parts, the **between-groups** variation and the **within-groups** variation.

For example, suppose sentence length is the dependent variable. Variance, you'll recall from chapter 7, is a measure of spread or dispersion. Part of its calculation, as shown in Appendix B, involves the subtraction of the mean from each score. Variance is, therefore, a measure of spread around a central value, the mean. The numerator of the variance formula is called **variation** or **sums of squares**. To calculate the variation or sums of squares in sentence length, we subtract the overall mean sentence length from each offender's sentence, square that result, and sum them all together. It is this statistic, the variation in the dependent variable, that ANOVA partitions into between-groups and within-groups variation.

The between-groups component of variation (or between-groups sums of squares) refers to how each group's mean departs from the dependent variable's overall mean. It measures the variation between the groups being compared. The calculation of the between-groups component of variation involves the subtraction of the overall mean from each group's mean.

The within-groups variation (or within-groups sums of squares) is a measure of variation within the groups being compared. To calculate within-groups variation, we subtract the group mean from each score in its group. The decomposition of the dependent variable's variation into these two components is shown in equation 1.

Equation 1: Total variation = Between groups + Within groups
(Score − Mean) = (Group mean − Mean) + (Score − Group mean)

Think about the implications of equation 1 for testing the null hypothesis that the group means are equivalent. Suppose all offenders in the low socioeconomic group receive about the same sentence, all offenders in the middle socioeconomic group receive about the same sentence, and all offenders in the high socioeconomic group receive about the same sentence. Furthermore, suppose that the high, middle, and low socioeconomic groups receive sentences that are different from each other. How does this situation apply to equation 1?

The within-groups variation, as described above, is negligible. Offenders within each group receive about the same sentence. The be-tween-groups variation accounts for the differences in sentence length. The total variation in the dependent variable, sentence length, is composed primarily of between-groups variation. In this example, offenders within socioeconomic groups receive similar sentences, and the average sentence differs among the groups. When the between-group variation is substantial relative to the within-group variation, it is an indication that the group means differ. This situation results in the rejection of the null hypothesis. What, however, do we mean by "substantial"?

Suppose there were 300 offenders, 100 in each group. Assume that the overall mean for sentence length was 44 months. Suppose the means for the low, middle, and high socioeconomic groups were 72, 40, and 20 months, respectively. Subtracting the overall mean (44) from each group mean gives the effect of socioeconomic status on sentence length. In this case the effects are 28, −4, and −24, for the low, middle, and high socioeconomic groups respectively. Are these effects important? Are they statistically significant?

To test the null hypothesis, the equal means hypothesis, we use the F ratio. In ANOVA the F ratio compares the between-groups variation (or between-groups sums of squares) to the within-groups variation (or within-groups sums of squares). Equation 2 shows the formula for the F ratio:

$$\text{Equation 2: } F = \frac{\text{Between sums of squares}/k - 1}{\text{Within sums of square}/N - k}$$

The numerator in equation 2 is often referred to as the **mean square between-group variance** and the denominator as the **mean square within-group variance**. The mean square statistic refers to the division of the variation or sums of squares by the appropriate degrees of freedom. In ANOVA, the F ratio is distributed with $k - 1$ and $N - k$ degrees of freedom, where k = the number of categories in the independent variable, and N = sample size.

Suppose we found that the F ratio for the sentencing problem equaled 22.3. What does that indicate? It means that the ratio of the between-groups to the within-groups variation is 22.3 to 1. Phrased slightly differently, the between-groups variation is 22.3 times as large as the within-groups variation. Is that "substantial"? In this case $k = 3$ and $N = 300$, and we are therefore working with an F distribution with 2 and 297 degrees of freedom. Look in Appendix E for the critical value of F for a test at the 0.05 level. You should find a critical value of 3.04.

Our calculated F ratio (22.3) exceeds the table's F ratio (3.04). That indicates that the between-groups variation is substantially greater than the within-groups variation. A between-groups variation that is 22.3 times greater than the within-groups variation is more of a difference than we would expect by chance. We therefore reject the null hypothesis. We conclude that the three means differ; sentence length differs among the three offender types. Remember, we do not know which means differ from each other using ANOVA.

Eta Squared

Eta squared (also called the **correlation ratio**) is a measure of the strength of the relationship between an interval- or ratio-level dependent variable and a nominal-level independent variable. Eta squared ranges from 0 to 1 and has a PRE interpretation. Zero indicates no relationship between the independent variable(s) and the dependent variable. Using the PRE interpretation, an eta squared of 0 indicates a 0 percent reduction in error in predicting the dependent variable from the independent variable. An eta squared of 1 indicates a perfect relationship, a 100 percent reduction in error in predicting the dependent variable from the independent variable.

Remember that a perfect relationship in ANOVA means that all the variation in the dependent variable is accounted for by between-group variation; there is no within-group variation. Remember too that when the between-group variation accounts for *all* the variation in the dependent variable, then the only differences are between groups. Before we apply the basics of ANOVA to a computer printout, try the following checkpoint.

C H E C K P O I N T

1. Interpret the following ANOVA *F* ratios:
   a. 2.31
   b. 10.45
   c. 45.98

2. Test the *F* ratios from the previous checkpoint question for statistical significance. Assume the sample size was 200, the independent variable was sex (male, female), and the dependent variable was income (measured in dollars). Test at the 0.05 and 0.01 levels.

3. Assume that eta squared for the above problem was 0.425. What does this mean?

SPSS^X: Analysis of Variance

The following set of commands illustrates a typical ANOVA program. What have we told the computer?

```
ANOVA MEMNUM BY DEGREE(0,4)
STATISTICS ALL
```

The ANOVA command tells the computer to run an analysis of variance. The variable(s) named prior to the BY keyword is(are) the dependent variable(s). The variable(s) listed after the BY keyword is(are) the independent variable(s). In this case we are working with one dependent variable, MEMNUM, and one independent variable, DEGREE. In this run we are examining whether people with different levels of education join, on the average, different numbers of organizations.

If we also wanted to know whether people with different educational levels watch the same number of hours of TV, on the average, we could add TVHOURS as a second dependent variable. The following commands allow us to examine MEMNUM BY DEGREE and TV HOURS BY DEGREE:

```
ANOVA MEMNUM,TVHOURS BY DEGREE(0,4)
STATISTICS ALL
```

The variable(s) named after BY is(are) the independent variable(s). We examined MEMNUM within categories of DEGREE. The numbers enclosed in parentheses after DEGREE are the range of values on the independent variable included in the ANOVA analysis. In this case (0,4) corresponds to less than high school (0), high school (1), associate or junior college (2), bachelor's degree (3), and graduate school (4). The range on DEGREE is therefore 0 to 4 (0,4). Suppose, however, that we wanted to do an ANOVA examining the average organizational membership for people without a graduate school degree. What could we do? We could list the range as (0,3). In doing so we omit the value 4, graduate school, from the analysis. Values not included in the range are ignored in the ANOVA analysis.

The STATISTICS command tells the computer to print selected statistics. In this case ALL the statistics associated with the ANOVA program were requested. The ANOVA program calculates three sets of statistics. You may ask for one or more of these statistics by using the keywords listed below:

- STATISTICS 1 prints a multiple classification analysis table.
- STATISTICS 2 prints the unstandardized regression coefficients.
- STATISTICS 3 prints a cell means table.
- STATISTICS ALL prints 1, 2, and 3 from above.

Let's examine a printout and these statistics together. Run the ANOVA program explained above for MEMNUM BY DEGREE and TVHOURS BY DEGREE. Your printout should look like the one in table 15-1.

The first part of the printout is CELL MEANS. From these statistics, we learn that the overall mean for the 247 cases included in the analysis was 1.6 organizations. The average number of organizational memberships increases as the degree level increases. The average number of organizations joined is 0.62, 1.77, 1.91, 2.47, and 2.56 for less than high school, high school, associate or junior college, bachelor's

Table 15-1 / One-Way Analysis of Variance: MEMNUM by DEGREE

```
                            CELL MEANS
TOTAL POPULATION
    1.60
    (247)
DEGREE
    0           1           2           3           4
  0.62        1.77        1.91        2.47        2.56
 ( 63)       (134)       ( 11)       ( 30)       (  9)
```

ANALYSIS OF VARIANCE

SOURCE OF VARIATION	SUM OF SQUARES	DF	MEAN SQUARE	F	SIGNIF OF F
MAIN EFFECTS	96.231	4	24.058	9.164	.0000
DEGREE	96.231	4	24.058	9.164	.0000
EXPLAINED	96.231	4	24.058	9.164	.0000
RESIDUAL	635.283	242	2.625		
TOTAL	731.514	246	2.974		

```
   249 CASES WERE PROCESSED.
     2 CASES (.8 PCT.) WERE MISSING
```

MULTIPLE CLASSIFICATION ANALYSIS

GRAND MEAN = 1.60

VARIABLE + CATEGORY	N	UNADJUSTED DEV'N	ETA
0	63	−.98	
1	134	.17	
2	11	.31	
3	30	.87	
4	9	.96	
			.36

degree, and graduate school, respectively. The numbers in parentheses indicate the number of cases within each category of the independent variable.

The second part of the printout is a "typical" ANOVA table. It is divided into four sources of variation: MAIN EFFECTS, EXPLAINED, RESIDUAL, and TOTAL variation. MAIN EFFECTS refers to the variation explained by each independent variable. EXPLAINED variation refers to between-group variation. RESIDUAL variation is another term for within-group variation. The TOTAL variation is the total variation in the dependent variable. From this ANOVA table we gain some interesting information about the relationship between MEMNUM and DEGREE.

First, we learn that the total variation in MEMNUM is 731.514. Second, we learn that the between-group variation, or the variation in MEMNUM accounted for by DEGREE, is 96.231. Third, we learn that the within-group variation, or that which is left unexplained or residual, is 635.283. To calculate F, we divide the between- and within-group variations by their corresponding degrees of freedom. This is automatically done by the SPSS^x program and labeled "mean square." The ratio of the between-group variation (explained) to the within-group variation (residual) is 9.164; that is, the between-group variation is 9.164 times greater than the within-group variation. Is this figure statistically significant?

There were five categories on the independent variable and 247 cases. We are working, therefore, with an F distribution with 4 $(k-1)$ and 242 $(N-k)$ degrees of freedom. Is that statistically significant at the 0.05 level? Yes. The SIGNIF OF F associated with an F ratio of 9.164 with 4 and 242 degrees of freedom is less than 0.0000. You can check this if you like by looking up the critical value of F at the 0.01 level with 4 and 242 degrees of freedom. You will find that the calculated F ratio exceeds the table's critical value. We therefore reject the null hypothesis and conclude that the average number of organizations joined differs by degree.

Notice once again the use of the term EXPLAINED and RESIDUAL in the printout. These terms should remind you of regression analysis. The between-group variation, or the explained variation, in ANOVA is analogous to the explained sums of squares in regression analysis. In both schemes these terms refer to the amount of variance in the dependent variable explained by the independent variable(s). In ANOVA the variation is explained by group membership, and in regression the variance is explained by the regression equation.

The within-group variation, or the residual variation, in ANOVA is analogous to the residual or error sums of squares in regression analysis. In both schemes these terms refer to the variance that is left unexplained by the independent variable(s). In ANOVA the unexplained variation is attributed to the within-group variation. In regression analysis the unexplained or error sums of squares is the variance the regression equation does not explain. To reduce the size of the residuals, researchers often add additional independent variables to their models.

The third part of the table in our printout is the MULTIPLE CLASSIFICATION ANALYSIS table. I won't explain all the statistics in this table's printout, but I have selected several to describe. First, the overall mean for the dependent variable is printed; it equals 1.6 organizations. Second, each category on degree is listed with its corresponding sample size. For example, 63 respondents had less than a high school education. Thus far, the information in the multiple classification table replicates the information printed in the CELL MEANS part of the printout. What additional information does it contain?

The UNADJUSTED DEV'N shows how the mean of each category deviates from the overall mean. A negative sign indicates that the category's mean is below the overall mean. A positive sign indicates that the category's mean is above the overall mean. For example, the organizational mean for people with less than a high school degree deviates from the overall mean by -0.98. Thus, the mean for people with less than a high school degree is below the overall mean of 1.6 by 0.98. The mean for them is 0.62 $(1.6 - 0.98)$. What is the mean for people with a high school degree? It is above the overall mean by 0.17, so it equals 1.77 $(1.6 + 0.17)$.

A comparison of entries in the UNADJUSTED DEV'N column indicates the effects of each DEGREE category. By looking at these effects, we learn that the mean for people with less than a high school degree deviates the most from the overall mean, followed by the mean for the graduate school category. The mean for the high school category deviates the least from the overall mean.

Eta is printed in this table; it equals 0.36. Eta squared is the PRE measure, and it equals 0.1296. This means that 12.96 percent of the variation in MEMNUM is explained by DEGREE. Although the information contained in the three tables of this printout often replicates, all three give us slightly different and important information about the relationship between an interval- or ratio-level dependent variable and a nominal- or ordinal-level independent variable. To see if we're together, do the following checkpoint.

C H E C K P O I N T

4. Write a set of SPSS^X commands to examine the impact of MAWORK on SIBS. As you write the commands, keep in mind that you think the average number of children in a family may differ according to whether or not a woman worked.

5. Table 15-1 contained printout information for MEMNUM BY DEGREE. In the MEMNUM BY DEGREE run we also ran an ANOVA for TVHOURS BY DEGREE. Interpret the ANOVA printout for TVHOURS BY DEGREE.

Two-Way ANOVA

Adding a second independent variable to an ANOVA results in a technique termed **two-way analysis of variance**, or **two-way ANOVA**. Let's add the variable SEX to the already examined one-way ANOVA of

MEMNUM BY DEGREE and TVHOURS BY DEGREE and see what happens. The following commands illustrate a two-way ANOVA:

```
ANOVA MEMNUM, TVHOURS BY DEGREE(0,4) SEX(1,2)
STATISTICS ALL
```

These commands tell the computer to run two two-way ANOVAs. One two-way ANOVA examines the effects of DEGREE and SEX on MEMNUM, and the other looks at the effects of DEGREE and SEX and TVHOURS. So far this sounds familiar. Although the commands look like the commands for a one-way ANOVA, our printout will look somewhat different. These commands tell the computer to check for an interaction between DEGREE and SEX.

Interaction refers to the idea that the effect of one independent variable may not be the same for all levels of the other independent variable. For example, the effect of SEX may be different at the different levels of DEGREE. At one level of degree, females may, on the average, join more organizations, and at another level of degree, males may join more organizations. Phrased slightly differently, the effect of DEGREE may differ for each SEX. The notion of interaction should sound familiar—it is similar to the idea of specification discussed in chapter 12. In reference to the partials, specification described the situation in which the effect of a variable held under certain circumstances but not under others. Why weren't we concerned with interaction in one-way ANOVA? We were not concerned because interaction can only occur when there are two or more independent variables. Let's see how interaction affects our printout and analysis.

The computer printout for the two-way ANOVA involving the effects of DEGREE and SEX on MEMNUM appears in table 15-2. Notice that the two-way ANOVA printout looks strikingly like the one-way printout. The first section contains cell means. The mean of the overall population and the means for each category of the two independent variables are shown. In addition, the means for the combined attributes of the two independent variables are printed. For example, the mean for males with less than a high school degree is 0.75 organizations, and the mean for females with a high school degree is 1.67 organizations. The numbers in parentheses indicate the number of cases within a particular category.

The ANOVA table in this printout differs slightly from the ANOVA table in the one-way printout. It contains five sources of variation: MAIN EFFECTS, 2-WAY INTERACTIONS, EXPLAINED, RESIDUAL, and TOTAL. Once again, TOTAL refers to the variation in the dependent variable. Notice that its numerical value is identical in tables 15-1 and 15-2. This is not a fluke. The variation in the dependent variable does not change for a particular sample.

MAIN EFFECTS refers to joint variation, the combined contribution of the independent variables to explaining the variation in the dependent variable. 2-WAY INTERACTION refers to whether an interaction between the two independent variables contributes to the

Table 15-2 / Two-Way Analysis of Variance: MEMNUM by Degree and Sex

```
                          CELL MEANS
TOTAL POPULATION
   1.60
   (247)

DEGREE
     0         1          2        3          4
   0.62      1.77       1.91     2.47       2.56
   (63)     (134)      ( 11)    ( 30)      (  9)

SEX
      1         2
   1.72      1.49
   (111)    (136)
```

```
                         SEX
DEGREE         1            2
   0          .75          .54
            ( 24)        ( 39)

   1         1.90         1.67
            ( 58)        ( 76)

   2         1.67         2.20
            (  6)        (  5)

   3         2.50         2.42
            ( 18)        ( 12)

   4         1.60         3.75
            (  5)        (  4)
```

ANALYSIS OF VARIANCE

SOURCE OF VARIATION	SUM OF SQUARES	DF	MEAN SQUARE	F	SIGNIF OF F
MAIN EFFECTS	96.636	5	19.327	7.366	.000
DEGREE	93.457	4	23.364	8.905	.000
SEX	.405	1	.405	.155	.695
2-WAY INTERACTIONS	13.030	4	3.258	1.242	.294
DEGREE SEX	13.030	4	3.258	1.242	.294
EXPLAINED	109.666	9	12.185	4.644	.000
RESIDUAL	621.848	237	2.624		
TOTAL	731.514	246	2.974		

```
   249 CASES WERE PROCESSED
     2 CASES (.8 PCT) WERE MISSING.
```

```
              MULTIPLE CLASSIFICATION ANALYSIS
```

GRAND MEAN = 1.60

			UNADJUSTED	
VARIABLE + CATEGORY		N	DEV'N	ETA
DEGREE				
0		63	−.98	
1		134	.17	
2		11	.31	
3		30	.87	
4		9	.96	
				.36
SEX				
1		111	.13	
2		136	−.10	
				.07

```
MULTIPLE R SQUARED   .132
MULTIPLE R           .363
```

variation in the dependent variable. In this case we're concerned with whether differences in DEGREE produce the same effect whether a respondent is male or female, and whether differences in SEX produce the same effect in all categories of DEGREE. If so, there is no interaction. EXPLAINED variation is that which is explained by the main effects and the interaction together. RESIDUAL variation is the variation in the dependent variable this is left unexplained by both the main effects and the interactions.

What do you conclude about this table from looking at the SIGNIF OF F column? Testing at the 0.05 level, you should conclude that the interaction is not statistically significant; that is, there is no indication that the means are statistically different within combinations of SEX and DEGREE. Under MAIN EFFECTS, only the DEGREE is statistically significant. The overall F ratio for the equation is significant. The significance level of 0.000 associated with the EXPLAINED source of variation indicates that we should reject the null hypothesis and conclude that the means differ.

The final table of the two-way analysis printout, the multiple classification table, indicates the effect of group membership. In addition, eta is shown for each of the independent variables. Eta squared is 0.1296 and 0.0049 for DEGREE and SEX, respectively. This means that degree explains 12.96 percent of the variation in MEMNUM, and SEX explains only 0.49 percent. Together the two variables explain 13.2 percent of the variation in MEMNUM, multiple R squared. See if you can interpret a two-way ANOVA by doing the following checkpoint.

C H E C K P O I N T

6. Table 15-2 is part of an SPSS[x] run. You should also have the two-way ANOVA printout for TVHOURS BY DEGREE and SEX. What does that analysis indicate?

In this chapter we discussed the analysis of an interval- or ratio-level dependent variable with a nominal- or ordinal-level independent variable. This chapter concludes our exploration of the world of research, computers, statistics, and SPSS[x]. One more chapter is included, however, to give you a brief wrap-up of everything we have covered.

chapter 16
Wrapping It All Up!

Now that you have completed this book, I hope you find the research world of the social scientist as exciting as I do! It is a world that changes almost every day. Calculations that took days to perform in the 1940s now take only fractions of a second! Computers have eliminated the time and drudgery from computations. They have not, however, replaced social scientists. We are the ones who decide on the areas of study, collect the data, program the computers, and interpret the results. Computers and statistics are an integral part of the social scientist's world.

My intention in writing this book was twofold. First, I wanted to provide you with a solid background in the interpretation of statistics. Second, I wanted to show you where these statistics come from. To accomplish these objectives, I have discussed how computers work, how to program in SPSS^X, and how to interpret selected statistics.

Whether you do social research or read the research produced by social scientists, you now have a solid base for evaluating the research. But don't close this book and think you know all there is to know about computers and statistics. We've only just begun! This book has laid the groundwork for both statistics and computer use, especially the use of SPSS^X. Now you're ready to take another course in research methods, or statistics, or computers.

It's your turn to do an analysis in an area that interests you. Look through the variables in Appendix A, or work with a data set selected by your instructor. Pick out variables that interest you, develop a hypothesis and do some analyses. How? Start by thinking about the question(s) you want answered. Then consider the following issues: How many variables are there? Is there a dependent variable? At what level are the variables measured? Would the sample or the population be more interesting to describe?

If you get stuck and can't decide what to do, refer to tables 16-1 and 16-2 for assistance. Good luck and good findings!

Table 16-1 / Summary Table: Descriptive Analyses

	Level of Measurement		
	Nominal	Ordinal	Interval/Ratio
Univariate			
Graphs	Bar graph	Bar graph	Histogram
SPSS^x command	FREQUENCIES BARCHART	FREQUENCIES BARCHART	FREQUENCIES HISTOGRAM
Measures of central tendency	Mode	Median	Mean
SPSS^x command	FREQUENCIES MODE	FREQUENCIES MEDIAN	FREQUENCIES MEAN
Measures of dispersion		Range	Standard deviation Variance
SPSS^x command		FREQUENCIES MINIMUM MAXIMUM	FREQUENCIES STDDEV VARIANCE
Bivariate			
Graphs	Crosstab table	Crosstab table	Scattergram
SPSS^x command	CROSSTABS	CROSSTABS	SCATTERGRAM
Measures of association or correlation	Contingency coefficient Phi Cramer's V Lambda	Gamma Somer's d Kendall's tau-b Kendall's tau-c	Pearson's product-moment r squared
SPSS^x command	CROSSTABS STATISTICS	CROSSTABS STATISTICS	CROSSTABS PEARSON CORR
Multivariate			
Graphs	Crosstab tables and partials		Regression line
SPSS^x command	CROSSTABS		SCATTERGRAM
Measures of association or correlation	Same as for the bivariate		Multiple R correlation coefficient
SPSS^x command	CROSSTABS STATISTICS	CROSSTABS STATISTICS	REGRESSION STATISTICS

Table 16-2 / Summary Table: Inferential Analyses

		Level of Measurement (Dependent Variable)		
		Nominal	Ordinal	Interval/Ratio
Level of Measurement (Independent Variable)	Nominal Ordinal Interval/Ratio	Chi square Chi square	Chi square Chi square	t test, ANOVA F ratios

General Social Survey

The General Social Survey is a biannual survey completed by the National Opinion Research Center. A probability sample of 1,468 persons was taken in 1980 using multistage cluster sampling with probabilities proportional to size. Standard Metropolitan Statistical Areas were selected first, Census blocks were selected second, households were selected third, and individuals were selected fourth. Stratification occurred at the first level (region and race), and at the second level (by geographic location, income, and race). A random sample of 249 cases was taken from the larger sample for this data set. The columns associated with each variable are located in parentheses under the variable name.

AGE
(1–2)

1. Age (determined by asking date of birth)
   18–90. Actual age
   98. Don't know (DK)   99. No answer (NA)

SIBS
(3–4)

2. How many brothers and sisters did you have? Please count those born alive, but no longer living, as well as those alive now. Also include stepbrothers and stepsisters, and children adopted by your parents.
   0–20. Actual number
   98. DK   99. NA

INCOME
(5–6)

3. In which of the following groups did your total FAMILY income, from ALL sources, fall last year before taxes, that is?
   1. Under $1,000
   2. $1,000 to $2,999
   3. $3,000 to $3,999
   4. $4,000 to $4,999
   5. $5,000 to $5,999
   6. $6,000 to $6,999
   7. $7,000 to $7,999
   8. $8,000 to $9,999
   9. $10,000 to $12,499
   10. $12,500 to $14,999
   11. $15,000 to $17,499
   12. $17,500 to $19,999

Source: Reprinted with permission of the National Opinion Research Company.

13. $20,000 to $22,499
14. $22,500 to $24,999
15. $25,000 to $49,999
16. $50,000 and over
17. Refused
98. DK   99. NA

MEMNUM
(7–8)

3. Here is a list of various kinds of organizations. Could you tell me whether or not you are a member of each type? (Number coded reflects total number of the following to which respondent belongs: fraternal groups, service clubs, veterans' groups, political clubs, labor unions, sports groups, youth groups, school service groups, hobby or garden clubs, school fraternities or sororities, nationality groups, farm organizations, literary/art/discussion/study groups, professional or academic societies, church groups, other).
0–16. Actual number
99. NA

TVHOURS
(9–10)

3. On the average day, about how many hours do you personally watch television?
0–18. Actual number
98. DK   99. NA

PRESTIGE
(11–12)

4. Hodge/Siegel/Rossi prestige scale score for respondent's occupation.
0. No score due to no job
12–89. Prestige scale score for job

WRKSTAT
(13)

5. Last week were you working full-time, part-time, going to school, keeping house, or what?
1. Working full-time
2. Working part-time
3. With a job, but not at work because of temporary illness, vacation, strike
4. Unemployed
5. Retired
6. In school
7. Keeping house
8. Other

MARITAL
(14)

6. Are your currently—married, widowed, divorced, separated, or have you never been married?
1. Married
2. Widowed
3. Divorced
4. Separated
5. Never married

CHILDS
(15)

7. How many children have you ever had? Please count all that were born alive at any time (including any you had from a previous marriage).

0–7. Actual number
8. Eight or more
9. NA

DEGREE
(16)

8. Highest degree.
   0. Less than high school
   1. High school
   2. Associate/junior college
   3. Bachelor's
   4. Graduate
   8. DK   9. NA

SEX
(17)

9. Sex (coded by interviewer).
   1. Male
   2. Female

RACE
(18)

10. What race do you consider yourself?
    1. White
    2. Black
    3. Other

MAWORK
(19)

11. Did your mother ever work for pay for as long as a year, after she was married?
    0. Did not live with mother
    1. Yes
    2. No
    8. DK   9. NA

REGION
(20)

12. Region of interview.
    1. New England
    2. Middle Atlantic
    3. East North Central
    4. West North Central
    5. South Atlantic
    6. East South Central
    7. West South Central
    8. Mountain
    9. Pacific

SRCBELT
(21)

13. Size/type of residence location.
    1. Central city of 12 largest Standard Metropolitan Statistical Areas (SMSAs)
    2. Central city of remainder of the 100 largest SMSAs
    3. Suburbs of 12 largest SMSAs
    4. Suburbs of the remaining 100 largest SMSAs
    5. Other urban (counties having towns of 10,000 or more)
    6. Other rural (counties having no towns of 10,000 or more)

RELIG
(22)

14. What is your religious preference? Is it Protestant, Catholic, Jewish, some other religion, or no religion?
    1. Protestant
    2. Catholic
    3. Jewish

4. None
5. Other
9. NA

ATTEND
(23)

15. How often do you attend religious services?
    0. Never
    1. Less than once a year
    2. About once or twice a year
    3. Several times a year
    4. About once a month
    5. 2–3 times a month
    6. Nearly every week
    7. Every week
    8. Several times a week
    9. DK/NA

CLASS
(24)

16. If you were asked to use one of four names for your social class, which would you say you belong in: the lower class, the working class, the middle class, or the upper class?
    1. Lower class
    2. Working class
    3. Middle class
    4. Upper class
    9. NA

UNEMP
(25)

17. At any time during the last ten years, have you been unemployed and looking for work for as long as a month?
    1. Yes
    2. No
    8. DK   9. NA

GOVAID
(26)

18. Did you ever—because of sickness, unemployment, or any other reason—receive anything like welfare, unemployment insurance, or other aid from governmental agencies?
    1. Yes
    2. No
    8. DK   9. NA

    We are faced with many problems in this country, none of which can be solved easily or inexpensively. I'm going to name some of these problems, and for each one I'd like you to tell me whether you think we're spending too much money on it, too little money, or about the right amount. Are we spending too much, too little, or about the right amount on . . .

NATEDUC
(27)

19. Improving the nation's educational system?
    1. Too little
    2. About right
    3. Too much
    8. DK   9. NA

NATFARE
(28)

20. Welfare?
    (same answers as NATEDUC, #19)

TAX
(29)

21. Do you consider the amount of federal income tax that you have to pay as too high, about right, or too low?
   1. Too high
   2. About right
   3. Too low
   8. DK   9. NA

SPKATH
(30)

22. If somebody who is against all churches and religion wanted to make a speech in your city/town/community against churches and religion, should he be allowed to speak, or not?
   1. Yes, allowed to speak
   2. Not allowed
   8. DK   9. NA

SPKCOM
(31)

23. Suppose a man who admits he is a Communist wanted to make a speech in your community. Should he be allowed to speak, nor not?
   (Same answers as SPKATH, #22)

SPKHOMO
(32)

24. Suppose a man who admits he is a homosexual wanted to make a speech in your community. Should he be allowed to speak, or not?
   (Same answers as SPKATH, #22)

CAPPUN
(33)

25. Do you favor or oppose the death penalty for persons convicted of murder?
   1. Favor
   2. Oppose
   8. DK   9. NA

GUNLAW
(34)

26. Would you favor or oppose a law which would require a person to obtain a police permit before he or she could buy a gun?
   (Same answers as CAPPUN, #25)

GRASS
(35)

27. Do you think the use of marijuana should be made legal or not?
   1. Should
   2. Should not
   8. DK   9. NA

COMMUN
(36)

28. Thinking about all the different kinds of government in the world today, which of these statements comes closest to how you feel about Communism as a form of government?
   1. It's the worst kind of all
   2. It's bad, but no worse than some others
   3. It's all right for some countries
   4. It's a good form of government
   8. DK   9. NA

HAPPY
(37)

29. Taken all together, how would you say things are these days—would you say that you are very happy, pretty happy, or not too happy?

1. Very happy
2. Pretty happy
3. Not too happy
8. DK   9. NA

HEALTH
(38)

30. Would you say your own health, in general, is excellent, good, fair, or poor?
    1. Excellent
    2. Good
    3. Fair
    4. Poor
    8. DK   9. NA

PARTYID
(39)

31. Generally speaking, do you usually think of yourself as a Republican, Democrat, Independent, or what?
    0. Strong Democrat
    1. Not very strong Democrat
    2. Independent, close to Democrat
    3. Independent (neither, no response)
    4. Independent, close to Republican
    5. Not very strong Republican
    6. Strong Republican
    7. Other party, refused to say
    8. DK   9. NA

POLVIEWS
(40)

32. I'm going to show you a seven-point scale on which the *political* views that people might hold are arranged from extremely liberal—point 1—to extremely conservative—point 7. Where would you place yourself on this scale?
    1. Extremely liberal
    2. Liberal
    3. Slightly liberal
    4. Moderate, middle of the road
    5. Slightly conservative
    6. Conservative
    7. Extremely conservative
    8. DK   9. NA

HELPFUL
(41)

33. Would you say that most of the time people try to be helpful, or that they are mostly just looking out for themselves?
    1. Try to be helpful
    2. Just look out for themselves
    3. Depends (volunteered)
    8. DK   9. NA

FAIR
(42)

34. Do you think most people would try to take advantage of you if they got a chance, or would they try to be fair?
    1. Would take advantage of you
    2. Would try to be fair
    3. Depends (volunteered)
    8. DK   9. NA

SATFAM
(43)

35. Tell me the number that shows how much satisfaction you get from your family life.
   1. A very great deal
   2. A great deal
   3. Quite a bit
   4. A fair amount
   5. Some
   6. A little
   7. None
   8. DK   9. NA

SATFRND
(44)

36. Tell me the number that shows how much satisfaction you get from your friendships.
   (Same answers as SATFAM, #35)

SATJOB
(45)

37. On the whole, how satisfied are you with the work you do—would you say you are very satisfied, moderately satisfied, a little dissatisfied, or very dissatisfied?
   0. Not applicable due to no job
   1. Very satisfied
   2. Moderately satisfied
   3. A little dissatisfied
   4. Very dissatisfied
   8. DK   9. NA

I am going to name some institutions in this country. As far as the *people running* these institutions are concerned, would you say that you have a great deal of confidence, only some confidence, or hardly any confidence at all in them?

CONEDUC
(46)

38. Education
   1. A great deal
   2. Only some
   3. Hardly any
   8. DK   9. NA

CONPRESS
(47)

39. Press
   (Same answers as CONEDUC, #38)

CONLEGIS
(48)

40. Congress
   (Same answers as CONLEGIS, #38)

AGED
(49)

41. As you know, many older people share a home with their grown children. Do you think this is generally a good idea or a bad idea?
   1. A good idea
   2. Bad idea
   3. Depends
   8. DK   9. NA

DRUNK
(50)

42. Do you sometimes drink more than you think you should?
   0. Total abstainer
   1. Yes

2. No
8. DK   9. NA

SMOKE   43. Do you smoke?
(51)   1. Yes
                     2. No
                     9. NA

ANOMIA1   44. In spite of what some people say, the lot/situation/con-
(52)   dition of the average man is getting worse, not better. Do
                     you more or less agree with that, or more or less disagree?
                     1. Agree
                     2. Disagree
                     8. DK   9. NA

ANOMIA2   45. It's hardly fair to bring a child into the world with the
(53)   way things look for the future.
                     (Same answers as ANOMIA1, #44)

ANOMIA3   46. Most public officials (people in public office) are not really
(54)   interested in the problems of the average man.
                     (Same answers as ANOMIA1, #44)

FINALTER   47. During the last few years, has your financial situation
(55)   been getting better, getting worse, or has it stayed the
                     same?
                     1. Getting better
                     2. Getting worse
                     3. Stayed the same
                     8. DK   9. NA

GETAHEAD   48. Some people say that people get ahead by their own hard
(56)   work; others say that lucky breaks or help from other
                     people are more important. Which do you think is most
                     important?
                     1. Hard work most important
                     2. Hard work, luck equally important
                     3. Luck most important
                     8. DK   9. NA

               Please tell me whether or not *you* think it should be pos-
               sible for a pregnant woman to obtain a *legal* abortion if. . . .

ABDEFECT   49. If there is a strong chance of serious defect in the baby?
(57)   1. Yes
                     2. No.
                     8. DK   9. NA

ABNOMORE   50. If she is married and does not want any more children?
(58)   (Same answers as ABDEFECT, #49)

ABHLTH   51. If the woman's health is seriously endangered by the
(59)   pregnancy?
                     (Same answers as ABDEFECT, #49)

ABPOOR
(60)

52. If the family has a very low income and cannot afford any more children?
(Same answers as ABDEFECT, #49)

ABRAPE
(61)

53. If she became pregnant as a result of rape?
(Same answers as ABDEFECT, #49)

ABSINGLE
(62)

54. If she is not married and does not want to marry the man?
(Same answers as ABDEFECT, #49)

The next questions are about pornography—books, movies, magazines, and photographs that show or describe sex activities. I'm going to read some opinions about the effects of looking at or reading such sexual materials. As I read each one, please tell me if you think sexual materials do or do not have that effect.

PORNMORL
(63)

55. Sexual materials lead to breakdown of morals.
1. Yes
2. No
8. DK   9. NA

PORNRAPE
(64)

56. Sexual materials lead people to commit rape.
(Same answers as PORNMORL, #55)

PORNOUT
(65)

57. Sexual materials provide an outlet for bottled-up impulses.
(Same answers as PORNMORL, #55)

XMOVIE
(66)

58. Have you seen an X-rated movie in the last year?
1. Yes
2. No
8. DK   9. NA

HIT
(67)

59. Have you ever been punched or beaten by another person?
1. Yes
2. No
8. DK   9. NA

HITOK
(68)

60. Are there any situations that you can imagine in which you would approve of a man punching an adult stranger?
1. Yes
2. No
8. Not sure
9. NA

FEAR
(69)

61. Is there any area right around here—that is, within a mile—where you would be afraid to walk alone at night?
1. Yes
2. No
8. DK   9. NA

OWNGUN
(70)

62. Do you happen to have in your home or garage any guns or revolvers?

1. Yes
2. No
3. Refused
8. DK   9. NA

TICKET
(71)

63. Have you ever received a ticket, or been charged by the police, for a traffic violation—other than for illegal parking?
(Same answers as OWNGUN, #62)

TRAUMA
(72)

64. Number of traumatic events (deaths, divorces, unemployments, and hospitalizations/disabilities) happening to respondent during the last five years.
0. Zero
1. One
2. Two
3. Three
4. Four
9. NA

DEFENSE
(73)

65. Some people believe that we should spend much less money for defense. Suppose these people are at one end of the scale at point number 1. Others feel that defense spending should be greatly increased. Suppose these people are at the other end, at point 7. And, of course, some other people have opinions somewhere in between at points 2,3,4,5, or 6. Where would you place yourself on this scale, or haven't you thought much about this?
0. Haven't thought much about this
1. Greatly decrease
7. Greatly increase
8. DK   9. NA

CUTSPEND
(74)

65. Some people think the government should provide fewer services, even in areas such as health and education, in order to reduce spending. Suppose these people are at one end of the scale at point number 1. Other people feel it is important for the government to continue the services it now provides even if it means no reduction in spending. Suppose these people are at the other end, at point 7. And, of course, some other people have opinions somewhere in between at points 2,3,4,5, or 6. Where would you place yourself on this scale, or haven't you thought much about this?
0. Haven't thought much about this
1. Government should reduce
7. Government should continue
8. DK   9. NA

Formulas for Selected Statistics

Mean $(\bar{X})$ $\quad \bar{X} = \dfrac{\Sigma X}{N}$ where X = scores on variable
$\quad\quad\quad\quad\quad\quad\quad\quad\quad\quad N$ = sample size

Standard deviation (s) $\quad (s) = \sqrt{\dfrac{\Sigma(X - \bar{X})^2}{N}}$

Variance (s^2) $\quad s^2 = \dfrac{\Sigma(X - \bar{X})^2}{N}$

Chi square (χ^2) $\quad \chi^2 = \Sigma\dfrac{(f_o - f_e)^2}{f_e}$ where f_o = observed frequency
$\quad\quad\quad\quad\quad\quad\quad\quad\quad\quad\quad\quad\quad f_e$ = expected frequency

Degrees of freedom for chi square $= (r - 1)(c - 1)$
$\quad\quad\quad\quad\quad\quad\quad\quad\quad\quad\quad\quad\quad$ where r = number of rows
$\quad\quad\quad\quad\quad\quad\quad\quad\quad\quad\quad\quad\quad\quad c$ = number of columns

Phi (ϕ) $\quad \phi = \sqrt{\dfrac{\chi^2}{N}}$

Contingency coefficient (C) $\quad C = \sqrt{\dfrac{\chi^2}{\chi^2 + N}}$

Cramer's v (v) $\quad v = \sqrt{\dfrac{\chi^2}{N(k - 1)}}$ where k = number of rows or columns, whichever is less

Lambda (λ) $\quad \lambda = \dfrac{E_1 - E_2}{E_1}$

Gamma (γ) $\quad \gamma = \dfrac{L - D}{L + D}$

Somer's d $\quad$ Somer's $d_{yx} = \dfrac{L - D}{L + D + T_y}$ where T_y = ties on y, when y is the dependent variable

187

Somer's d Somer's $d_{xy} = \dfrac{L - D}{L + D + T_x}$ where T_x = ties on x, when x is the dependent variable

Kendall's tau-b Tau-$b = \dfrac{L - D}{\sqrt{(L + D + T_y)(L + D + T_x)}}$

Kendall's tau-c Tau-$c = \dfrac{2k(L - D)}{N^2(k - 1)}$ where k = number of rows or columns, whichever is less

Pearson's r (r) $r = \dfrac{\Sigma(X - \bar{X})(Y - \bar{Y})}{\sqrt{[\Sigma(X - \bar{X})^2][\Sigma(Y - \bar{Y})^2]}}$

Regression coefficient (b) $b_{yx} = \dfrac{\Sigma(X - \bar{X})(Y - \bar{Y})}{\Sigma(X - \bar{X})^2}$

Standardized regression coefficient (β) $\beta_{yx} = b_{yx}\dfrac{s_x}{s_y}$

t test for unequal variances $t = \dfrac{\bar{X}_1 - \bar{X}_2}{s_{\bar{x}_1 - \bar{x}_2}}$

where $\bar{X}_1, \bar{X}_2$ = sample means for groups 1 and 2 respectively

$s_{\bar{x}_1 - \bar{x}_2}$ = standard error of the difference between the two means, calculated using the following formula:

$$s_{\bar{x}_1 - \bar{x}_2} = \sqrt{\dfrac{s_1^2}{N_1 - 1} + \dfrac{s_2^2}{N_2 - 1}}$$

where s_1^2, s_2^2 = variances for groups 1 and 2, respectively

N_1, N_2 = sample size for groups 1 and 2, respectively

Areas under the normal curve

Fractional parts of the total area (10,000) under the normal curve, corresponding to distances between the mean and ordinates which are Z standard-deviation units from the mean.

Z	.00	.01	.02	.03	.04	.05	.06	.07	.08	.09
0.0	0000	0040	0080	0120	0159	0199	0239	0279	0319	0359
0.1	0398	0438	0478	0517	0557	0596	0636	0675	0714	0753
0.2	0793	0832	0871	0910	0948	0987	1026	1064	1103	1141
0.3	1179	1217	1255	1293	1331	1368	1406	1443	1480	1517
0.4	1554	1591	1628	1664	1700	1736	1772	1808	1844	1879
0.5	1915	1950	1985	2019	2054	2088	2123	2157	2190	2224
0.6	2257	2291	2324	2357	2389	2422	2454	2486	2518	2549
0.7	2580	2612	2642	2673	2704	2734	2764	2794	2823	2852
0.8	2881	2910	2939	2967	2995	3023	3051	3078	3106	3133
0.9	3159	3186	3212	3238	3264	3289	3315	3340	3365	3389
1.0	3413	3438	3461	3485	3508	3531	3554	3577	3599	3621
1.1	3643	3665	3686	3718	3729	3749	3770	3790	3810	3830
1.2	3849	3869	3888	3907	3925	3944	3962	3980	3997	4015
1.3	4032	4049	4066	4083	4099	4115	4131	4147	4162	4177
1.4	4192	4207	4222	4236	4251	4265	4279	4292	4306	4319
1.5	4332	4345	4357	4370	4382	4394	4406	4418	4430	4441
1.6	4452	4463	4474	4485	4495	4505	4515	4525	4535	4545
1.7	4554	4564	4573	4582	4591	4599	4608	4616	4625	4633
1.8	4641	4649	4656	4664	4671	4678	4686	4693	4699	4706
1.9	4713	4719	4726	4732	4738	4744	4750	4758	4762	4767
2.0	4773	4778	4783	4788	4793	4798	4803	4808	4812	4817
2.1	4821	4826	4830	4834	4838	4842	4846	4850	4854	4857
2.2	4861	4865	4868	4871	4875	4878	4881	4884	4887	4890
2.3	4893	4896	4898	4901	4904	4906	4909	4911	4913	4916
2.4	4918	4920	4922	4925	4927	4929	4931	4932	4934	4936
2.5	4938	4940	4941	4943	494f	4946	4948	4949	4951	4952
2.6	4953	4955	4956	4957	4959	4960	4961	4962	4963	4964
2.7	4965	4966	4967	4968	4969	4970	4971	4972	4973	4974
2.8	4974	4975	4976	4977	4977	4978	4979	4980	4980	4981
2.9	4981	4982	4983	4984	4984	4984	4985	4985	4986	4986
3.0	4986.5	4987	4987	4988	4988	4988	4989	4989	4989	4990
3.1	4990.0	4991	4991	4991	4992	4992	4992	4992	4993	4993
3.2	4993.129									
3.3	4995.166									
3.4	4996.631									
3.5	4997.674									
3.6	4998.409									
3.7	4998.922									
3.8	4999.277									
3.9	4999.519									
4.0	4999.683									
4.5	4999.966									
5.0	4999.997133									

SOURCE: Harold O. Rugg, Statistical Methods Applied to Education, pp. 389–390. Copyright © 1917, renewal 1945 by Houghton Mifflin Company. Used by permission.

appendix D
Distribution of χ^2

Probability

df	.99	.98	.95	.90	.80	.70	.50	.30	.20	.10	.05	.02	.01	.001
1	$.0^3157$	$.0^3628$	$.0^2393$	.0158	.0642	.148	.455	1.074	1.642	2.706	3.841	5.412	6.635	10.827
2	.0201	.0404	.103	.211	.446	.713	1.386	2.408	3.219	4.605	5.991	7.824	9.210	13.815
3	.115	.185	.352	.584	1.005	1.424	2.366	3.665	4.642	6.251	7.815	9.837	11.341	16.268
4	.297	.429	.711	1.064	1.649	2.195	3.357	4.878	5.989	7.779	9.488	11.668	13.277	18.465
5	.554	.752	1.145	1.610	2.343	3.000	4.351	6.064	7.289	9.236	11.070	13.388	15.086	20.517
6	.872	1.134	1.635	2.204	3.070	3.828	5.348	7.231	8.558	10.645	12.592	15.033	16.812	22.457
7	1.239	1.564	2.167	2.833	3.822	4.671	6.346	8.383	9.803	12.017	14.067	16.622	18.475	24.322
8	1.646	2.032	2.733	3.490	4.594	5.527	7.344	9.524	11.030	13.362	15.507	18.168	20.090	26.125
9	2.088	2.532	3.325	4.168	5.380	6.393	8.343	10.656	12.242	14.684	16.919	19.679	21.666	27.877
10	2.558	3.059	3.940	4.865	6.179	7.267	9.342	11.781	13.442	15.987	18.307	21.161	23.209	29.588
11	3.053	3.609	4.575	5.578	6.989	8.148	10.341	12.899	14.631	17.275	19.675	22.618	24.725	31.264
12	3.571	4.178	5.226	6.304	7.807	9.034	11.340	14.011	15.812	18.549	21.026	24.054	26.217	32.909
13	4.107	4.765	5.892	7.042	8.634	9.926	12.340	15.119	16.985	19.812	22.362	25.472	27.688	34.528
14	4.660	5.368	6.571	7.790	9.467	10.821	13.339	16.222	18.151	21.064	23.685	26.873	29.141	36.123
15	5.229	5.985	7.261	8.547	10.307	11.721	14.339	17.322	19.311	22.307	24.996	28.259	30.578	37.697
16	5.812	6.614	7.962	9.312	11.152	12.624	15.338	18.418	20.465	23.542	26.296	29.633	32.000	39.252
17	6.408	7.255	8.672	10.085	12.002	13.531	16.338	19.511	21.615	24.769	27.587	30.995	33.409	40.790
18	7.015	7.906	9.390	10.865	12.857	14.440	17.338	20.601	22.760	25.989	28.869	32.346	34.805	42.312
19	7.633	8.567	10.117	11.651	13.716	15.352	18.338	21.689	23.900	27.204	30.144	33.687	36.191	43.820
20	8.260	9.237	10.851	12.443	14.578	16.266	19.337	22.775	25.038	28.412	31.410	35.020	37.566	45.315
21	8.897	9.915	11.591	13.240	15.445	17.182	20.337	23.858	26.171	29.615	32.671	36.343	38.932	46.797
22	9.542	10.600	12.338	14.041	16.314	18.101	21.337	24.939	27.301	30.813	33.924	37.659	40.289	48.268
23	10.196	11.293	13.091	14.848	17.187	19.021	22.337	26.018	28.429	32.007	35.172	38.968	41.638	49.728
24	10.856	11.992	13.848	15.659	18.062	19.943	23.337	27.096	29.553	33.196	36.415	40.270	42.980	51.179
25	11.524	12.697	14.611	16.473	18.940	20.867	24.337	28.172	30.675	34.382	37.652	41.566	44.314	52.620
26	12.198	13.409	15.379	17.292	19.820	21.792	25.336	29.246	31.795	35.563	38.885	42.856	45.642	54.052
27	12.879	14.125	16.151	18.114	20.703	22.719	26.336	30.319	32.912	36.741	40.113	44.140	46.963	55.476
28	13.565	14.847	16.928	18.939	21.588	23.647	27.336	31.391	34.027	37.916	41.337	45.419	48.278	56.893
29	14.256	15.574	17.708	19.768	22.475	24.577	28.336	32.461	35.139	39.087	42.557	46.693	49.588	58.302
30	14.953	16.306	18.493	20.599	23.364	25.508	29.336	33.530	36.250	40.256	43.773	47.962	50.892	59.703

For larger values of df, the expression $\sqrt{2\chi^2} - \sqrt{2df - 1}$ may be used as a normal deviate with unit variance, remembering that the probability for χ^2 corresponds with that of a single tail of the normal curve.

SOURCE: I am grateful to the Literary Executor of the late Sir Ronald A. Fisher, F. R. S., to Dr. Frank Yates, F. R. S., and to Longman Group Ltd., London, for permission to reprint Table IV from their book *Statistical Tables for Biological, Agricultural, and Medical Research* (6th Edition, 1974).

appendix E
Critical Values of F

The obtained F is significant at a given level if it is equal to or *greater than* the value shown in the table. 0.05 (light row) and 0.01 (dark row) points for the distribution of F.

Degrees of freedom for greater mean square (variance). Values shown as 0.05 (light) / 0.01 (dark).

df (lesser)	1	2	3	4	5	6	7	8	9	10	11	12	14	16	20	24	30	40	50	75	100	200	500	∞
1	161 / 4052	200 / 4999	216 / 5403	225 / 5625	230 / 5764	234 / 5859	237 / 5928	239 / 5981	241 / 6022	242 / 6056	243 / 6082	244 / 6106	245 / 6142	246 / 6169	248 / 6208	249 / 6234	250 / 6258	251 / 6286	252 / 6302	253 / 6323	253 / 6334	254 / 6352	254 / 6361	254 / 6366
2	18.51 / 98.49	19.00 / 99.01	19.16 / 99.17	19.25 / 99.25	19.30 / 99.30	19.33 / 99.33	19.36 / 99.34	19.37 / 99.36	19.38 / 99.38	19.39 / 99.40	19.40 / 99.41	19.41 / 99.42	19.42 / 99.43	19.43 / 99.44	19.44 / 99.45	19.45 / 99.46	19.46 / 99.47	19.47 / 99.48	19.47 / 99.48	19.48 / 99.49	19.49 / 99.49	19.49 / 99.49	19.50 / 99.50	19.50 / 99.50
3	10.13 / 34.12	9.55 / 30.81	9.28 / 29.46	9.12 / 28.71	9.01 / 28.24	8.94 / 27.91	8.88 / 27.67	8.84 / 27.49	8.81 / 27.34	8.78 / 27.23	8.76 / 27.13	8.74 / 27.05	8.71 / 26.92	8.69 / 26.83	8.66 / 26.69	8.64 / 26.60	8.62 / 26.50	8.60 / 26.41	8.58 / 26.30	8.57 / 26.27	8.56 / 26.23	8.54 / 26.18	8.54 / 26.14	8.53 / 26.12
4	7.71 / 21.20	6.94 / 18.00	6.59 / 16.69	6.39 / 15.98	6.26 / 15.52	6.16 / 15.21	6.09 / 14.98	6.04 / 14.80	6.00 / 14.66	5.96 / 14.54	5.93 / 14.45	5.91 / 14.37	5.87 / 14.24	5.84 / 14.15	5.80 / 14.02	5.77 / 13.93	5.74 / 13.83	5.71 / 13.74	5.70 / 13.69	5.68 / 13.61	5.66 / 13.57	5.65 / 13.52	5.64 / 13.48	5.63 / 13.46
5	6.61 / 16.26	5.79 / 13.27	5.41 / 12.06	5.19 / 11.39	5.05 / 10.97	4.95 / 10.67	4.88 / 10.45	4.82 / 10.27	4.78 / 10.15	4.74 / 10.05	4.70 / 9.96	4.68 / 9.89	4.64 / 9.77	4.60 / 9.68	4.56 / 9.55	4.53 / 9.47	4.50 / 9.38	4.46 / 9.29	4.44 / 9.24	4.42 / 9.17	4.40 / 9.13	4.38 / 9.07	4.37 / 9.04	4.36 / 9.02
6	5.99 / 13.74	5.14 / 10.92	4.76 / 9.78	4.53 / 9.15	4.39 / 8.75	4.28 / 8.47	4.21 / 8.26	4.15 / 8.10	4.10 / 7.98	4.06 / 7.87	4.03 / 7.79	4.00 / 7.72	3.96 / 7.60	3.92 / 7.52	3.87 / 7.39	3.84 / 7.31	3.81 / 7.23	3.77 / 7.14	3.75 / 7.09	3.72 / 7.02	3.71 / 6.99	3.69 / 6.94	3.68 / 6.90	3.67 / 6.88
7	5.59 / 12.25	4.74 / 9.55	4.35 / 8.45	4.12 / 7.85	3.97 / 7.46	3.87 / 7.19	3.79 / 7.00	3.73 / 6.84	3.68 / 6.71	3.63 / 6.62	3.60 / 6.54	3.57 / 6.47	3.52 / 6.35	3.49 / 6.27	3.44 / 6.15	3.41 / 6.07	3.38 / 5.98	3.34 / 5.90	3.32 / 5.85	3.29 / 5.78	3.28 / 5.75	3.25 / 5.70	3.24 / 5.67	3.23 / 5.65
8	5.32 / 11.26	4.46 / 8.65	4.07 / 7.59	3.84 / 7.01	3.69 / 6.63	3.58 / 6.37	3.50 / 6.19	3.44 / 6.03	3.39 / 5.91	3.34 / 5.82	3.31 / 5.74	3.28 / 5.67	3.23 / 5.56	3.20 / 5.48	3.15 / 5.36	3.12 / 5.28	3.08 / 5.20	3.05 / 5.11	3.03 / 5.06	3.00 / 5.00	2.98 / 4.96	2.96 / 4.91	2.94 / 4.88	2.93 / 4.86
9	5.12 / 10.56	4.26 / 8.02	3.86 / 6.99	3.63 / 6.42	3.48 / 6.06	3.37 / 5.80	3.29 / 5.62	3.23 / 5.47	3.18 / 5.35	3.13 / 5.26	3.10 / 5.18	3.07 / 5.11	3.02 / 5.00	2.98 / 4.92	2.93 / 4.80	2.90 / 4.73	2.86 / 4.64	2.82 / 4.56	2.80 / 4.51	2.77 / 4.45	2.76 / 4.41	2.73 / 4.36	2.72 / 4.33	2.71 / 4.31
10	4.96 / 10.04	4.10 / 7.56	3.71 / 6.55	3.48 / 5.99	3.33 / 5.64	3.22 / 5.39	3.14 / 5.21	3.07 / 5.06	3.02 / 4.95	2.97 / 4.85	2.94 / 4.78	2.91 / 4.71	2.86 / 4.60	2.82 / 4.52	2.77 / 4.41	2.74 / 4.33	2.70 / 4.25	2.67 / 4.17	2.64 / 4.12	2.61 / 4.05	2.59 / 4.01	2.56 / 3.96	2.55 / 3.93	2.54 / 3.91
11	4.84 / 9.65	3.98 / 7.20	3.59 / 6.22	3.36 / 5.67	3.20 / 5.32	3.09 / 5.07	3.01 / 4.88	2.95 / 4.74	2.90 / 4.63	2.86 / 4.54	2.82 / 4.46	2.79 / 4.40	2.74 / 4.29	2.70 / 4.21	2.65 / 4.10	2.61 / 4.02	2.57 / 3.94	2.53 / 3.86	2.50 / 3.80	2.47 / 3.74	2.45 / 3.70	2.42 / 3.66	2.41 / 3.62	2.40 / 3.60
12	4.75 / 9.33	3.88 / 6.93	3.49 / 5.95	3.26 / 5.41	3.11 / 5.06	3.00 / 4.82	2.92 / 4.65	2.85 / 4.50	2.80 / 4.39	2.76 / 4.30	2.72 / 4.22	2.69 / 4.16	2.64 / 4.05	2.60 / 3.98	2.54 / 3.86	2.50 / 3.78	2.46 / 3.70	2.42 / 3.61	2.40 / 3.56	2.36 / 3.49	2.35 / 3.46	2.32 / 3.41	2.31 / 3.38	2.30 / 3.36
13	4.67 / 9.07	3.80 / 6.70	3.41 / 5.74	3.18 / 5.20	3.02 / 4.86	2.92 / 4.62	2.84 / 4.44	2.77 / 4.30	2.72 / 4.19	2.67 / 4.10	2.63 / 4.02	2.60 / 3.96	2.55 / 3.85	2.51 / 3.78	2.46 / 3.67	2.42 / 3.59	2.38 / 3.51	2.34 / 3.42	2.32 / 3.37	2.28 / 3.30	2.26 / 3.27	2.24 / 3.21	2.22 / 3.18	2.21 / 3.16

Degrees of freedom for lesser mean square (variance)

SOURCE: I am grateful to the Literary Executor of the late Sir Ronald A. Fisher, F. R. S., to Dr. Frank Yates, F. R. S., and to Longman Group Ltd., London, for permission to reprint Table V from their book, *Statistical Tables for Biological, Agricultural and Medical Research* (6th edition, 1974).

Degrees of freedom for greater mean square (variance)

Each cell shows the 5% point (top) and the 1% point (bold, bottom).

df (lesser)	1	2	3	4	5	6	7	8	9	10	11	12	14	16	20	24	30	40	50	75	100	200	500	∞
14	4.60 **8.86**	3.74 **6.51**	3.34 **5.56**	3.11 **5.03**	2.96 **4.69**	2.85 **4.46**	2.77 **4.28**	2.70 **4.14**	2.65 **4.03**	2.60 **3.94**	2.56 **3.86**	2.53 **3.80**	2.48 **3.70**	2.44 **3.62**	2.39 **3.51**	2.35 **3.43**	2.31 **3.34**	2.27 **3.26**	2.24 **3.21**	2.21 **3.14**	2.19 **3.11**	2.16 **3.06**	2.14 **3.02**	2.13 **3.00**
15	4.54 **8.68**	3.68 **6.36**	3.29 **5.42**	3.06 **4.89**	2.90 **4.56**	2.79 **4.32**	2.70 **4.14**	2.64 **4.00**	2.59 **3.89**	2.55 **3.80**	2.51 **3.73**	2.48 **3.67**	2.43 **3.56**	2.39 **3.48**	2.33 **3.36**	2.29 **3.29**	2.25 **3.20**	2.21 **3.12**	2.18 **3.07**	2.15 **3.00**	2.12 **2.97**	2.10 **2.92**	2.08 **2.89**	2.07 **2.87**
16	4.49 **8.53**	3.63 **6.23**	3.24 **5.29**	3.01 **4.77**	2.85 **4.44**	2.74 **4.20**	2.66 **4.03**	2.59 **3.89**	2.54 **3.78**	2.49 **3.69**	2.45 **3.61**	2.42 **3.55**	2.37 **3.45**	2.33 **3.37**	2.28 **3.25**	2.24 **3.18**	2.20 **3.10**	2.16 **3.01**	2.13 **2.96**	2.09 **2.89**	2.07 **2.86**	2.04 **2.80**	2.02 **2.77**	2.01 **2.75**
17	4.45 **8.40**	3.59 **6.11**	3.20 **5.18**	2.96 **4.67**	2.81 **4.34**	2.70 **4.10**	2.62 **3.93**	2.55 **3.79**	2.50 **3.68**	2.45 **3.59**	2.41 **3.52**	2.38 **3.45**	2.33 **3.35**	2.29 **3.27**	2.23 **3.16**	2.19 **3.08**	2.15 **3.00**	2.11 **2.92**	2.08 **2.86**	2.04 **2.79**	2.02 **2.76**	1.99 **2.70**	1.97 **2.67**	1.96 **2.65**
18	4.41 **8.28**	3.55 **6.01**	3.16 **5.09**	2.93 **4.58**	2.77 **4.25**	2.66 **4.01**	2.58 **3.85**	2.51 **3.71**	2.46 **3.60**	2.41 **3.51**	2.37 **3.44**	2.34 **3.37**	2.29 **3.27**	2.25 **3.19**	2.19 **3.07**	2.15 **3.00**	2.11 **2.91**	2.07 **2.83**	2.04 **2.78**	2.00 **2.71**	1.98 **2.68**	1.95 **2.62**	1.93 **2.59**	1.92 **2.57**
19	4.38 **8.18**	3.52 **5.93**	3.13 **5.01**	2.90 **4.50**	2.74 **4.17**	2.63 **3.94**	2.55 **3.77**	2.48 **3.63**	2.43 **3.52**	2.38 **3.43**	2.34 **3.36**	2.31 **3.30**	2.26 **3.19**	2.21 **3.12**	2.15 **3.00**	2.11 **2.92**	2.07 **2.84**	2.02 **2.76**	2.00 **2.70**	1.96 **2.63**	1.94 **2.60**	1.91 **2.54**	1.90 **2.51**	1.88 **2.49**
20	4.35 **8.10**	3.49 **5.85**	3.10 **4.94**	2.87 **4.43**	2.71 **4.10**	2.60 **3.87**	2.52 **3.71**	2.45 **3.56**	2.40 **3.45**	2.35 **3.37**	2.31 **3.30**	2.28 **3.23**	2.23 **3.13**	2.18 **3.05**	2.12 **2.94**	2.08 **2.86**	2.04 **2.77**	1.99 **2.69**	1.96 **2.63**	1.92 **2.56**	1.90 **2.53**	1.87 **2.47**	1.85 **2.44**	1.84 **2.42**
21	4.32 **8.02**	3.47 **5.78**	3.07 **4.87**	2.84 **4.37**	2.68 **4.04**	2.57 **3.81**	2.49 **3.65**	2.42 **3.51**	2.37 **3.40**	2.32 **3.31**	2.28 **3.24**	2.25 **3.17**	2.20 **3.07**	2.15 **2.99**	2.09 **2.88**	2.05 **2.80**	2.00 **2.72**	1.96 **2.63**	1.93 **2.58**	1.89 **2.51**	1.87 **2.47**	1.84 **2.42**	1.82 **2.38**	1.81 **2.36**
22	4.30 **7.94**	3.44 **5.72**	3.05 **4.82**	2.82 **4.31**	2.66 **3.99**	2.55 **3.76**	2.47 **3.59**	2.40 **3.45**	2.35 **3.35**	2.30 **3.26**	2.26 **3.18**	2.23 **3.12**	2.18 **3.02**	2.13 **2.94**	2.07 **2.83**	2.03 **2.75**	1.98 **2.67**	1.93 **2.58**	1.91 **2.53**	1.87 **2.46**	1.84 **2.42**	1.81 **2.37**	1.80 **2.33**	1.78 **2.31**
23	4.28 **7.88**	3.42 **5.66**	3.03 **4.76**	2.80 **4.26**	2.64 **3.94**	2.53 **3.71**	2.45 **3.54**	2.38 **3.41**	2.32 **3.30**	2.28 **3.21**	2.24 **3.14**	2.20 **3.07**	2.14 **2.97**	2.10 **2.89**	2.04 **2.78**	2.00 **2.70**	1.96 **2.62**	1.91 **2.53**	1.88 **2.48**	1.84 **2.41**	1.82 **2.37**	1.79 **2.32**	1.77 **2.28**	1.76 **2.26**
24	4.26 **7.82**	3.40 **5.61**	3.01 **4.72**	2.78 **4.22**	2.62 **3.90**	2.51 **3.67**	2.43 **3.50**	2.36 **3.36**	2.30 **3.25**	2.26 **3.17**	2.22 **3.09**	2.18 **3.03**	2.13 **2.93**	2.09 **2.85**	2.02 **2.74**	1.98 **2.66**	1.94 **2.58**	1.89 **2.49**	1.86 **2.44**	1.82 **2.36**	1.80 **2.33**	1.76 **2.27**	1.74 **2.23**	1.73 **2.21**
25	4.24 **7.77**	3.38 **5.57**	2.99 **4.68**	2.76 **4.18**	2.60 **3.86**	2.49 **3.63**	2.41 **3.46**	2.34 **3.32**	2.28 **3.21**	2.24 **3.13**	2.20 **3.05**	2.16 **2.99**	2.11 **2.89**	2.06 **2.81**	2.00 **2.70**	1.96 **2.62**	1.92 **2.54**	1.87 **2.45**	1.84 **2.40**	1.80 **2.32**	1.77 **2.29**	1.74 **2.23**	1.72 **2.19**	1.71 **2.17**
26	4.22 **7.72**	3.37 **5.53**	2.98 **4.64**	2.74 **4.14**	2.59 **3.82**	2.47 **3.59**	2.39 **3.42**	2.32 **3.29**	2.27 **3.17**	2.22 **3.09**	2.18 **3.02**	2.15 **2.96**	2.10 **2.86**	2.05 **2.77**	1.99 **2.66**	1.95 **2.58**	1.90 **2.50**	1.85 **2.41**	1.82 **2.36**	1.78 **2.28**	1.76 **2.25**	1.72 **2.19**	1.70 **2.15**	1.69 **2.13**
27	4.21 **7.68**	3.35 **5.49**	2.96 **4.60**	2.73 **4.11**	2.57 **3.79**	2.46 **3.56**	2.37 **3.39**	2.30 **3.26**	2.25 **3.14**	2.20 **3.06**	2.16 **2.98**	2.13 **2.93**	2.08 **2.83**	2.03 **2.74**	1.97 **2.63**	1.93 **2.55**	1.88 **2.47**	1.84 **2.38**	1.80 **2.33**	1.76 **2.25**	1.74 **2.21**	1.71 **2.16**	1.68 **2.12**	1.67 **2.10**

Degrees of freedom for lesser mean square (variance)

Degrees of freedom for greater mean square (variance)

Degrees of freedom for lesser mean square (variance)	1	2	3	4	5	6	7	8	9	10	11	12	14	16	20	24	30	40	50	75	100	200	500	∞
28	4.20 / 7.64	3.34 / 5.45	2.95 / 4.57	2.71 / 4.07	2.56 / 3.76	2.44 / 3.53	2.36 / 3.36	2.29 / 3.23	2.24 / 3.11	2.19 / 3.03	2.15 / 2.95	2.12 / 2.90	2.06 / 2.80	2.02 / 2.71	1.96 / 2.60	1.91 / 2.52	1.87 / 2.44	1.81 / 2.35	1.78 / 2.30	1.75 / 2.22	1.72 / 2.18	1.69 / 2.13	1.67 / 2.09	1.65 / 2.06
29	4.18 / 7.60	3.33 / 5.42	2.93 / 4.54	2.70 / 4.04	2.54 / 3.73	2.43 / 3.50	2.35 / 3.32	2.28 / 3.20	2.22 / 3.08	2.18 / 3.00	2.14 / 2.92	2.10 / 2.87	2.05 / 2.77	2.00 / 2.68	1.94 / 2.57	1.90 / 2.49	1.85 / 2.41	1.80 / 2.32	1.77 / 2.27	1.73 / 2.19	1.71 / 2.15	1.68 / 2.10	1.65 / 2.06	1.64 / 2.03
30	4.17 / 7.56	3.32 / 5.39	2.92 / 4.51	2.69 / 4.02	2.53 / 3.70	2.42 / 3.47	2.34 / 3.30	2.27 / 3.17	2.21 / 3.06	2.16 / 2.98	2.12 / 2.90	2.09 / 2.84	2.04 / 2.74	1.99 / 2.66	1.93 / 2.55	1.89 / 2.47	1.84 / 2.38	1.79 / 2.29	1.76 / 2.24	1.72 / 2.16	1.69 / 2.13	1.66 / 2.07	1.64 / 2.03	1.62 / 2.01
32	4.15 / 7.50	3.30 / 5.34	2.90 / 4.46	2.67 / 3.97	2.51 / 3.66	2.40 / 3.42	2.32 / 3.25	2.25 / 3.12	2.19 / 3.01	2.14 / 2.94	2.10 / 2.86	2.07 / 2.80	2.02 / 2.70	1.97 / 2.62	1.91 / 2.51	1.86 / 2.42	1.82 / 2.34	1.76 / 2.25	1.74 / 2.20	1.69 / 2.12	1.67 / 2.08	1.64 / 2.02	1.61 / 1.98	1.59 / 1.96
34	4.13 / 7.44	3.28 / 5.29	2.88 / 4.42	2.65 / 3.93	2.49 / 3.61	2.38 / 3.38	2.30 / 3.21	2.23 / 3.08	2.17 / 2.97	2.12 / 2.89	2.08 / 2.82	2.05 / 2.76	2.00 / 2.66	1.95 / 2.58	1.89 / 2.47	1.84 / 2.38	1.80 / 2.30	1.74 / 2.21	1.71 / 2.15	1.67 / 2.08	1.64 / 2.04	1.61 / 1.98	1.59 / 1.94	1.57 / 1.91
36	4.11 / 7.39	3.26 / 5.25	2.86 / 4.38	2.63 / 3.89	2.48 / 3.58	2.36 / 3.35	2.28 / 3.18	2.21 / 3.04	2.15 / 2.94	2.10 / 2.86	2.06 / 2.78	2.03 / 2.72	1.98 / 2.62	1.93 / 2.54	1.87 / 2.43	1.82 / 2.35	1.78 / 2.26	1.72 / 2.17	1.69 / 2.12	1.65 / 2.04	1.62 / 2.00	1.59 / 1.94	1.56 / 1.90	1.55 / 1.87
38	4.10 / 7.35	3.25 / 5.21	2.85 / 4.34	2.62 / 3.86	2.46 / 3.54	2.35 / 3.32	2.26 / 3.15	2.19 / 3.02	2.14 / 2.91	2.09 / 2.82	2.05 / 2.75	2.02 / 2.69	1.96 / 2.59	1.92 / 2.51	1.85 / 2.40	1.80 / 2.32	1.76 / 2.22	1.71 / 2.14	1.67 / 2.08	1.63 / 2.00	1.60 / 1.97	1.57 / 1.90	1.54 / 1.86	1.53 / 1.84
40	4.08 / 7.31	3.23 / 5.18	2.84 / 4.31	2.61 / 3.83	2.45 / 3.51	2.34 / 3.29	2.25 / 3.12	2.18 / 2.99	2.12 / 2.88	2.07 / 2.80	2.04 / 2.73	2.00 / 2.66	1.95 / 2.56	1.90 / 2.49	1.84 / 2.37	1.79 / 2.29	1.74 / 2.20	1.69 / 2.11	1.66 / 2.05	1.61 / 1.97	1.59 / 1.94	1.55 / 1.88	1.53 / 1.84	1.51 / 1.81
42	4.07 / 7.27	3.22 / 5.15	2.83 / 4.29	2.59 / 3.80	2.44 / 3.49	2.32 / 3.26	2.24 / 3.10	2.17 / 2.96	2.11 / 2.86	2.06 / 2.77	2.02 / 2.70	1.99 / 2.64	1.94 / 2.54	1.89 / 2.46	1.82 / 2.35	1.78 / 2.26	1.73 / 2.17	1.68 / 2.08	1.64 / 2.02	1.60 / 1.94	1.57 / 1.91	1.54 / 1.85	1.51 / 1.80	1.49 / 1.78
44	4.06 / 7.24	3.21 / 5.12	2.82 / 4.26	2.58 / 3.78	2.43 / 3.46	2.31 / 3.24	2.23 / 3.07	2.16 / 2.94	2.10 / 2.84	2.05 / 2.75	2.01 / 2.68	1.98 / 2.62	1.92 / 2.52	1.88 / 2.44	1.81 / 2.32	1.76 / 2.24	1.72 / 2.15	1.66 / 2.06	1.63 / 2.00	1.58 / 1.92	1.56 / 1.88	1.52 / 1.82	1.50 / 1.78	1.48 / 1.75
46	4.05 / 7.21	3.20 / 5.10	2.81 / 4.24	2.57 / 3.76	2.42 / 3.44	2.30 / 3.22	2.22 / 3.05	2.14 / 2.92	2.09 / 2.82	2.04 / 2.73	2.00 / 2.66	1.97 / 2.60	1.91 / 2.50	1.87 / 2.42	1.80 / 2.30	1.75 / 2.22	1.71 / 2.13	1.65 / 2.04	1.62 / 1.98	1.57 / 1.90	1.54 / 1.86	1.51 / 1.80	1.48 / 1.76	1.46 / 1.72
48	4.04 / 7.19	3.19 / 5.08	2.80 / 4.22	2.56 / 3.74	2.41 / 3.42	2.30 / 3.20	2.21 / 3.04	2.14 / 2.90	2.08 / 2.80	2.03 / 2.71	1.99 / 2.64	1.96 / 2.58	1.90 / 2.48	1.86 / 2.40	1.79 / 2.28	1.74 / 2.20	1.70 / 2.11	1.64 / 2.02	1.61 / 1.96	1.56 / 1.88	1.53 / 1.84	1.50 / 1.78	1.47 / 1.73	1.45 / 1.70
50	4.03 / 7.17	3.18 / 5.06	2.79 / 4.20	2.56 / 3.72	2.40 / 3.41	2.29 / 3.18	2.20 / 3.02	2.13 / 2.88	2.07 / 2.78	2.02 / 2.70	1.98 / 2.62	1.95 / 2.56	1.90 / 2.46	1.85 / 2.39	1.78 / 2.26	1.74 / 2.18	1.69 / 2.10	1.63 / 2.00	1.60 / 1.94	1.55 / 1.86	1.52 / 1.82	1.48 / 1.76	1.46 / 1.71	1.44 / 1.68
55	4.02 / 7.12	3.17 / 5.01	2.78 / 4.16	2.54 / 3.68	2.38 / 3.37	2.27 / 3.15	2.18 / 2.98	2.11 / 2.85	2.05 / 2.75	2.00 / 2.66	1.97 / 2.59	1.93 / 2.53	1.88 / 2.43	1.83 / 2.35	1.76 / 2.23	1.72 / 2.15	1.67 / 2.06	1.61 / 1.96	1.58 / 1.90	1.52 / 1.82	1.50 / 1.78	1.46 / 1.71	1.43 / 1.66	1.41 / 1.64

Degrees of freedom for greater mean square (variance)

df (lesser)	1	2	3	4	5	6	7	8	9	10	11	12	14	16	20	24	30	40	50	75	100	200	500	∞
60	4.00 / **7.08**	3.15 / **4.98**	2.76 / **4.13**	2.52 / **3.65**	2.37 / **3.34**	2.25 / **3.12**	2.17 / **2.95**	2.10 / **2.82**	2.04 / **2.72**	1.99 / **2.63**	1.95 / **2.56**	1.92 / **2.50**	1.86 / **2.40**	1.81 / **2.32**	1.75 / **2.20**	1.70 / **2.12**	1.65 / **2.03**	1.59 / **1.93**	1.56 / **1.87**	1.50 / **1.79**	1.48 / **1.74**	1.44 / **1.68**	1.41 / **1.63**	1.39 / **1.60**
65	3.99 / **7.04**	3.14 / **4.95**	2.75 / **4.10**	2.51 / **3.62**	2.36 / **3.31**	2.24 / **3.09**	2.15 / **2.93**	2.08 / **2.79**	2.02 / **2.70**	1.98 / **2.61**	1.94 / **2.54**	1.90 / **2.47**	1.85 / **2.37**	1.80 / **2.30**	1.73 / **2.18**	1.68 / **2.09**	1.63 / **2.00**	1.57 / **1.90**	1.54 / **1.84**	1.49 / **1.76**	1.46 / **1.71**	1.42 / **1.64**	1.39 / **1.60**	1.37 / **1.56**
70	3.98 / **7.01**	3.13 / **4.92**	2.74 / **4.08**	2.50 / **3.60**	2.35 / **3.29**	2.32 / **3.07**	2.14 / **2.91**	2.07 / **2.77**	2.01 / **2.67**	1.97 / **2.59**	1.93 / **2.51**	1.89 / **2.45**	1.84 / **2.35**	1.79 / **2.28**	1.72 / **2.15**	1.67 / **2.07**	1.62 / **1.98**	1.56 / **1.88**	1.53 / **1.82**	1.47 / **1.74**	1.45 / **1.69**	1.40 / **1.62**	1.37 / **1.56**	1.35 / **1.53**
80	3.96 / **6.96**	3.11 / **4.88**	2.72 / **4.04**	2.48 / **3.56**	2.33 / **3.25**	2.21 / **3.04**	2.12 / **2.87**	2.05 / **2.74**	1.99 / **2.64**	1.95 / **2.55**	1.91 / **2.48**	1.88 / **2.41**	1.82 / **2.32**	1.77 / **2.24**	1.70 / **2.11**	1.65 / **2.03**	1.60 / **1.94**	1.54 / **1.84**	1.51 / **1.78**	1.45 / **1.70**	1.42 / **1.65**	1.38 / **1.57**	1.35 / **1.52**	1.32 / **1.49**
100	3.94 / **6.90**	3.09 / **4.82**	2.70 / **3.98**	2.46 / **3.51**	2.30 / **3.20**	2.19 / **2.99**	2.10 / **2.82**	2.03 / **2.69**	1.97 / **2.59**	1.92 / **2.51**	1.88 / **2.43**	1.85 / **2.36**	1.79 / **2.26**	1.75 / **2.19**	1.68 / **2.06**	1.63 / **1.98**	1.57 / **1.89**	1.51 / **1.79**	1.48 / **1.73**	1.42 / **1.64**	1.39 / **1.59**	1.34 / **1.51**	1.30 / **1.46**	1.28 / **1.43**
125	3.92 / **6.84**	3.07 / **4.78**	2.68 / **3.94**	2.44 / **3.47**	2.29 / **3.17**	2.17 / **2.95**	2.08 / **2.79**	2.01 / **2.65**	1.95 / **2.56**	1.90 / **2.47**	1.86 / **2.40**	1.83 / **2.33**	1.77 / **2.23**	1.72 / **2.15**	1.65 / **2.03**	1.60 / **1.94**	1.55 / **1.85**	1.49 / **1.75**	1.45 / **1.68**	1.39 / **1.59**	1.36 / **1.54**	1.31 / **1.46**	1.27 / **1.40**	1.25 / **1.37**
150	3.91 / **6.81**	3.06 / **4.75**	2.67 / **3.91**	2.43 / **3.44**	2.27 / **3.13**	2.16 / **2.92**	2.07 / **2.76**	2.00 / **2.62**	1.94 / **2.53**	1.89 / **2.44**	1.85 / **2.37**	1.82 / **2.30**	1.76 / **2.20**	1.71 / **2.12**	1.64 / **2.00**	1.59 / **1.91**	1.54 / **1.83**	1.47 / **1.72**	1.44 / **1.66**	1.37 / **1.56**	1.34 / **1.51**	1.29 / **1.43**	1.25 / **1.37**	1.22 / **1.33**
200	3.89 / **6.76**	3.04 / **4.71**	2.65 / **3.38**	2.41 / **3.41**	2.26 / **3.11**	2.14 / **2.90**	2.05 / **2.73**	1.98 / **2.60**	1.92 / **2.50**	1.87 / **2.41**	1.83 / **2.34**	1.80 / **2.28**	1.74 / **1.17**	1.69 / **2.09**	1.62 / **1.97**	1.57 / **1.88**	1.52 / **1.79**	1.45 / **1.69**	1.42 / **1.62**	1.35 / **1.53**	1.32 / **1.48**	1.26 / **1.39**	1.22 / **1.33**	1.19 / **1.28**
400	3.86 / **6.70**	3.02 / **4.66**	2.62 / **3.83**	2.39 / **3.36**	2.23 / **3.06**	2.12 / **2.85**	2.03 / **2.69**	1.96 / **2.55**	1.90 / **2.46**	1.85 / **2.37**	1.81 / **2.29**	1.78 / **2.23**	1.72 / **2.12**	1.67 / **2.04**	1.60 / **1.92**	1.54 / **1.84**	1.49 / **1.74**	1.42 / **1.64**	1.38 / **1.57**	1.32 / **1.47**	1.28 / **1.42**	1.22 / **1.32**	1.16 / **1.24**	1.13 / **1.19**
1000	3.85 / **6.66**	3.00 / **4.62**	2.61 / **3.80**	2.38 / **3.34**	2.22 / **3.04**	2.10 / **2.82**	2.02 / **2.66**	1.95 / **2.53**	1.89 / **2.43**	1.84 / **2.34**	1.80 / **2.26**	1.76 / **2.20**	1.70 / **2.09**	1.65 / **2.01**	1.58 / **1.89**	1.53 / **1.81**	1.47 / **1.71**	1.41 / **1.61**	1.36 / **1.54**	1.30 / **1.44**	1.26 / **1.38**	1.19 / **1.28**	1.13 / **1.19**	1.08 / **1.11**
∞	3.84 / **6.64**	2.99 / **4.60**	2.60 / **3.78**	2.37 / **3.32**	2.21 / **3.02**	2.09 / **2.80**	2.01 / **2.64**	1.94 / **2.51**	1.88 / **2.41**	1.83 / **2.32**	1.79 / **2.24**	1.75 / **2.18**	1.69 / **2.07**	1.64 / **1.99**	1.57 / **1.87**	1.52 / **1.79**	1.46 / **1.69**	1.40 / **1.59**	1.35 / **1.52**	1.28 / **1.41**	1.24 / **1.36**	1.17 / **1.25**	1.11 / **1.15**	1.00 / **1.00**

Degrees of freedom for lesser mean square (variance)

Distribution of t

df	Level of significance for one-tailed test					
	.10	.05	.025	.01	.005	.0005
	Level of significance for two-tailed test					
	.20	.10	.05	.02	.01	.001
1	3.078	6.314	12.706	31.821	63.657	636.619
2	1.886	2.920	4.303	6.965	9.925	31.598
3	1.638	2.353	3.182	4.541	5.841	12.941
4	1.533	2.132	2.776	3.747	4.604	8.610
5	1.476	2.015	2.571	3.365	4.032	6.859
6	1.440	1.943	2.447	3.143	3.707	5.959
7	1.415	1.895	2.365	2.998	3.499	5.405
8	1.397	1.860	2.306	2.896	3.355	5.041
9	1.383	1.833	2.262	2.821	3.250	4.781
10	1.372	1.812	2.228	2.764	3.169	4.587
11	1.363	1.796	2.201	2.718	3.106	4.437
12	1.356	1.782	2.179	2.681	3.055	4.318
13	1.350	1.771	2.160	2.650	3.012	4.221
14	1.345	1.761	2.145	2.624	2.977	4.140
15	1.341	1.753	2.131	2.602	2.947	4.073
16	1.337	1.746	2.120	2.583	2.921	4.015
17	1.333	1.740	2.110	2.567	2.898	3.965
18	1.330	1.734	2.101	2.552	2.878	3.922
19	1.328	1.729	2.093	2.539	2.861	3.883
20	1.325	1.725	2.086	2.528	2.845	3.850
21	1.323	1.721	2.080	2.518	2.831	3.819
22	1.321	1.717	2.074	2.508	2.819	3.792
23	1.319	1.714	2.069	2.500	2.807	3.767
24	1.318	1.711	2.064	2.492	2.797	3.745
25	1.316	1.708	2.060	2.485	2.787	3.725
26	1.315	1.706	2.056	2.479	2.779	3.707
27	1.314	1.703	2.052	2.473	2.771	3.690
28	1.313	1.701	2.048	2.467	2.763	3.674
29	1.311	1.699	2.045	2.462	2.756	3.659
30	1.310	1.697	2.042	2.457	2.750	3.646
40	1.303	1.684	2.021	2.423	2.704	3.551
60	1.296	1.671	2.000	2.390	2.660	3.460
120	1.289	1.658	1.980	2.358	2.617	3.373
∞	1.282	1.645	1.960	2.326	2.576	3.291

SOURCE: I am grateful to the Literary Executor of the late Sir Ronald Fisher, F. R. S., to Dr. Frank Yates, F. R. S., and to Longman Group Ltd., London, for permission to reprint Table III from their book, *Statistical Tables for Biological, Agricultural and Medical Research* (6th edition, 1974).

C H A P T E R   1

1. (a) 3, 5 **(b)** 2, 5 **(c)** 1, 2, 5 **(d)** 4, 5 **(e)** 6

2. (1) b **(2)** c **(3)** a **(4)** d

C H A P T E R   2

1. Plumber (A)
Female (A)
Religion (V)
Occupation (V)
High School (A)
Educational level (V)
Republican (A)
Political party preference (V)
Jewish (A)
Gender (V)

2. Maybe. If the university or college has no graduate students, the attribute scheme fulfills both criteria. However, if graduate students attend the school, the scheme fails to meet the exhaustive criterion. This could be resolved by adding either a graduate student attribute or another category.

3. (a) R **(b)** O **(c)** N **(d)** O **(e)** N **(f)** R

4. These are suggested schemes; other possibilities exist. **(a)** Code number as stated from 0 to highest number stated. **(b)** Small = 1; medium = 2; large = 3 **(c)** Schlitz = 1; Budweiser = 2; Coors = 3; other = 4 **(d)** Strongly agree = 1; agree = 2; undecided = 3; disagree = 4; strongly disagree = 5 **(e)** Never married = 1; married = 2; widowed = 3; divorced = 4; separated = 5 **(f)** Code number as stated from 0 to highest number stated.

5. Variable   **Columns**
   (a) ID number   1–3
   (b) Card number   4

(c) Sex   5
(d) P.P.P.   6
(e) Age   7–9
(f) Education   10–11
(g) Number of siblings   12–13

6. (a) Age is ratio; education is ratio; birth sign is nominal; gender is nominal; belief in UFOs is ordinal. (b) Age: code as the number stated Education: code as the number stated   Birth sign: Libra = 1; Gemini = 2; Scorpio = 3; Capricorn = 4; Aquarius = 5; Sagittarius = 6; Pisces = 7; Leo = 8; Aries = 9; Taurus = 10; Cancer = 11; Virgo = 12   Sex: male = 1; female = 2   Belief in UFOs: strongly believe = 1; believe = 2; undecided = 3; disbelieve = 4; strongly disbelieve = 5

(c)

Variable	Columns
Age	1–3
Education	4–5
Birth sign	6–7
Gender	8
UFO belief	9

(d) 021120411
    054160323
    010040112
    038120225
    032160222

C H A P T E R 3

1. The data are in fixed format and are part of the SPSS^x program. There are three cards (records) per case. For all cases the first card contains data on ID in columns 1 through 5, SEX in column 6, RACE in column 7, AGE in columns 8 and 9, and SALARY in columns 10 through 17. The SALARY variable is coded with two implied decimal points. Card 2 contains data on PRACTICE in column 5, FIRM in column 6, and YEARS in columns 7, 8, and 9. Column 9 for the variable YEARS follows an implied decimal point. Card 3, column 1 contains information on the variable SAT.

2. DATA LIST FILE=INFILE RECORDS=1
     /1 AGE 1–2 SIBS 3–4 WRKSTAT 13 REGION 20 SMOKE 51
     TRAUMA 72

3. The 98 and 99 codes are declared missing on AGE. The 99999997 and 99999998 are declared missing on SALARY. The 4 code is declared missing on PRACTICE, and the 6 and 7 codes are declared missing on FIRM.

4. MISSING VALUES AGE(98,99) SIBS(98,99) TVHOURS(98,99)

5. In the printout we will see AGE referred to as "AGE AT LAST BIRTHDAY"; SALARY as "NET INCOME FROM LAW PRACTICE"; PRACTICE as "DOMINANT TYPE OF CASES"; FIRM as "NUMBER OF ATTORNEYS IN FIRM"; and YEARS as "YEARS SINCE LAW SCHOOL GRADUATION."

6. VARIABLE LABELS SIBS "N BROTHERS & SISTERS"
     INCOME "FAMILY INC ALL SOURCES" MEMNUM "N"
     + "ORGANIZATIONS" WRKSTAT "LAST WEEK WORK"

7. For the variable SEX 1 represents female and 2 male. On RACE 1 represents white and 2 nonwhite. On FIRM 1 represents a sole practitioner, 2 indicates two to five lawyers, 3 indicates six or more attorneys, and 4 is a refusal to answer.

8. VALUE LABELS SEX 1 'MALE' 2 'FEMALE'/
   WRKSTAT 1 'FULLTIME' 2 'PARTTIME' 3 'JOB, IVS'
   4 'UNEMP' 5 'RETIRED' 6 'SCHOOL' 7 'HOUSE'/
   MARITAL 1 'MARRIED' 2 'WIDOWED' 3 'DIVORCED'
   4 'SEPARATE' 5 'NEVER'/DEGREE 0 'LESS HS'
   1 'HS' 2 'ASSOC' 3 'BACHELOR' 4 'GRAD' 8 'DK'
   9 'NA'

9. It would assist in labeling only the don't know and no answer codes. The other codes are interval or ratio variables, which do not require value labels.

10. Initially, we're checking the run with the EDIT command. The run's name is "A FREQUENCIES RUN ON THE OCCUPATIONAL MOBILITY DATA, 1983, N = 2500." The data are in fixed format and are attached to the SPSS^x program. There are five cards per respondent. The first card contains ID in columns 1 through 4, SEX in 5, RACE in 6, and AGE in columns 7 through 9, with column 9 reserved for parts of years. Card 2 contains data on ED in columns 10 and 11 and PAED in columns 12 and 13. Card 3 contains information on MAED in columns 12 and 13 and SIBS in column 14. Card 4 has data on ROCC in column 8, POCC in column 9, and MOCC in column 10. Card 5 contains data on STATUS in column 8 and INCOME in column 9. The codes declared as missing are stated for AGE, ED, PAED, MAED, SIBS, ROCC, POCC, MOCC, STATUS, and INCOME. The variables are labeled. For example, we know that INCOME refers to whether R (an abbreviation often used for respondent) paid income taxes in 1983. The codes on the variables are named. For example, a 1 on SIBS is yes and a 2 is no. The FREQUENCIES command is used. The data are attached to the SPSS^x program, and the computer is told BEGIN DATA and END DATA.

C H A P T E R 4

1. Yes. Reading from left to right, the first command recodes all 0's to 1's, then all 1's to 2's, and then all 2's to 3's. If these are the only codes on the variable, three codes are left after the RECODE procedure 1, 2, 3. The second command recodes the 2's to 3's, then the 1's to 2's, and then the 0's to 1's. The RECODE command changes codes 0, 1, and 2 to codes 1, 2, and 3.

2. **(a)** The codes on the variable SAT are recoded such that 0 and 2 become 1, 3 becomes 2, and 4 and 5 become 3. **(b)** Same as 2a, except the new coding scheme is retained as a new variable called SAT1. The old coding scheme is kept as the original SAT variable. **(c)** Two variables are recoded. On INCOME all codes of 0 to 10000 are recoded to 1. The codes of 10001 to 20000 are recoded to 2. The new coding scheme is retained as a new variable called LOWMID. The old scheme is saved as the original INCOME variable. The codes of 7 and 8 on the variable FUN are treated as a 9.

3. RECODE·SIBS (1 THRU 3=1) (4 THRU 8=2) (9 THRU 11=3)
   (12 THRU 20=4)
   RECODE INCOME (1 THRU 8=1) (9 THRU 12=2)
   (13 THRU 16=3) (17,98,99=4) INTO INC1

4. Yes. In the first set of instructions a new variable is developed called ORGS, which is based on a recoding of MEMNUM. Although the code of 99 on MEMNUM is missing, it does not retain a mssing value status on the new variable ORGS. In the second set of instructions the 99 code is declared missing on both MEMNUM and ORGS.

5. **(a)** A variable HOURS is constructed by summing together the values on the three variables, DAY1, DAY2, and DAY3. **(b)** A variable AGESQ is computed by multiplying AGE by itself. **(c)** A variable INCOME is computed by dividing the variable GROSSINC by 12.

6. They give two different results. In the first case the SALARY, DIVIDEND, and INTEREST variables are added together, and the result is divided by 12. In the second case the INTEREST variable is divided by 12, and that result is added to SALARY and DIVIDEND.

7. COMPUTE SEXRATIO = (NMALES/NFEMS)*100

8. MISSING VALUES CONDEDUC TO CONLEGIS (8,9)
   COMPUTE CONFID=(CONEDUC + CONPRESS + CONLEGIS)

   8 & 9 MISSING ON CONEDUC or CONPRESS or CONLEGIS

   Case 1:   .
   Case 2:   9
   Case 3:   6

9. **(a)** Selects cases when INCOME is less than 9 or less than $10,000. **(b)** Selects cases where SIBS is greater than or equal to 1; results in selecting cases where the respondents have or had one or more siblings. **(c)** Selects cases from New England that are either married, widowed, divorced, or separated. **(d)** Selects cases that are either from New England or are married, widowed, divorced, or separated.

10. SELECT IF (MARITAL EQ 1 AND WRKSTAT EQ 1)

11. SELECT IF (DEGREE EQ 1 OR 3)

12. **(a)** Saves a file called FIRST. This file contains the variables SAT, JOB1, and INCOME1. **(b)** Saves a file called JOBS. This file contains the variables JOB1, JOB2, AND JOB3. To be sure the correct variables were saved, the variables' names were requested. **(c)** Saves a file called HOURS with all the variables.

13. **(a)** Retrieve a file called TIME. **(b)** Retrieve a file called HOURS.

14. This run is called "AN EXAMPLE OF SAVING AN SPSS^x SYSTEM FILE." There are three records per case, the data are in fixed format, and they are part of the SPSS^x job. The locations of the variables are described, and variable labels and value labels are used. A new variable, HRLYINC, is computed by dividing INCOME by HOURS. A second new variable, NEWED, is constructed by collapsing the categories of the old ED variable

such that the groupings are as follows: less than high school (1), high school (2), some college (3), and college (4). Codes of 98 and 99 are declared missing for the NEWED variable. The computer is told to do a frequency run. We keep a file and call it TRIAL. On this file we keep three variables, HRLYINC, NEWED, and SEX.

15. This run retrieves a file called TRIAL. Cases are selected for the analysis when SEX equals 2. If code 2 represents females, then only females are used in the analysis.

C H A P T E R 5

1. MISSING VALUES SIBS(98,99) RELIG(9)
FREQUENCIES VARIABLES=SIBS RELIG RACE
The codes are legitimate on all three variables. We learn, for example, that there are 159 Protestants, 60 Catholics, 5 Jews, 21 of no religious preference, and 5 others in the sample.

2. FREQUENCIES VARIABLES=MARITAL
Yes, most are married. Of the 249 respondents, 167 are currently married. Ten of these are separated from their spouses.

3. SELECT IF (SEX EQ 1)
FREQUENCIES VARIABLES=INCOME

4. FREQUENCIES VARIABLES=AGE/HISTOGRAM/
FREQUENCIES VARIABLES=RACE/BARCHART/
You should select the histogram for age, since age is a ratio variable, and the bar chart for race, since race is a nominal variable.

5. The AGE histogram indicates that the largest categories are 36 and 33 years of age. The RACE bar chart indicates that the largest category is white.

C H A P T E R 6

1. (a) 2, 5 **(b)** 1, 5 **(c)** 3, 4, 5

2. (a) Median **(b)** Mode **(c)** Mode **(d)** Median **(e)** Mean
(f) Median **(g)** Mean

3. RECODE TVHOURS (0 THRU 2=1) (3 THRU 6=2) (7 THRU 18=3)
INTO TVNEW
MISSING VALUES TVHOURS(98,99) SPKATH(8,9) SPKCOM(8,9)
SPKHOMO(8,9) TVNEW(98,99)
FREQUENCIES VARIABLES=TVHOURS SPKATH SPKCOM SPKHOMO
TVNEW/
STATISTICS=MEAN MEDIAN MODE

4. TVHOURS is a ratio variable, and therefore you can interpret its mode, median, and mean. The largest category for TVHOURS is 2—more people watch two hours of TV than any other number of hours (the mode). Half the sample watches more than two hours of TV, and half watches less than two hours (the median). On the average, people watch 2.854 hours of TV, the mean.

SPKATH, SPKCOM, and SPKHOMO are nominal variables, and therefore only the mode should be interpreted. The mode for all three variables is 1—yes, they should be allowed to speak.

TVNEW is an ordinal variable constructed from the ratio variable TVHOURS. The mean cannot be interpreted. The mode is code 1, which represents two or fewer hours. The median is also code 1: half watch more than zero to two hours of TV, and half watch less.

C H A P T E R   7

1. **(a)** 2, 5 **(b)** 1, 3, 5 **(c)** 2, 4, 5

2. **(a)** 0.4525 **(b)** 0.4904 **(c)** 0.4525 **(d)** 0.3106

3. **(a)** 2.13 and -2.13 **(b)** 0.13 and -0.13 **(c)** 1.34 and -1.34 are the closest

4. **(a)** $43 + 1(6)$, or 37 to 49 **(b)** same as a **(c)** $43 + 1.28(6)$, or 35.32 to 50.68

5. Constructs frequency distributions for three variables, AGE, EDUC, and TRIAL. In addition, summary measures of central tendency (mode, median, and mean) and dispersion (standard deviation, minimum, and maximum) are printed.

6. MISSING VALUES (98,99) DEGREE(8,9)
FREQUENCIES VARIABLES=AGE DEGREE/
  STATISTICS = MODE MEDIAN MEAN STDDEV MINIMUM MAXIMUM/

7. AGE is a ratio variable, and therefore all the statistics are meaningful. The most frequently occurring age is 36 (the mode). Half the sample was older than 39 and half was younger (the median). The average was 44.312 years. DEGREE is an ordinal variable. The modal category is high school. Half the sample had less than a high school degree, and half the sample had more.

C H A P T E R   8

1. **(a)** R **(b)** N **(c)** R **(d)** N **(e)** L **(f)** L

2. **(a)** C + **(b)** C − **(c)** C **(d)** Cov

3. **(a)** Children who watch violence on TV tend to be more violent than children who do not watch violence on TV. **(b)** There is no difference in the violence of children who watch and children who do not watch violence on TV. **(c)** Rejecting a true null. You tell people that children who watch violence tend to be more violent than children who do not, and this is not true. **(d)** Failure to reject a false null. You tell people that TV has no impact on children's violence, and this is not true. **(e)** 0.01—probability of rejecting a true null is 0.01, or you'll risk rejecting a true null 1 time in 100.

0.4—probability of rejecting a true null is 0.4, or you'll risk rejecting a true null 4 times in 10.

C H A P T E R   9

1.

	Variable A		
	1	2	3
Variable B 1			
2			
3			
4			

2. 12, 4, 12, 12

3. (a) 3 **(b)** 3 **(c)** Percentage of fun categories that have blonde hair, brown hair, or red hair. For example, 25 percent of the "lots" of fun category are blonde. **(d)** Percentage of hair color categories that have fun. For example, 50 percent of the blondes have "lots" of fun. **(e)** Column. The old adage "Blondes have more fun" claims that hair color affects fun. Therefore, hair color is the independent variable. By the way, this table indicates that people with brown hair have the most fun.

4. In the five remaining tables SEX is the independent variable and happens to be the row variable. Therefore, the row percentages are the most interesting.

SEX BY ABNOMORE: There is little difference between males and females, 52.3 percent versus 49.6 percent for males and females, respectively, supporting abortion under this circumstance.

SEX BY ABHLTH: There is little difference between males and females, 95.3 percent versus 87.4 percent for males and females, respectively, supporting abortion under this circumstance.

SEX BY ABPOOR: There is little difference between males and females, 56.1 percent versus 48.4 percent for males and females, respectively, supporting abortion under this circumstance.

SEX BY ABRAPE: There is a difference of more than 10 percentage points between males and females supporting abortion under this circumstance, 90.7 percent versus 80.6 percent for males and females, respectively.

SEX BY ABSINGLE: There is almost no difference between males and females who support abortion under this circumstance, 49.1 percent versus 49.6 percent for males and females, respectively.

5. Declare the values 8 and 9 missing on DEGREE, SPKATH, SPKCOM, and SPKHOMO. Declare the value 9 missing on SMOKE. Construct four crosstab tables: DEGREE BY SPKATH, DEGREE BY SPKCOM, DEGREE BY SPKHOMO, and SEX BY SMOKE. Print all the percentage information. The dummy tables are shown below.

		SPKATH		
		Yes	No	Total
	Less H.S.			
	H.S.			
DEGREE	Assoc.			
	Bachelor's			
	Grad			
	Total			

		SPKCOM		
		Yes	No	Total
	Less H.S.			
	H.S.			
DEGREE	Assoc.			
	Bachelor's			
	Grad			
	Total			

	SPKHOMO		
	Yes	No	Total
DEGREE Less H.S.			
H.S.			
Assoc.			
Bachelor's			
Grad			
Total			

	SMOKE		
	Yes	No	Total
SEX Male			
Female			
Total			

6. Use the row percentages for the DEGREE BY SPKATH, DEGREE BY SPKCOM, and DEGREE BY SPKHOMO tables. The researcher is interested in whether education influences attitude toward allowing people to speak.
DEGREE BY SPKATH: As education increases, so too does the belief in allowing an atheist to speak. However, people with graduate degrees break this pattern. People with graduate degrees are slightly more willing than people with high school degrees to let atheists speak. It is only among those with less than a high school education that a majority say no to allowing atheists to speak.
DEGREE BY SPKCOM: Same as above. As education increases, people are more willing to allow communists to speak. However, people with graduate degrees are less likely than people with bachelor's degrees to say yes. Only among those with less than a high school education do the majority say no.
DEGREE BY SPKHOMO: Approximately the same pattern as above. However, the people with associate degrees are slightly less likely than those with high school degrees to say yes to allowing homosexuals to speak. Once again, those with graduate degrees are less likely to say yes than those with bachelor's degrees.
SEX BY SMOKE: Examine the row percentages to determine the impact of sex on smoking behavior. Men are more likely to say they smoke than are women, 56.3 percent versus 39.4 percent.

7. At the 0.05 level SEX BY ABHLTH shows a statistically significant relationship: chi square equals 4.53 and significance level equals 0.033.
At the 0.05 level SEX BY ABRAPE shows a statistically significant relationship: chi square equals 4.73 and significance level equals 0.029.
At the 0.1 levels SEX BY ABHLTH and SEX BY ABRAPE remain the only statistically sigificant relationships.

C H A P T E R   10

1. (a) Ordinal, asymmetric **(b)** Nominal, asymmetric **(c)** Nominal, symmetric **(d)** Ordinal, symmetric

2 (a) CLASS is ordinal and HEALTH is ordinal. If we hypothesize that CLASS influences HEALTH, we could choose Somer's d. If we simply think the two variables are related, we could use gamma. **(b)** MARITAL is nominal and AGED is nominal. Assuming MARITAL influences AGED, asymmetric lambda might be a good choice. **(c)** CAPPUN is nominal and GRASS is nominal. If neither variable is considered the dependent variable, phi squared is a good choice, since both variables are dichotomized.

3. RECODE MARITAL (3,4=2) (5=3)
   MISSING VALUES CLASS(9) HEALTH(8,9) AGED(8,9)
    CAPPUN(8,9) GRASS(8,9)
   VALUE LABELS MARITAL 1 'MARRY' 2 'WDS' 3 'NEVER'
   CROSSTABS TABLES=CLASS BY HEALTH/MARITAL BY AGED/
    CAPPUN BY GRASS
   STATISTICS ALL
   OPTIONS 18

   CLASS BY HEALTH: Both are ordinal. Somer's *d* indicates that there is a 15.34 percent reduction in error in predicting HEALTH from CLASS. In addition, its negative sign means that the variables have a negative relationship: as CLASS increases, HEALTH declines. Gamma indicates a 22.35 percent reduction in error in predicting one variable from the other. Remember, gamma is larger than Somer's *d* because gamma ignores ties. The sign of gamma is also negative, indicating a negative relationship between the variables. The appropriate statistic depends on whether or not the hypothesis is causal.

   MARITAL BY AGED: A nominal measure is appropriate. AGED is being treated as the dependent variable. The idea that marital status may influence how people feel about living with their parents is being considered. Lambda with AGED dependent indicates a 4.6 percent reduction in error in predicting AGED from MARITAL.

   CAPPUN BY GRASS: A nonimal measure is appropriate, since both are nominal variables. It is thought that the two are related, but no claim is made that one is the independent variable and the other the dependent variable. The relationship is simply one of covariation. Phi is an appropriate measure, and if we square phi we learn that there is a 0.9 percent reduction in error in predicting one variable from the other.

4. MISSING VALUES HEALTH(8,9) SMOKE(9) FEAR(8,9)
   VALUE LABELS HEALTH 1 'EXCELL' 2 'GOOD' 3 'BAD' 4 'POOR'/
    SEX 1 'MALE' 2 'FEMALE'/
    SMOKE 1 'YES' 2 'NO'/
    FEAR 1 'YES' 2 'NO'
   CROSSTABS TABLES=HEALTH BY SMOKE/FEAR BY SEX
   STATISTICS ALL
   OPTIONS 18

   HEALTH BY SMOKE: Examine the column percentages. The people in excellent health tend to be nonsmokers. Those in good health tend to be smokers. Those in fair health tend to be nonsmokers. Those in poor health tend to be smokers. Since SMOKE is nominal and HEALTH is ordinal, a nominal-based measure of association could be examined. We could use lambda with HEALTH dependent. However, we know from the data that that will equal zero, since the modal categories are always good health. We could use Cramer's *V* or the contingency coefficient. The former is the better choice, since its upper limit is presumably 1. It indicates a weak relationship between the two variables, 0.106.

FEAR BY SEX: Examine the column percentages. Women are far more likely than men to claim that they fear, 24.3 percent versus 61.8 percent saying yes on fear for men and women, respectively. Report lambda with FEAR dependent. It indicates a 28.8 percent reduction in error in predicting FEAR from SEX.

C H A P T E R   11

1.

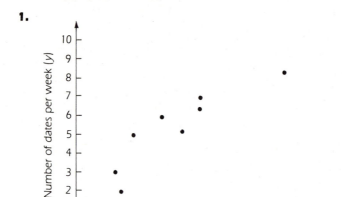

2. MISSING VALUES AGE(98,99) MEMNUM(99) TVHOURS(98,99)
SCATTERGRAM AGE WITH MEMNUM/MEMNUM WITH TVHOURS
OPTIONS 4 7
STATISTICS ALL

3. Both scattergrams indicate very little relationship between the two variables. The MEMNUM = TVHOURS relationship appears to be negative.

4. **(a)** The intercept is 9 and the slope is −0.5. The intercept indicates that for people with zero education, the desired family size is nine; it is the point where the regression line crosses the y-axis. The −0.5 slope indicates that, for each additional year of education, desired family size declines by one-half person. **(b)** The intercept is 1 and the slope is 1. The intercept is the point where the regression line crosses the y-axis. It indicates that, for people with no age, the sentence length is one year. The slope of 1 indicates that for each additional year of age, sentence length increases by one year.

5. For respondents with a twelfth-grade education, desired family size equals 3. For those with an eighth-grade education, desired family size equals 5. For those with a fourth-grade education, desired family size equals 7.

6. **(a)** r squared has a PRE interpretation; 40 percent of the variance in the dependent variable is explained by the independent variable. **(b)** The relationship is positive and "fairly strong," "moderate," or "weak," depending on the correlations found in prior research. The sign of the relationship is positive: increases in values on one variable are accompanied by increases in values on the other variable.

7. They are both the same in strength. Both correlation coefficients show a 25 percent in error in predicting the dependent variable from the independent variable. The two relationships differ in sign: one is positive and the other negative.

8. MISSING VALUES MEMNUM(99) TVHOURS(98,99) AGE(98,99)
SCATTERGRAM TVHOURS WITH AGE/MEMNUM WITH AGE
OPTIONS 4 7
STATISTICS ALL

TV HOURS = 2.53 + (0.0069 AGE)

$r = 0.050$, a positive relationship
r squared = 0.0025, a 0.25 percent reduction in error in predicting TV HOURS from AGE

MEMNUM = 1.83 − (0.005 AGE)

$r = -0.048$, a negative relationship
r squared = 0.0023, a 0.23 percent reduction in error in predicting MEMNUM from AGE

C H A P T E R 12

1. (a) Age (A); Race (A); Income (A) **(b)** Skills (I); Aspirations (A); Parents' income (A) **(c)** Sex ratio (A)

2. Table 12–5a is the original table, and tables 12–5b and 12–5c are partials. The control variable is miles driven. Partial 12–5b shows the original relationship when miles driven is less than 5000 per year. Partial 12–5c shows the original relationship when miles driven is 5000 or more per year.

3. The original table, table 12–5a, indicates that men have more accidents than women, 30 percent versus 10 percent. The partials indicate no relationship between sex and accident rate. When mileage is controlled, men are no more or less likely to have accidents than women. A comparison of the partial tables to the original illustrates vanishing partials. Vanishing partials may be considered either interpretation or explanation. The two differ in theoretical model, not statistics. Tables 12–5a, 12–5b, and 12–5c illustrate interpretation: sex influences miles driven, and miles driven influences accident rate.

4. Original table:

		SMOKE		
		Yes	No	Total
HEALTH	Excell			
	Good			
	Fair			
	Poor			
	Total			

Partial tables:

For Women Only
SMOKE

		Yes	No	Total
	Excell			
HEALTH	Good			
	Fair			
	Poor			
	Total			

For Men Only
SMOKE

		Yes	No	Total
	Excell			
HEALTH	Good			
	Fair			
	Poor			
	Total			

5. MISSING VALUES HAPPY(8,9) HEALTH(8,9) SMOKE(9)
VALUE LABELS SMOKE 1 'YES' 2 'NO'/
  HEALTH 1 'EXCELL' 2 'GOOD' 3 'FAIR' 4 'POOR'/
  HAPPY 1 'VERY' 2 'PRETTY' 3 'NOT TOO'
CROSSTABS TABLES=HAPPY BY HEALTH/HAPPY BY HEALTH
  BY SMOKE
STATISTICS ALL
OPTIONS 18

In general, there seems to be a positive relationship between the two variables: as happiness increases, so too do reports of better health. For example, among those reporting excellent health, 41.5 percent said they were very happy, as compared to 30.8 percent who said they were pretty happy, as compared to 24.2 percent who said they were not too happy. Among the good health respondents, many report that they are pretty happy. Among the fair health respondents, many report that they are not too happy, and the same holds true for the poor health respondents. There is a 16.68 percent reduction in error, as measured by Somer's d, in predicting HEALTH from HAPPY. The relationship is not statistically significant at the 0.05 level.

The partials for women and men replicate the original table. Although the percentages are not identical to those in the original table, the general patterns seem similar. Neither partial shows a statistically significant relationship at the 0.05 level, and the relationship for men is slightly weaker than the relationship for women. Somer's d equals 0.2177 and 0.1117 for women and men, respectively.

C H A P T E R 13

1. (a) Intercept = 1500: when age and education are zero, the predicted income is $1500. For each additional year of school, an increase of $250 is predicted in income. For each additional year in age, an increase of $35 is predicted in income. **(b)** Intercept = 15: when there are no children, and people have been married zero years, the predicted marital happiness score is 15. For every additional year of marriage, an increase of 2 points is predicted in marital happiness. Children reduce marital happiness. Each child reduces marital happiness by 1 point.

2. (a) $6375 **(b)** 53

3. (a) A one-unit change in education increases income by three units, whereas a one-unit change in age increases income by only one-half unit. Education is the better predictor of income. **(b)** A one-unit change in years married increases marital happiness by four units. A one-unit increase in children decreases marital happiness by two and a half units. Years married is the better predictor of marital happiness.

4. (a) R is the multiple correlation coefficient. It indicates a "weak" or "moderate" relationship. R squared shows that 14.4 percent of the variance in the dependent variables is explained by the independent variables. **(b)** An R of 0.82 indicates a "strong" or "very strong" relationship. R squared indicates that 67.2 percent of the variance in the dependent variables is explained by the independent variables.

5. (a) At the 0.05 level the critical value of F at 8, 4191 degrees of freedom is approximately 1.95. The calculated F (34.56) exceeds the critical value (1.95), and therefore we reject the null hypothesis. We conclude that the relationship expressed in the sample was not due solely to chance and that it is unlikely that our sample was drawn from a population in which R equaled zero. **(b)** At the 0.01 level the critical value of F at 4, 215 degrees of freedom is approximately 3.41. The calculated F ratio (2.18) does not equal or exceed the critical value (3.41). Therefore we fail to reject the null hypothesis. We conclude that our sample could have been drawn from a population in which R equaled zero.

6. (a) At the 0.05 level the critical value of F at 1, 224 degrees of freedom is approximately 3.86. The calculated F ratio is 39.06. Since the calculated exceeds the critical value of F, we reject the null hypothesis. We conclude that the regression coefficient for age is statistically significant and that it is probably greater than zero in the population. **(b)** At the 0.05 level the critical value of F at 1, 468 degrees of freedom is approximately 3.86. The calculated F ratio is 878.37. Since the calculated exceeds the critical value of F, we reject the null hypothesis. We conclude that the regression coefficient for hours studied is statistically significant and that it is probably greater than zero in the population.

7. `MISSING VALUES MEMNUM(99) AGE(98,99) TVHOURS(98,99)`
   `CHILDS(9)`
`REGRESSION VARIABLES=MEMNUM,AGE,TVHOURS,CHILDS/`
   `STATISTICS=ALL/`
   `DEPENDENT=MEMNUM/STEPWISE`

Of the three possible independent variables, only TVHOURS is entered into the regression equation. The regression equation is

`MEMNUM = 2.05 - (0.155 × TVHOURS)`

The other variables did not meet the statistical criteria. The overall regression equation is statistically significant at the 0.01 level. R squared is 0.043

and indicates that TVHOURS explains 4.3 percent of the variance in MEM-NUM.

C H A P T E R   14

1. (a) M **(b)** I

2. (a) At the 0.05 level at 400, 100 degrees of freedom, the critical value of F is approximately 1.30. The calculated F ratio exceeds the critical value, and therefore we reject the null hypothesis. We conclude that the variances for the two groups are probably unequal in the population. **(b)** At the 0.01 level the critical value of F at 130, 80 degrees of freedom is approximately 1.65. The calculated F ratio of 2.78 exceeds the critical value, and therefore we reject the null hypothesis. We conclude that the variances for the two groups are probably unequal in the population.

3. (a) One-tailed **(b)** Two-tailed **(c)** One-tailed **(d)** Two-tailed

4. (a) Compare the married and the never married respondents on average organizational membership. **(b)** Compare the graduate degree respondents with the others on average occupational prestige.

5. T–TEST GROUPS=RELIG(1,2)/VARIABLES=PRESTIGE

6. We fail to reject the null hypotheses for equality of variances. Therefore we conclude that the variances for males and females are probably not different in the population. We use a t test that assumes equal variances, the pooled variance estimate. Our hypothesis indicates a two-tailed test. Testing at the 0.05 level, we fail to reject the null hypothesis using a two-tailed test. We conclude that the MEMNUM mean hours could be the same for males and females.

C H A P T E R   15

1. (a) The between-groups variation is 2.31 times as large as the within-groups variation. **(b)** The between-groups variation is 10.45 times as large as the within-groups variation. **(c)** The between-groups variation is 45.98 times as large as the within-groups variation.

2. At 1, 198 degrees of freedom, the critical value of F at the 0.05 level is approximately 3.89, and at the 0.01 level it is approximately 6.76. At the 0.05 level, the F ratio for b and c are statistically significant. These same ratios are statistically significant at the 0.01 level. Only the F ratio for a, 2.31, is not statistically significant at either level.

3. It means that 42.5 percent of the variance in income is explained by sex.

4. ANOVA SIBS BY MAWORK(1,2)
STATISTICS ALL

5. For the 247 cases the average number of TVHOURS was 2.85. Looking at the means for the different DEGREES, we find that the average number of TVHOURS seems to decline as DEGREE increases. The people with bachelor's degrees violate that pattern, however. The ANOVA table for TVHOURS and DEGREE shows that at the 0.05 level no effects are statistically significant. We conclude that the average number of TVHOURS does not vary by

DEGREE. The MCA part of the table shows that the people with an associate degree and a graduate degree depart the most from the overall TVHOURS mean.

6. At the 0.05 level no effects are statistically significant. TVHOURS do not differ by DEGREE, by SEX, or by a combination of DEGREE and SEX.

references

Rosenberg, Morris. 1968. The logic of survey analysis. New York: Basic Books.

SPSS, Inc. SPSS[x] user's guide. New York: McGraw-Hill.